JUSTUS S. STEARNS

Great Lakes Books
A complete listing of the books in this series
can be found online at wsupress.wayne.edu

JUSTUS S. STEARNS

Michigan Pine King and Kentucky Coal Baron, 1845–1933

MICHAEL W. NAGLE

WAYNE STATE UNIVERSITY PRESS
DETROIT

ISBN 978-0-8143-4882-6 (paperback)
ISBN 978–0-8143-4126-1 (cloth)
ISBN 978–0-8143-4127-8 (ebook)

Library of Cataloging Control Number: 2015934524

Designed and typeset by Adam B. Bohannon
Composed in Adobe Caslon

Wayne State University Press rests on Waawiyaataanong, also referred to as Detroit, the ancestral and contemporary homeland of the Three Fires Confederacy. These sovereign lands were granted by the Ojibwe, Odawa, Potawatomi, and Wyandot nations, in 1807, through the Treaty of Detroit. Wayne State University Press affirms Indigenous sovereignty and honors all tribes with a connection to Detroit. With our Native neighbors, the press works to advance educational equity and promote a better future for the earth and all people.

Wayne State University Press
Leonard N. Simons Building
4809 Woodward Avenue
Detroit, Michigan 48201-1309

Visit us online at wsupress.wayne.edu

For my parents,
Larry and Janice Nagle

CONTENTS

PREFACE AND ACKNOWLEDGMENTS

In 1996, I came to Ludington, Michigan, to be interviewed for a position on the faculty at West Shore Community College. While on this visit, I saw Lake Michigan for the first time. I could not believe how large it was; after all, it was "just a lake." I had grown up in the Seattle area near Puget Sound, but this was much different. As I looked out at the water, I was struck by its vastness. Walking along the city's main beach at the end of Ludington Avenue, I had to convince myself that this was not saltwater. I put my finger in the water to taste it; the water was not salty.

At the time, I had no idea that the beach was named Stearns Park Beach. Over the next several years I returned to this beach on many occasions, sometimes

Crowds of people visit Stearns Beach to watch the fireworks show each year. Notice Ludington's lighthouse and the SS *Badger* car ferry in the background. (Courtesy of Todd and Brad Reed)

alone, but usually with family and friends to walk to the lighthouse, to watch the fireworks on the Fourth of July, or to swim in the cool waters of Lake Michigan on a hot, summer day. Over time, I learned the beach was named in honor of Justus S. Stearns, the man who donated this valuable piece of property to the city of Ludington. Nearly fifteen years after my initial "taste test" I began to research Stearns's life, a project that was both exciting and nerve-racking. On the one hand, I was eager to study someone with so many achievements. At the same time, I feared that researching and writing a book while maintaining a full teaching load would require sacrificing time I wanted to spend with my family.

Undertaking this project has provided me with several unique opportunities. Research trips have taken me to the National Archives in Washington, DC; Maryland; and Atlanta, along with visits to the Bentley Historical Library in Ann Arbor and the University of Kentucky, in Lexington. One family vacation to Wisconsin included a trip to the Ojibwe Museum and Cultural Center, located in Lac du Flambeau. On the way home from a vacation to New York City, we stopped in Fredonia, New York, the birthplace of Justus Stearns. I also traveled to Stearns, Kentucky, twice to conduct research. I was greatly impressed when I took the Big South Fork Scenic Railway to the Blue Heron Mine, which at one time was operated by the Stearns Coal and Lumber Company; now it is a historic site operated by the National Park Service. I had traveled to Kentucky in the past, but was captivated by the Big South Fork National River and Recreation area. When I began the project, I was familiar with Stearns's legacy for the city of Ludington, but I slowly began to learn how wide-ranging his legacy had been for communities in the South and throughout the entire region of the Great Lakes.

I am indebted to the great number of people whose encouragement and assistance helped to facilitate the completion of this work. The spark that prompted me to begin this project was a phone call from Robert E. Gable, the great-grandson of Justus Stearns. He offered encouragement, related oral traditions handed down over the years, and provided unrestricted access to numerous Stearns family materials. Several individuals took the time to read all or some of this manuscript; their thoughts and observations have only improved this work. Bill Anderson has been a valuable mentor whenever I had a question or sought counsel. Don Whisenhunt read the manuscript closely and volunteered to complete the index. My friend and colleague Seán Henne challenged me to become a more thoughtful writer. Jim Jensen and Hal Filter offered several helpful suggestions. Ned Nordine deserves special thanks. Many years ago Ned identified and copied newspaper articles that mentioned Justus Stearns and his companies that appeared in various Ludington newspapers. His work greatly facilitated my own research endeavors. The staff at Wayne State University Press has been great to work with. I would like to offer thanks to Kathryn Wildfong; Kristina Stonehill; the anonymous reviewers; Dawn Hall, whose observations and suggestions as copyeditor were of great value; and many others who have offered their assistance and critical analysis of this work.

Many archivists and librarians have helped to uncover valuable resources. I fear that by including a list of names, some will be left out, but I still would like to recognize the efforts of key individuals and institutions. These include Mary Frances Ronan from the National Archives in Washington, DC; Amy Reytar of the National Archives in College Park, Maryland; Zina Rhone, Maureen Hill, and Cathy Miller at the National Archives in Atlanta; Gordon Hogg, Special Collections Library director at the University of Kentucky Libraries; the staffs at the Bentley Historical Library in Ann Arbor, the Grand Rapids Public Library, the McCreary County Library in Kentucky, New York's Darwin R. Barker Historical Museum, and the Michigan State Archives in Lansing. Ron Wood, Neva Wood, Kate Arbogast, and Carmen Tiffany facilitated research at Historic White Pine Village, while Amy Combs provided valuable assistance at the McCreary County Museum. Jeanne Briggs, Mike Hypio, and Renee Snodgrass processed numerous interlibrary loan requests from West Shore's William M. Anderson Library.

Many other individuals also furnished assistance. William "Doc" Coffee graciously sat for an interview and answered questions about life for coal miners and the coal mining industry, Louise Legeza researched the family of Paulina Lyon Stearns in Ohio, and David K. Petersen answered questions and generously offered the use of several photos that have enhanced the manuscript. Bruce Micinski, president of the Lake County Historical Society, spent the day helping with some research and showed me the location of historic Stearns Siding. Mike Hankwitz, John Holcomb, and Bruce and Cindy Bosley provided valuable photos while Bruce and Cindy also allowed me to access the correspondence between Matt Stevensen and Ingeborg Clomen, two residents of Stearns Siding. Gunver Lodge translated their correspondence as it was written in Norwegian. John Poindexter facilitated the preparation of many photos while John Wolff provided editorial assistance; Rebecca Mott prepared two maps. Others deserving thanks include Michael Birdwell, Diane L. Englebrecht, Mark Fedder, Caryl Ferguson, David and Thom Hawley, Steve Hunt, Steve Koss, Geoff Kramer, Nick Krieger, Deborah Luskin, Mason County Historical Society, McCreary County Museum, Jim Newkirk, Darlene Ponko, Matt Sanderson, Connie Schwass,

Douglas Shepard, Duane Wolf, West Shore Community College, and all of my colleagues at West Shore who offered support and counsel in many ways.

As I became engaged in this research project, my family learned more historical trivia than they ever cared to know. My sister and brother, Lori and Doug, provided encouragement over time; my in-laws, Elizabeth Karella and Bernd Werny, offered comments as they read initial drafts of the manuscript. I need to offer an apology to my daughters, Maggie and Elizabeth. They have heard more stories about Justus Stearns and spent more family vacations visiting historical locations than I am able to count. Thank you both for your patience. My wife, Buffy, was the first to read every single chapter. This project never would have been completed without her constant and unflinching support. I am a better person because of her.

While many individuals have contributed mightily to this work, any errors in fact or interpretation are mine alone.

Introduction

Justus S. Stearns was an important Michigan timber baron who at one time served as the state's largest producer of manufactured lumber; however, he was more than that. He was a "Pine King" with an astounding range of accomplishments. He also founded the Stearns Coal and Lumber Company, along with the town of Stearns, Kentucky, in 1902. For much of his lifetime, Stearns's company was one of Kentucky's largest producers of coal, and prior to the sale of its largest mine in the 1970s, it stood as the state's oldest continuous mining operation. Throughout his career in business, Stearns expanded his timber empire outside of Michigan and into Wisconsin, Kentucky, Tennessee, Florida, and even Washington State. He was an active member of the Republican Party who served one term as Michigan's secretary of state and ran for governor on three occasions. Stearns also founded or owned more than thirty additional businesses.

Justus Stearns either lived in or operated businesses at several locations in the Great Lakes region. (Courtesy of Rebecca Mott)

Furthermore, he was a generous benefactor who gave back much of his wealth to communities in both Michigan and Kentucky. The more I studied his life, the more fascinated I became with his impressive array of business ventures, political activities, and philanthropy.

Although his wide range of accomplishments was noteworthy, Stearns's business empire never reached the level of a John D. Rockefeller or Andrew Carnegie; nor did he influence political discourse like a Theodore Roosevelt or Woodrow Wilson. Yet his story was an important one and his impact still can be felt today. The United States experienced a capitalist revolution in the late nineteenth century, as the nation was transformed from an agrarian-based society into an industrial power. Justus Stearns was one of many captains of industry operating at the local and regional levels whose ambition and innovation brought the United States into this industrial age, which ultimately raised the standard of living for those living within the nation's borders.[1]

Stearns's business activities can be seen as a bridge that connects the late 1800s and the Gilded Age to the 1930s and the era of the Great Depression. His career began to flourish in 1880 when he founded the lumber town of Stearns Siding. By the late 1890s he had moved his base of operations to Ludington when he organized the Stearns Salt and Lumber Company. In the first decade of the 1900s, he established the Stearns Coal and Lumber Company in Kentucky and then diversified his business investments; he owned a hotel, electric company, and other manufacturing organizations, including the business that evolved into the Stearns Motor Manufacturing Company. Most of his endeavors continued to prosper during the First World War. By the 1920s his hotel was expanded, and while his sawmill in Ludington had closed down, his lumber operations continued in multiple locations inside and outside of Michigan. Meanwhile, in 1929 his Kentucky operations included a coal company that produced nearly one million tons of coal, his mills manufactured twenty million feet of lumber, and his Kentucky and Tennessee Railway transported coal, employees, lumber, and other cargo throughout the local area. Conditions had changed dramatically by the early 1930s. As the nation suffered from the Great Depression, the Stearns Motor Manufacturing Company had closed, and production at the Stearns Coal and Lumber Company had dropped significantly as a result of a sharp decrease in the demand for coal.

For much of the era between the Gilded Age and the Great Depression, American business owners often were influenced by two divergent philosophies; some acted in a paternalistic manner, while others were influenced by the principles of Social Darwinism. Paternalistic business owners considered themselves to be like fathers who developed a genuine interest in their employees and attempted to ensure adequate housing and safe working conditions, and contributed to the communities in which their workers lived. Social Darwinists emphasized competition and the need for a laissez faire, or "hands off," approach to the economy, while rejecting the belief they had a responsibility to help the less fortunate in society. Advocates of this view argued that success came to those in society who had special talent and worked hard, while advancement was open to anyone willing to adopt a hard work ethic and live a frugal life. Of Michigan's lumber barons, Charles Hackley can be seen as paternalistic in his actions. Hackley operated in Muskegon for several decades in the late nineteenth century and eventually became famous for his numerous business interests and philanthropic contributions to that city. Henry Sage, who owned a large sawmill in Bay City, was more reflective of a lumberman influenced by Social Darwinism. He continually worked to maintain control over his workforce and believed "responsibility for his workers ended . . . with the payment of their wages."[2]

It would be far too simplistic to argue the actions of business leaders can be placed only into these two categories. Even the most benevolent owners strove to earn a profit, while most others were not so coldhearted as to be completely unconcerned with the conditions their employees faced. Those in the business community held many common traits. Most worked to maintain as much control over their workforce as possible. Alcohol abuse, absenteeism, and sloppy work habits were not to be tolerated. Owners, including Stearns, wanted the power to hire their workers and fire them if they caused problems. Probably the greatest sin an employee could commit involved union organizing. Stearns's contemporaries in the coalfields of the South were among the most ardent opponents of unionization. Some even argued it was part of a movement "to destroy the American form of government and American way of life."[3]

Historian Jeremy Kilar has demonstrated that another factor that influenced the attitudes and actions of American business leaders, lumbermen in particular, was whether they were absentee or resident owners. Individuals who resided in the towns where their companies were located had a strong sense of city loyalty. They worked to start new local businesses and helped to diversify the economies of their hometowns. Additionally, they also made substantive philanthropic contributions in the form of parks, libraries, schools, hospitals, churches, and such. Absentee owners felt no such loyalty. When natural resources, such as trees, were gone, they simply moved to the next town and established a new sawmill. Resident owners also became involved in the political and civic life of the towns where they lived, whereas absentee owners at times alienated themselves from the communities where their businesses were located. After all, because they didn't live there, absentee owners did not have as much of a stake in the community; they may have visited a few times during the year, but they were there strictly for profit.[4]

This work argues that the actions of Justus Stearns demonstrated the influence of both paternalism and Social Darwinism; however, the majority of his activities reflected his paternalism. Furthermore, Stearns was both a resident and absentee owner. Following his relocation to Ludington in 1876, Stearns continued to live there for the rest of his life. He was a resident owner of several businesses in Ludington, and for many years the anchor of his holdings in that city was the Stearns Salt and Lumber Company. The Stearns Empire spread to many additional states throughout the country, but two of his primary operations outside of Michigan were in Wisconsin and Kentucky. He was an absentee owner in Wisconsin, where he cut timber and established a sawmill on two Indian reservations, as well as in Kentucky; however, his activities in the Bluegrass State were more complex. He did not simply hire a manager to oversee the Kentucky operations. Instead, his son Robert L. Stearns relocated to Stearns and lived there for many years. Subsequent generations of Stearns family members also lived in Kentucky, became involved in the community, and oversaw the company's operations. Stearns's activities in Ludington, Michigan, and in Stearns, Kentucky, demonstrate his success as a business entrepreneur, but they also show the positive impact Stearns had on these communities as each struggled to enter the industrial age.

Organization of the Book

This work is divided into nine chapters. The first two chapters address key events in the first few decades of Stearns's life and his initial foray into the lumber industry. He was born on a farm in rural New York where his father operated a sawmill; here he received his early training in business. Eventually, he moved with his family to Conneaut, Ohio, where he met and married Paulina Lyon. With her family's business connections and assistance, he later moved to Ludington, Michigan, and established his own lumber town named Stearns Siding. The early history of Ludington, which was characterized by periodic booms and busts, also will be chronicled. Stearns's investment in the community sparked an economic revival for the city, and by 1899 he became the largest producer of manufactured lumber in Michigan.

Chapters 3 and 4 address Stearns's political career and his timber operations in Wisconsin. Stearns was a lifelong Republican who was influenced by the ideals of the Progressive movement, which sometimes put him at odds with some members of his own party.[5] While he never served in a statewide office beyond his single term as secretary of state, his advocacy for the use of political primaries to replace party conventions influenced political discourse in Michigan, resulting in the expansion of democracy throughout the state. Stearns also established lumber operations on two Wisconsin Indian reservations beginning in the early 1890s. These were very successful and allowed him to expand his timber empire; however, they also demonstrate the failed Indian policies of this era the federal government adopted; by the time Stearns left Wisconsin, life on the reservations was plagued by unemployment and poverty.

The next three chapters (5, 6, and 7) detail Stearns's coal, lumber, and railroad operations in Kentucky and Tennessee. Stearns founded the Stearns Coal and Lumber Company, the Kentucky and Tennessee Railway, and the coal-company town of Stearns, Kentucky, in the first decade of the twentieth century. His actions brought employment and opportunity to a depressed region of the country along with access to education, electricity, and medical care. Life for miners and their families working for Stearns also is discussed. While mining remained a dirty and dangerous occupation, Stearns's employees were among the first in the state to have access to washhouses at the mines, and even though accidents did occur, company officials implemented strict operating rules designed to promote safety in the mines. Like many of his contemporaries, Stearns was no lover of unions. Conflict developed between striking workers and Stearns Company officials in 1908, which eventually resulted in the murder of a United States marshal in 1908 by union members. This era of conflict and violence will be juxtaposed with the time period from 1915 to 1929 when the business experienced its greatest prosperity and the Stearns Coal and Lumber Company became the third-largest producer of coal in the state.

Chapter 8 shows that while the Stearns Salt and Lumber Company may have been the anchor of Stearns's Michigan holdings in the early twentieth century, Stearns founded or purchased many other businesses, such as an electric company, hotel, and firms that manufactured game boards and kitchen utensils. He also founded the Stearns Motor Manufacturing Company, which produced high-end motors for boats and tractors. Furthermore, Stearns was a generous philanthropist who contributed to numerous causes, including the resort community of Epworth Heights and Ludington's first hospital. To the city he gave a significant stretch of beachfront property along Lake Michigan, which eventually was named Stearns Park in his honor.

The final chapter offers an overview and analysis of Stearns's lifetime of accomplishments.

Goal

The goal of this work is not simply to produce the history of one man's achievements. Instead, Stearns's life story can be used as a window to highlight key events from the years in which he lived (1845–1933). Readers will come to a greater understanding of the lumber and coal mining industries along with key events in the early histories of Ludington, Michigan, and Stearns, Kentucky. The failed Indian policies the US government adopted will be explored as well as characteristics of Michigan's political history, particularly Stearns's activity in what was known as the Progressive movement (1890s–1917). Justus Stearns led an interesting and eventful life. His achievements help to show how one man's career in business can demonstrate the ways in which life in America was transformed in the late nineteenth and early twentieth centuries when the nation became a manufacturing giant.

1

Early Life and Family Connections

I think as we advance to extreme age, the things which appeal to us most are those that happened in our younger days.

Letter from Justus Stearns (age eighty-four) to William Stearns, March 27, 1930 (Mason County Historical Society Archive, Ludington, Michigan)

Although he was born and raised on a farm in Chautauqua County, New York, Justus Stearns developed his early business skills while working in Pennsylvania and Ohio and later earned his fortune in states such as Michigan, Wisconsin, Kentucky, and Tennessee. He did not receive a formal education beyond his teens; nevertheless, throughout his formative years, his family connections played a central role in what would become a successful career in business. Several of his ancestors were involved in the lumber business, including his father. His marriage to Paulina Lyon in 1868, and subsequent business dealings with members of her family, resulted in his move to Michigan and proved to be crucial to his later success. After working several years in the timber industry for others, in 1880 he established his own lumbering operation in Lake County, Michigan, at a town called Stearns Siding. In retrospect, one can view the actions in his early life as the formal education he never received, enabling him to develop the knowledge and experience necessary to become one of Michigan's leading lumber barons. However, Stearns struggled at times during his early career, and at no time was his success a foregone conclusion.

Abraham Lincoln and Grace Bedell

A series of events involving Abraham Lincoln, and a little girl named Grace Bedell, can help to provide insight into the character of Justus Stearns and explain some of the actions he undertook later in life. In February 1861 Stearns was fifteen years old and lived on Van Buren Point in New York, while Lincoln had just been elected to his first term as president. As the president-elect made his way to the nation's capital via train, he stopped in numerous towns where crowds of well-wishers greeted him. He made a special stop in Westfield, New York, as this was the hometown of Grace Bedell, a young girl with whom he had carried on a unique correspondence.

Lincoln's communication with Miss Bedell began in October 1860 when the eleven-year-old girl sent a letter to Lincoln, who at the time was the Republican nominee for president. She mentioned she had four brothers and asked if he had any daughters. She continued by letting him know she was working to generate support for his candidacy, and that if she were a man she would vote for him, but also suggested that he grow a beard as then, "you would look a great deal better for your face is so thin."[1] Lincoln was charmed by this letter and replied within one week by writing, "My dear little Miss: Your very agreeable letter of the 15th is received. I regret the necessity of saying I have no daughter. . . . As to the whiskers, having never worn any, do you not think people would call it a piece of silly affection if I were to begin it now?"[2] While he seemed to discount the idea of growing a beard, following his victory in the fall election, as early as December 1860, he no longer remained clean shaven.

When it was announced that Lincoln's train was scheduled to stop in the nearby town of Westfield, Justus Stearns, along with his father and a group of other farmers, made the twelve-mile trip to catch a glimpse of the incoming president. As Lincoln arrived at the Westfield train station, he asked if the Bedell family was present. Young Grace then was rushed to the platform where she planned to offer Mr. Lincoln some flowers, but he surprised her by rubbing his beard and telling her, "I let these whiskers grow for you, Grace."[3] He then gave the girl a kiss and continued on his way to Washington, DC, and his first inauguration. Young Justus Stearns was present when Lincoln arrived at the train station and observed the encounter between Lincoln and Bedell. He later recalled that Lincoln wore a stovepipe hat and was, "of unusual height, having to stoop considerably in order to get through the door out onto the platform, and had immensely large hands and feet."[4] The incident must have left a remarkable impression on the young man, which was evident by a letter he wrote seventy years later to Grace Bedell. By that time, she was eighty-two years old, living in Kansas, and was known as Mrs. Grace Billings. The eighty-six-year-old Stearns addressed this touching letter to, "My dear Mrs. Billings." He "remembered well" her meeting with Lincoln and recalled his own journey to the train station that day, "as of yesterday."[5] He also remembered the days following Lincoln's assassination when the fallen president's body was transported from Washington, DC, to Illinois. Stearns traveled to one of Cleveland's public parks and joined a crowd that had gathered to show their respect for Mr. Lincoln. Most onlookers were driven to tears as the casket was opened and mourners filed past. Stearns did not expect a reply from Mrs. Billings, but wanted her to know that while the incident had taken place many years previously, by 1931 there was at least one living witness to her meeting with Lincoln back in 1861.[6]

That Stearns would take the time to write this letter at the age of eighty-six truly was remarkable and revealed the caring nature of Stearns's actions taken over the course of his lifetime. In the late 1800s and early 1900s, his thoughtfulness was demonstrated as he worked to develop a strong sense of community in the settlements he founded in Stearns Siding, Michigan, and Stearns, Kentucky. He also showed tremendous loyalty to his adopted hometown of Ludington, Michigan, as he became an active booster and philanthropist on behalf of the city for many years. Furthermore, it reflected the attention to detail that characterized the manner in which he operated his businesses. Finally, this incident can help to explain Stearns's lifelong affiliation with the Republican Party, as the details of this encounter with the nation's first Republican president remained with him decades after the events took place.

Stearns's Early Life and Family

The father of Justus Stearns was Heman Swift Stearns, who was born in 1819 in Bennington, Vermont. Heman Stearns's parents were Joseph and Susan (Rogers) Stearns. The Stearns family could trace its roots back to Nathaniel Stearns who originally settled in Dedham, Massachusetts, in 1647 as part of the "Great Migration" that ultimately brought thousands of Puritans to New England. Most members of the Stearns family were farmers, but one ancestor, Ebenezer Stearns Jr., appeared to be the first of the Stearns men to become a lumberman; he owned and operated large sawmills in Lanesboro, Massachusetts. By the 1840s, Heman Stearns had moved to Fredonia, New York, where he lived with his family.[7]

Justus Stearns's mother was Mabel W. Smith, who was born in Connecticut in 1823. Her own mother also was named Mabel Smith and her father was Perry Smith. Census records indicate that Mabel W. Smith and her family moved to Fredonia, New York, about 1832. Mabel had at least one other sibling, a brother named Justus. Mabel, both parents, and her brother were members of Fredonia's Presbyterian Church. Unfortunately, the life of Justus Smith was cut short when his body was found floating in the Ohio River in 1841, an apparent victim of a boating accident. Perry Smith, Mabel's father, often was referred to as "Captain" Smith. An advertisement that appeared in the *Fredonia Censor* indicated that Captain Smith operated a large storehouse and wharf on Van Buren Harbor where he declared he would maintain "the strictest care and attention . . . on all Goods landed to his care and liberal advances made on Goods received on consignment."[8]

Heman Stearns and Mabel Smith both lived in the Van Buren Harbor area of Fredonia. The two met and the couple was married April 19, 1842, and three years later, their only child, Justus Smith Stearns, was born April 10, 1845. He was named for his uncle who had died so suddenly just a few years before. As a young boy without siblings, Justus Stearns learned that growing up on a farm involved many responsibilities. Each day he was expected to milk twelve cows before he walked more than three miles to school in Cordova, where a cousin also was enrolled. His chores had to be completed regardless of the weather. As he grew older, his responsibilities increased, and every Saturday he worked at his father's sawmill where he wheeled away sawdust and stacked seemingly endless boards of lumber. It is unclear exactly when he stopped attending school, but as work at his father's mill increased, Justus spent more time tallying, piling, and loading lumber and less time at school. Heman Stearns later commented that it was during these formative years that the lumber business was "thoroughly pounded into him" (meaning his son Justus). It was no wonder that when Justus grew older, he would pursue a career in the lumber industry. Other than a business course he took in Poughkeepsie, Justus's formal schooling ended in his early teens. From that time on, his education came from his broad firsthand business experiences.[9]

Not all of young Justus's time was spent working, and years later he retained many fond memories of his youth. When shown a postcard of a landmark from his hometown, he reminisced about Van Buren Point and recalled, "I used to fish there as a boy" along with "many of the men from Fredonia [who] used to come down there to do their fishing."[10] His uncle's family lived nearby, and Justus often spent time with these relatives as he later complained he did not have many other places to visit. Uncle Sidney Stearns had four daughters. The closest in age to Justus was Alice, with whom he attended school. He frequently spent the night at his cousins' home and once recalled having to share a bed with his cousins Alice, Jane, and Annette when he was about eight years old because the house was so crowded with guests.[11] Justus remembered "Grant Grocery store very well as my mother used to make nearly all of her purchases there—and Harry Parker, who had a store just west or nearby the Grant Store." When in town, he remembered the ritual of calling on other families as life could become quite isolated on a rural farm. Located in the center of town was a large park. Decades later, Stearns remembered that as a boy he listened to a speech delivered by New York senator William H. Seward as he campaigned for the Republican nomination for president against a field of aspirants including Abraham Lincoln. Seward would go on to serve with distinction in Lincoln's cabinet. Opposite the park was the Presbyterian Church young Justus occasionally attended with his mother. However, as far as he was concerned at the time, they attended services more often than he preferred. Years later, Stearns related a story involving his mother, his aunt, and a "colored barber" from his hometown that sheds light on his youth and personality: "I remember the old hotel, the Johnson House, and that there was a colored barber in the lower part of it. Up until the time that I was eight or nine years old my mother did all my hair-cutting. My aunt Mary . . . accused my mother of putting a bowl on top of my head and cutting around the bottom of that. This annoyed me somewhat and by the time I had to have another hair-cut, I had managed to save up enough change so that I could go down to the colored barber and get a regular hair-cut."[12]

That Stearns was "annoyed" about the quality of his hairstyle at the age of eight or nine may have foreshadowed concerns he had about his appearance when he grew older. Photos taken over the years show Stearns with a full head of hair well into old age, but when he was in his fifties his head was shaved bald for a time. This change in his appearance over the years might indicate he wore a toupee for the last twenty-five years of his life.[13]

Census data and tax rolls provide insight into the economic status of Justus Stearns's family while he was growing up in Fredonia. The census conducted by the state of New York in 1855 listed his father's occupation as "lumberman," while the family lived in a brick home valued at about $500. In addition to his parents, others living in the household that year included a cousin, a servant, and his grandmother, Mabel Smith. The assessment rolls for the town of Pomfret from 1855 indicated that Heman Stearns owned over 330 acres of property and a sawmill, worth a combined value of about $5,000. The United States Census, conducted five years later in 1860, listed Heman as a "farmer" with real estate valued at $8,000. Justus turned fifteen that year, and he "attended school." The fact that Heman was described as both a "farmer" and "lumberman" recognized his engagement in both industries, and the value of his property showed that while the family may not have been the most prominent in the region, their holdings were quite extensive.[14]

Stearns's family background and origins can be compared to other nineteenth-century timber pioneers. Two previously published studies of leading lumbermen, by Frederick Kohlmeyer and Barbara Benson, showed that nearly 90 percent of those who established operations in Michigan and the Great Lakes were born in the United States. Very few, less than 3 percent, were born in

Michigan. Interestingly enough, the largest number came from the state of New York, while very few hailed from affluent families. The fact that Stearns grew up on a family farm was typical; over half the lumbermen studied were the sons of farmers; some combined farming with lumbering, as was the case in the Stearns's household. More than three-quarters attended only common schools, although some received additional vocational or academic training. Taken collectively, these studies demonstrate that Stearns's background and experiences were typical when compared to many of his contemporaries in the timber industry.[15]

In 1861, Heman Stearns sold his farm and mill at Van Buren Point and the family moved to Erie, Pennsylvania, where he established a retail lumber business. Justus, who was sixteen years old, became his assistant. That same year, Mr. Stearns partnered with a man named Finn, and the two started an oil refining operation. The lumberyard proved to be lucrative, but the oil industry was much less predictable. Heman Stearns invested at least $8,000 of his own capital in the company. It had operated about four years when, as Justus Stearns put it years later, "they lost everything they had."[16] Following the failure of this business in 1864, the family moved to Conneaut, Ohio, when Justus was nineteen. Once again father and son engaged in the manufacture and sale of lumber. Their more

Justus and Paulina Stearns were married for thirty-six years, until Paulina's untimely death in 1904. (Courtesy of Robert E. Gable)

successful endeavors involved purchasing large amounts of lumber from several small mills in town. The two then shipped large quantities to eastern markets where the demand and price was higher. Heman and Justus worked together in Conneaut for about ten years. While he was living in the area, Justus came to know his future wife, Miss Paulina Lyon.[17]

Paulina was the daughter of Robert Bond Lyon and Clarissa (Kellogg) Lyon. Robert was born September 27, 1796, in Elizabeth, New Jersey, and married Catherine Bacon, his first wife, in Bath, New York, in 1822. In 1831 the Lyons moved to Salem (now Conneaut), Ohio, where they raised five children until Catherine's death in 1840. Robert married Clarissa Kellogg shortly thereafter in January 1841. Clarissa had been born in Kelloggsville, Ohio, October 12, 1819, and was twenty-two years old at the time of her marriage. Clarissa and Robert had four children of their own. Paulina was their third child; she was born November 24, 1849.[18]

Robert Lyon was a very successful businessman. Soon after he moved to Conneaut in 1831 he opened a general store with an associate from New York. The business continued for several years, at times with other partners, until it simply became known as the Robert Lyon Firm. Mr. Lyon was noted for his "unusual business ability, integrity, and for his readiness in forwarding any plan for the general good."[19] He was a devoted father and husband involved in many public activities in his community. While he never aspired to public office, he was considered the leading merchant in Conneaut until he sold his business holdings in 1854. Unfortunately, he died shortly thereafter at the age of fifty-eight, following a tragic accident. He was standing in a wagon pulled by a horse when a loud train whistle was heard. The noise frightened the horse and it started unexpectedly with a jump, throwing Mr. Lyon out of the wagon. His back was injured in the fall and he died within the week.[20]

Each of the children born from this second marriage between Robert and Clarissa Lyon became quite successful. Catherine, their oldest child, married Eber Brock Ward, a famed industrialist. Ward initially succeeded as a steamboat man shipping cargo throughout the Great Lakes, but then established an enormous iron mill at Wyandotte, Michigan, with a blast furnace and rolling mills. Ward built another mill in Chicago and a third in Milwaukee. He always employed the latest techniques in his plants; Ward was the first in America to manufacture steel using the Bessemer process. Additionally, he owned several thousand acres of prime timberland near Ludington, Michigan. At the time of his death in 1875, he was considered the richest man in Michigan. The second child was Clarissa Lyon, who married James F. Wade, the son of Ohio senator

Benjamin Wade. James Wade was commissioned a first lieutenant in the Sixth Ohio Cavalry during the Civil War and was made a major general during the Spanish-American War of 1898. He later commanded troops stationed in the Philippines. Paulina's younger brother was Thomas Rice Lyon. In the early 1870s he moved to Ludington to work as a clerk in the offices of his brother-in-law, Eber Ward. Following Ward's death, he assumed the management of Ward's Ludington operations, eventually becoming a major manufacturer of lumber in his own right. The Ward interests in Ludington eventually brought Justus and Paulina to that city.[21]

Paulina Lyon and Justus Stearns were married at the home of Paulina's mother in Conneaut, Ohio, March 4, 1868.[22] At the time of their wedding, Justus was twenty-two and Paulina was eighteen. Census records from 1870 indicate the young couple lived with Paulina's mother that year, along with Paulina's sixteen-year-old brother Thomas and a domestic servant. Paulina remained close to her mother for many years, even after her family's move to Michigan in the 1870s. She and her mother traveled back and forth between Ohio and Michigan on numerous occasions to maintain their family ties, until her mother's death in 1896. Paulina also traveled a great deal with her sister Clarissa and brother Thomas. While living in Conneaut, Robert Lyon Stearns, the couple's only child, was born March 12, 1872. The fact that Justus lived in the home of his mother-in-law was significant and indicated that he married into a well-to-do family. Clarissa Lyon was a widow in 1870, but that year's census indicated her home had a value of $3,000 while her personal estate was valued at $10,000. No value was

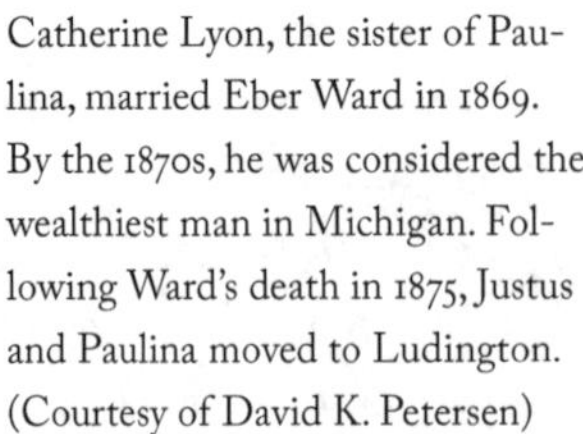

Catherine Lyon, the sister of Paulina, married Eber Ward in 1869. By the 1870s, he was considered the wealthiest man in Michigan. Following Ward's death in 1875, Justus and Paulina moved to Ludington. (Courtesy of David K. Petersen)

listed for the personal items owned by Justus and Paulina, but Justus's parents, Heman and Mabel Stearns, were living in the same town as their son in 1870. Heman's occupation was listed as "lumber dealer" and the value of his personal estate was estimated to be $500.[23] In subsequent years, Stearns continued to live in close proximity to members of Paulina's family, and their business interests often intertwined.

Following his marriage, Justus continued in the lumber business in Conneaut, but he also cut hardwood timber, probably on a contract basis, twelve miles outside of Toledo near the Black Swamp. However, disaster struck in 1875 after Stearns had contracted to provide several clients in Conneaut with lumber. Stearns planned to acquire the necessary lumber from his brother-in-law, Eber Ward, whose Michigan mills were quite extensive by this time. In January 1875 Ward died suddenly of apoplexy (a stroke). This came at a difficult interval for Stearns; Ward's vast estate was complicated and remained in litigation for three years. In the ensuing chaos, production dropped at Ward's mills, and Stearns was unable to deliver the lumber under contract. Ward's death also came in the aftermath of a financial panic that began in 1873 as the entire nation experienced a major economic downturn. This unsettled several industries in the United States, including the lumber market, and caused problems for many families. For Stearns, it was a devastating turn of events; the death of his brother-in-law combined with a nationwide crisis forced him into bankruptcy. To make matters even worse, Justus's mother, Mabel, died in 1875 at the age of fifty-three. This certainly was a low point for Justus's family. The following year Stearns traveled to Ludington to assist his widowed sister-in-law Catherine with the development of the Ward operations. Here he not only found employment but also financial success. Years later, Stearns returned to Conneaut. His mission was to track down those with whom he had contracted debts, just as he had located Grace Bedell to send her a note several decades following her encounter with President Lincoln. Stearns repaid the creditors he found, even though the bankruptcy laws legally freed him from doing so.[24]

Ludington

By the time Justus and Paulina Stearns arrived in 1876, Ludington already had established itself as a thriving lumber town. Located in Mason County, Ludington originally was known as the settlement of Pere Marquette. It was named for the Jesuit missionary and explorer Jacques Marquette, who died at Ludington's Buttersville Peninsula in 1675.[25] The first permanent white settlers arrived in the 1840s, and the region's first sawmill was built on Pere Marquette Lake in

1849, by Hiram Baird of the firm Baird and Bean. It was a rustic mill, and in 1851 Charles Mears established another farther north in a settlement originally named Little Sauble. George Ford purchased Baird and Bean's mill, but by 1859 it was transferred to James Ludington, for whom the town later was renamed. Charles Mears operated James Ludington's mill for two years under contract, during which time he oversaw the construction of a new channel linking Pere Marquette Lake to Lake Michigan. This facilitated access to vast forests of timber along the Pere Marquette River to the east. While the new channel allowed for the eventual expansion of lumbering in the region, Stearns recalled, "none of the early lumbermen could afford to cut timber that was more than a quarter-mile back from the river. The expense of getting it to the water [and mills] was too great."[26] In later years narrow gauge railroads transformed lumbering operations by allowing crews to cut timber anywhere, rather than simply along the banks of large rivers. James Ludington sold his interests in 1869 due to failing health, and his mill was reorganized as the Pere Marquette Lumber Company. By 1873 Ludington boasted as many as eight sawmills that cut over eighty-three million board feet of lumber that year. In addition to the mill operated by the Pere Marquette Lumber Company, other manufacturers included Eber Ward, Danaher and Melendy, George Roby (which later was purchased by Pardee, Cook, and Company), Oliver Taylor, Butters and Peters, and Cartier and Filer.[27]

The vast timber empire established by Eber Ward, who had been married to Paulina Stearns's sister Catherine prior to his death, drew Justus and Paulina to work in Ludington. Ward began purchasing large tracts of timber in Mason County as early as 1852. By 1869 he held at least 70,000 acres of pine-covered land along the Pere Marquette River, which made him the single largest timber baron in Ludington. He also operated two of the largest sawmills on Pere Marquette Lake. His first mill, generally referred to as North Mill, was constructed in 1870 at an estimated cost of $60,000 and had a capacity of 100,000 feet of lumber per day. The operation was large and modern for its time. It even included facilities to fight fires and could operate at night. When Ward's South Mill opened in 1872 it was considered "the model mill of Michigan at that time." It was even larger than the North Mill (the main building was 56 x 160 feet as compared to the North Mill, which was 50 x 130 feet) and cost an estimated $125,000. It too was built using the latest technologies. Ward also served as the president of the Flint and Pere Marquette Railway, which then was under construction. He ensured the railroad would terminate in Ludington, which it did in 1874, further demonstrating his influence on the city's development. Chicago had a tremendous demand for lumber, particularly following the Great Fire of

Justus relocated to Ludington in 1876, when he was in his thirties, about the time this photo was taken. (Courtesy of Dale Peterson)

1871 and the subsequent reconstruction of so many buildings in the city that had been destroyed. Over the years the Ward operations developed a unique method to ensure their lumber would be delivered efficiently. The company owned three enormous scows, which were loaded with lumber and towed to Chicago. At peak capacity, the goal was always to have one unloading in Chicago, another loading in Ludington, with the third on its way to or from Chicago. Each scow had the capacity to carry 700,000 feet of lumber.[28]

When Stearns arrived to work for the Ward estate, he was thirty-one years old. Initially, he served as a clerk in the company supply store. As he described it, "I came here in 1876, bringing my wife and baby son, to work for my sister-in-law, Mrs. Ward, at a salary of $75.00 a month, my wife doing her own house work and we paying $6.00 a month rental for our home."[29] They lived as boarders at the Elliott House, located in Ludington's Fourth Ward neighborhood on the 600 block of South James Street. This would be the future site of a planing mill Stearns would own. The salary of $75 per month was quite modest. While his in-laws helped Justus and Paulina to regain their financial stability, they were provided no additional favors. Stearns would have to prove his worth before he advanced in the family business. Their income did not allow for a life of luxury, but Justus, Paulina, and young Robert enjoyed their new surroundings. These were remembered as carefree, happy days, which ensured their continued residence in Ludington.[30]

Following the death of Eber Ward in 1875, his Ludington mills were operated by John S. Woodruff, who served as agent for the estate. Due to the death of her husband and the tough economic situation following the Panic of 1873, Ward's widow, Mrs. Catherine Ward, initially considered selling the large tracts of timber and two sawmills that produced fifty million feet of lumber each year. The majority of lumber was shipped to warehouses in Chicago and Milwaukee, but the price was so low from 1874 to 1877 they routinely operated at a loss or barely broke even. She was willing to sell the holdings for $250,000 and was concerned she could lose everything when no one was willing or able to purchase the business. Stearns later recalled,

> Times were so hard and banks had so little money to loan we had to get trusted from merchants in Chicago and Milwaukee for supplies to carry us through the winter months. In this way we were able to cut our timber, load it on sleighs and get it into the streams. There were no railroads then through the northern part of the peninsula. We could pay no money to our help for services they rendered. All were paid from merchandise at our store for which we had gotten trusted at Chicago. If our men had to have money they took an order payable on the first of the following June. Many of these were discounted by the banks at 25 per cent. for four to six months' use of the money.[31]

At the time, average pay for a ten-hour day was 90 cents for men working in the mills; however, by 1879 the nation's economy began to recover and the price of lumber increased. This made the operations much more profitable, and the company was able to increase compensation for workers to $1.25 a day. By 1878 Ward's estate had been settled and the Ludington operations were reorganized under the control of Catherine Lyon Ward, John B. Lyon (Catherine's half-brother), and her other brother Thomas R. Lyon. T. R. Lyon, as he was most often known, became the managing agent for the business when he was only twenty-four years old. With the continued increase in the price of lumber, Stearns later estimated Mrs. Ward eventually earned "profits over $6,000,000.00 from what she had offered to sell for $250,000.00."[32]

Conditions improved for Justus at the same time the company was reorganized, and his actions merited attention. Not long after he was hired, he worked with five or six men loading supplies for a lumber camp. He reorganized their duties and eliminated redundancies in such a way that he, with the help of just one man, was able to complete the required work just as efficiently as the group of men had before. His leadership skills, helped undoubtedly by his family connections, earned him a promotion in 1878 from clerk to cashier in the main office of the lumber firm. This put him into daily contact with the likes of Lucius K. Baker, John S. Woodruff, and his brother-in-law, T. R. Lyon. Baker operated as the head clerk at the company's store, and about twenty-five years later would serve as a pallbearer at the funeral of Paulina Stearns. Following its reorganization, Woodruff remained with the firm as supervisor of mills, vessels, and stores. T. R. Lyon oversaw the entire operation. Stearns's promotion coincided with his increased involvement in the region's lumbering industry. For example, he circulated a petition that asked Congress to increase its appropriations for Ludington's harbor, and in February 1879 Stearns was elected to the board of directors of the Pere Marquette Boom Company. As a member of the board he was required at times to leave town and conduct business in Lansing.[33]

The Pere Marquette Boom Company was organized in 1872 and ensured cut timber reached mills properly. Trees were felled along the shores of the Pere Marquette River in the winter. They then were cut into logs about sixteen feet in length; a brand was applied to each log that signified ownership. Following the spring thaw, logs were floated downstream to booms and then placed into large rafts as they continued their journey down the river toward the mills on Pere Marquette Lake. They would then be sorted, and each company's logs were put into booms that were towed to each owner's mill. At times, the huge quantities of lumber in the river created tremendous logjams. Longtime resident Dell Reed remembered observing "log jams from Scottville to Ludington" along the Pere Marquette River, a distance of about eight miles. The company played a large role in the region's early harvest of pine, as these logs easily floated in the water. In later years, when companies began to harvest hardwoods that would not float, railroads, rather than rivers, provided the primary means to transport logs from the forests to sawmills.[34]

By the late 1870s Justus Stearns emerged as an active member of the lumbering community in Mason County. He also was ambitious and became determined to embark on his own. He did so in 1880, at the age of thirty-five, when he established his own lumbering operation about thirty miles east of Ludington at a settlement commonly referred to as Stearns Siding.

Stearns Siding

Stearns Siding demonstrated the first of Justus Stearns's independent business endeavors after he partially severed his connections with the Ward operations.

In 1880, at the age of thirty-five, Justus established the lumber town of Stearns Siding, located in Lake County, Michigan. (Courtesy of Bruce and Cindy Bosley)

With the help of Catherine Ward, who advanced him some money and credit, he built a sawmill and secured a tract of pineland in Lake County, near its border with Mason County, just east of Branch. Several considerations must have been going through his mind as he established Stearns Siding. Only five years earlier he had been forced into bankruptcy, and in the past his father had made poor investments; however, he became determined to make it on his own. As construction on the mill began in the spring of 1880, the *Mason County Record* was careful to note its progress. In April, the paper reported, "J. S. Stearns' mill situation near Reno in Lake County is progressing." Three weeks later, it announced, "Stearns will have his mill in readiness to cut lumber on trial to-morrow. Next week the mill will get down to business."[35] When it was complete, his mill was capable of cutting 35,000 feet of lumber per day, and he initially employed about thirty men. By June, Stearns was ready to ship finished lumber to Ludington. His first mill was located about two miles from the Flint and Pere Marquette railroad, where it operated about two years. Once the lumber was cut, horse and mule teams hauled it by means of the "big wheels" that were placed on wooden tracks laid along the route from the site of the mill to the railroad. After two years at the original site, the mill was moved to a location along the tracks of the Pere Marquette Railroad to facilitate the transportation of finished lumber to market. At this time the settlement came to be known as Stearns Siding because the mill was placed just to the "side" of the railroad. While the village may have been known by most as Stearns Siding, its official name was Bennett. It was named for D. W. Bennett who served as postmaster and station agent for many years.[36]

From a modest start, Stearns's operations in Lake County grew. He expanded the mill site and continued to purchase standing pine and hardwood whenever he was able. Before long, Stearns Siding included "a sawmill, planing mill, box factory, store, post office, cook shanty [and] houses serving the dwellings of the families of lumberjacks."[37] At its height, Stearns Siding was a thriving village with as many as 2,700 inhabitants. His increased business activity in Lake County prompted Stearns to first lease, and then purchase, a store located in between Ludington and Stearns Siding, in the city of Scottville. Stearns's partner in the endeavor was J. N. Mack, and in 1882 they opened a general store to supply lumber camps and settlers in the area. Their business was named Stearns and Mack, which operated until Stearns sold his interest to Mack in 1900. Stearns Siding also was where another partnership began for Stearns; this one involved Wilmer (W. T.) Culver and lasted several decades. Culver and his wife Sarah moved to the settlement in its early years, and for months they made up one of its only English-speaking families. W. T. Culver worked in a variety of capacities in the village, but eventually became Stearns's vice president in numerous business enterprises. Things must have been going well for Stearns, as in 1882, just six years after relocating to Ludington, he began construction of what was described as an "elegant residence" in the city's Fourth Ward neighborhood on South Washington Avenue. That same winter, he traveled to Europe with his wife and brother-in-law, T. R. Lyon.[38]

Stearns even overcame adversity when a fire in 1882 destroyed his mill not long after the move to its new location. The fire started on a pleasant day in which Sarah Culver had been working on a variety of tasks. She had just been given some fresh venison and hoped to use it in a mincemeat pie. The meat had been carefully cooked over a large kettle for much of the day and was set aside to cool. She also had baked several loaves of bread when the fire was discovered. It quickly began to spread. Before long, "It fanned into flames, [and] soon became a roaring conflagration, threatening mill houses, lumber yards and timberland; all of the men of the camp turned out to fight the fire. They fought valiantly for many hours and the women carried refreshments to them as they fought, first one and then another stopping just long enough to eat a hasty bite. The pot of venison and the newly-made bread all went into sandwiches for the fire-fighters that night and the mincemeat never was made."[39] Once again faced with potential disaster, Stearns would not be discouraged, and he worked quickly to build another mill. Stearns Siding remained the base of Stearns's operations in Michigan until he purchased T. R. Lyon's holdings in Ludington in 1898.

A strong sense of community developed at Stearns Siding, as seen in the reaction to the 1882 fire. As one resident described it, "We were all happy out at Stearns Siding, or so it seemed back to that time. I don't remember anything we did to make such good times as we seem to have had, but we were young then, everything was new and novel and the youth and the novelty cast a glamour over everything we did."[40] This comment may have been clouded by a bit of nostalgia, but events from that era also demonstrated the sense of togetherness. In addition to the fire, another example of the community's spirit was shown by its reaction to the disappearance of a young boy. He was only seven years old when his mother raised the alarm he was missing. The entire village joined the search for the youngster. The mill even shut down. Later it was found the "little scamp" had boarded a train and traveled all the way across the state from Stearns Siding to Saginaw from where he was sent home. Another factor that created the unique bond in Stearns Siding was the presence of so many families. One resident recalled there were men who "would put up cabins and bring their families in. They were allowed $10 dollars a month extra for boarding themselves. Some of these women would do the men's washing for $1 dollar a month." The legacy of these cabins still could be seen decades later; a large clearing remained where the residences had been located along the north side of the railroad tracks. Several "basement holes" identified the location of what must have been the cabins described above.[41]

Justus Stearns's operations at Stearns Siding provided employment opportunities for many recent immigrants to the United States. A large number were from Sweden, while several others hailed from Norway; English became a second language for numerous inhabitants. An example of one such immigrant was Matt Stevensen, who arrived from Norway in 1888. For years Stevensen engaged in correspondence with Ingeborg Clomen, who continued to reside in Norway, as he tried to convince her to move to Michigan and hinted that she might become his bride. He complained that in the United States, "I cannot find anyone, here no one will have me. I am waiting for someone to come and propose to me, but I may have to wait a long time." She described herself as the "most simple girl" in town. He replied, "we have no use for the word 'simple' because we are equal" in the United States. After a long-distance courtship of eight years, and numerous letters, Stevensen purchased Ingeborg a ticket. He then was required to "wait longingly" for his "dearest girlfriend" while she made the trip across the

Matt and Ingeborg (Clomen) Stevensen were immigrants from Norway who settled in Stearns Siding. They are shown here with their four children. (Courtesy of Bruce and Cindy Bosley)

Atlantic Ocean. She arrived at Stearns Siding safely in the summer of 1896. The two were married July 8, 1896, raised four children, and lived in the area for the remainder of their lives.[42]

As early as 1882 the settlement included a school. One of the first teachers was Miss Louisa Sanger. She taught at Stearns Siding for at least two years, and her evaluations described her as an excellent teacher who managed the children well. Another teacher was Victor Vestling, the son of a popular pastor at a Swedish Lutheran Church in Ludington. The first child born in the village was Robert Ekstrom. At the age of five he was excited for the first day of school, yet he went home crying that afternoon because there was no seat for him. His parents promised to provide a chair from home in the future. Overall, the presence of a school seemed to demonstrate an investment in the community's future. In later years, residents recalled that Sunday school lessons were regularly held in the schoolhouse.[43]

Numerous employees were able to earn good wages working for Justus Stearns at Stearns Siding. C. C. Peck was an experienced sorter who traveled to Baldwin by rail and then to Stearns Siding by foot. In a letter to his mother, he wrote,

"We then walked six miles in to Bennett. We was tired when we reached here. We started from Baldwin at ten minutes to four and reached here at fifteen to six."[44] He approached the foreman at the mill in the afternoon and was happy to report to his mother, "I've got a job, the same one I had at Wyman's assorting. I guess I'll get one dollar and a quarter a day." He paid $3 a month in board and was glad to have the food; he continued, "Gosh, but the chuck is great. Milk three times a day."[45]

Stearns employed Stephen Darke for many years. His father had worked in the mills at the old lumber town of Lincoln. Darke remembered his father walking home on Saturday nights carrying a twenty-pound sack of flour and other groceries. At an early age his father "taught him how to cut, skid, and haul logs."[46] He started working for pay when he was fourteen years old, earning 50 cents a day. When he was sixteen, he worked for a father and son who had contracted to cut lumber for Stearns. That winter they cut a lot of cedar, which was used to pave the streets in Ludington. In later years he worked cutting logs for a Stearns camp near Ford Lake, which he described as "some of the best pine I ever saw." The following winter he worked for Stearns again, under Tom Conklin, who served as foreman. He discovered several changes when he arrived at camp, which had been moved close to a different lake. This must have been a large undertaking for Stearns's employees because the new camp "consisted of an Office where you could get anything from a needle to a bottle of pain killer, a Cook Shanty, a Teamster Shanty, a Men's Shanty, a Blacksmith Shop and the Horse Barn which was big enough to hold 3 or 4 car loads of hay and several hundred bushel of oats." Darke lived into his eighties and looked back on his experiences with fond memories. He also remembered the lyrics to a song they used to sing:

> Their a merry set of fellows
> So merry and so fine
> Who've left their home and dear ones
> To work among the pine.
>
> The Doctor and the Lawyer
> Likewise mechanic to
> For it takes alsorts of tradesmen
> To form a Lumbering crew.[47]

James Miller was born in Denmark in 1865 and came to the United States in 1889. He arrived at Stearns Siding in 1890 looking for work. He held a variety of positions: he cut trees in the woods, worked as a sorter on the rivers, and even spent time in the mills. He remembered camp life as being lively at night. Only men were allowed in the camp where they cut trees all day long. But things could become active at night, as there was music, dancing, and a lot of card playing. His logging camp was located in Carr Settlement where Bill Murphy was foreman. One night John McDonald, the cook, called them in to eat where the table was set. They ate until smoke was noticed in the woods to the south. They tried to put out the fire, but high winds made it impossible to stop. The men hurried back to create a burn zone and save their camp. The smoke was so intense they could not see one another even though only ten feet separated them. He described it as "a beautiful fire display at night, but very destructive to see those flames up in the tops of those tall pines."[48] It demonstrated the precarious nature of the lumber industry; fire could destroy months of work and investment in a moment. Businessmen like Stearns undertook great risks when they invested in lumbering operations like those at Stearns Siding.

Of course, not all operations proceeded as planned at every step. In 1888 Justus found himself a defendant in a lawsuit brought by John Danaher. The basis of Danaher's suit involved a set of pine logs he apparently had lost in December 1887. Initially, Danaher had cut some pine (about twenty thousand feet valued at about $100) in Pleasant Plains Township, located in Lake County. By late February the next year Danaher discovered Stearns was in possession of this timber. According to court documents, Danaher requested that Stearns return the property to him, but Stearns refused. In a letter to Danaher, Stearns responded to a threatened lawsuit by writing, "All I have to say is go ahead with your suit."[49] Danaher accepted the challenge and pursued his lawsuit.

The justice of the peace of Lake County, Edgar Campbell, presided over the case. A hearing was held on September 6, 1888, in Pleasant Plains Township. Danaher and his attorney were present, but Stearns failed to appear; he also did not enter a plea. Campbell rendered his judgment five days later on September 11 and issued a ruling in favor of Danaher. Stearns was ordered to pay Danaher $96.50 in damages and $2.90 for costs. Stearns filed paperwork to appeal the decision, but there is no record he ever went forward with the appeal.[50]

Stearns's final actions in this case remain unclear because the written records end at this point, but it is possible to draw some conclusions. It is likely that Stearns did not appear at the trial because he was liable for the charges leveled against him, or maybe he just decided not to bother with a $100 lawsuit. Danaher originally was in possession of the cut logs in the woods of Lake County December 31, 1887, and lost them. This probably was due to conditions in the forest. It was the middle of the winter and the weather could have prevented him from knowing exactly where the pine was located after it was cut. By February it had found its way to Stearns's possession. When Danaher discovered Stearns had the timber, he tried to claim ownership, but initially Stearns ignored him. Stearns later may have tried to intimidate Danaher into dropping the issue altogether by challenging him simply to "go ahead" with the lawsuit. After all, he was the largest lumberman in the immediate area, founder of Stearns Siding, and the value of the logs in the dispute was only about $100. But when the case came to trial, Stearns did not continue to contest the charges. A controversy like this over timber cut in the woods was not uncommon; lumber companies were known to steal logs and timber from one another. However, an investigation into the court records of the state of Michigan demonstrates this type of charge filed against Stearns for misappropriating logs cut by others was unique. Instead, maybe the Danaher case shows that at this time in his career Stearns, like many others in timber communities, was willing to take risks when it came to the "discovery" of another lumberman's logs. To put the dispute behind him, although it was more likely that his employees rather than Justus himself who stole the logs, he likely paid what was required and moved on, because the employees had been working on his behalf.[51]

For about twenty years Stearns Siding was a thriving community. By the mid-1890s, Stearns's mills produced about twenty-five to thirty million feet of lumber each year and employed an average of two hundred to three hundred men, depending upon the season. His payroll for the winter of 1895/96 reached about $7,000 per month; however, by the late 1890s much of the forested area he controlled in Lake County had been cut. In 1898, at the age of fifty-three, Stearns moved his base of operations to Ludington when he jumped at the opportunity to acquire a large mill and access to additional timberland by buying out his brother-in-law T. R. Lyon. Stearns's enterprises were successful because he demonstrated an ability to adapt and incorporate new technologies into his business methods. He began by using the traditional technique of transporting logs by river. Over time he made use of railroads to service the lumber camps; by the early 1900s he would transport logs over one hundred miles from Kalkaska to his mill in Ludington via rail. After Stearns moved his operations to Ludington, the population of Stearns Siding dwindled. A fire then destroyed what remained of the settlement on October 31, 1899, and Stearns Siding became a ghost town.[52]

Conclusion

Stearns's first attempt to strike out on his own was a huge success. By the 1890s, he had come a long way from his childhood on a farm in New York. The early years with his father served as an apprenticeship that offered quite an education. His marriage to Paulina Lyon, and subsequent dealings with T. R. Lyon and the Ward estate, helped him get started, and he would maintain close business connections with family members for years. Through his vision and guidance, a strong sense of community was established at Stearns Siding, just as he had shown a deep level of concern for Grace Bedell when he acknowledged her encounter with Abraham Lincoln. He also exhibited determination and leadership by establishing himself as a successful captain of industry in his own right, overcoming such adversities as his bankruptcy and the 1882 fire that destroyed his mill. He would build upon these successes throughout the 1890s and subsequent years as he later expanded his lumbering operations beyond Stearns Siding to other parts of Michigan and even into Wisconsin, Kentucky, Florida, and Washington State.

2

Booms, Busts, and a Benefactor for Ludington

But by far the most interesting word that has yet to come to the people of the Fourth ward and of the entire city, was the news that the T. R. Lyon plant had been purchased by Mr. J. S. Stearns. It was already a forgone conclusion that this plant, giving employment to a very large number of men and being perhaps the largest single institution in the city, must close its doors within a year or two and join the steadily increasing van of departing millmen. . . . With the change of ownership comes a new hope. . . . Our city will take on new life and there will be fresh hope for the future.

"Encouraging Prospects," *Ludington Appeal*, 1898

It was when the fighting spirit of the town was at its lowest ebb that The Stearns Salt & Lumber Company began operations. Its influence began at once to be felt. Ludington rose, like the Phoenix, from the ashes of despair and today, it is one of the prettiest and most prosperous cities in the state.

"The Influences That Made Ludington Come Back," *Michigan Manufacturer and Financial Record*, 1915

Justus and Paulina Stearns arrived in Michigan in the 1870s, just after they had been forced into bankruptcy. They relocated because they needed to connect with family to bring about their financial recovery. As previously seen, beginning in 1880 Stearns successfully established his own lumbering operations east of Ludington at the town called Stearns Siding; however, the couple continued to maintain their residence in the city of Ludington, close to a network of family and friends. This chapter will demonstrate how Stearns maintained close ties with his family and the social interaction he and Paulina had with others in the Ludington community, as he expanded his lumber operations in that city. His hometown of Ludington faced economic difficulties, particularly in the decade of the 1890s, as many lumber manufacturers left the region for larger tracts of untouched forests. Community leaders sought a benefactor to invest in the city

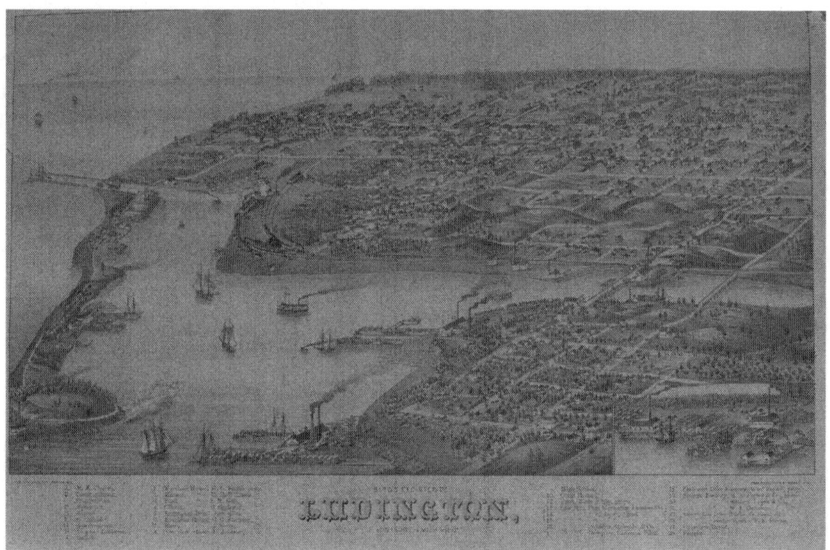

This map identifies key landmarks in the city of Ludington in 1880, about the time Justus and Paulina arrived to live there. (Archives of the Mason County Historical Society)

and lead it into the new century. Stearns stepped forward in 1898 to become the city's patron when he purchased the Ward interests from T. R. Lyon and transferred his business operations from Stearns Siding to Ludington. These actions sparked an economic revival for the city, and by 1899 Stearns became the leading manufacturer of lumber in the state of Michigan. Very soon afterward, Stearns expanded his business investments into additional industries, a practice that would typify his actions for the remainder of his life. With his continued success, Stearns began to contribute to many causes in the community where he lived, foreshadowing his extensive philanthropy in later years. Just as the city of Ludington overcame obstacles and matured in this era, the same would be true for the man who came to be considered the city's greatest benefactor.

Ludington

Ludington may have been recognized as a thriving lumber town when Stearns first arrived, but by the 1880s, many aspects of the city continued to remain unrefined. In the early years of the decade, cows wandered the streets, and yards surrounding homes often contained numerous outbuildings, barns, chicken coops, and outhouses. In some areas, pigsties could be seen. Crews graded county roads and covered them with logs in wet areas to ease transportation, but attempts also were made to pave streets within the city; as early as 1887 Ludington Avenue had a stretch of about 1.5 miles of paved surface. The city's business center could be found at the intersection of Ludington Avenue and James Street where several shops served customers' needs. Some boasted lanterns to attract evening patrons, and much of James Street was lined with plank sidewalks. The town's sandy beaches reflected the importance of lumbering to the local economy as butts of logs, wooden planks, and other refuse floated from booms near the mills and into Lake Michigan, littering the shoreline. The cold, long winters slowed down, or brought to a close, much of the city's activity. The mills shut down while men entered the forests to cut new timber, taking advantage of a snow-covered landscape that facilitated the skidding of logs. Waterways froze, which made transportation of goods difficult, if not impossible; however, one industry continued throughout the winter months. Gangs of workers cut large blocks of ice, which were then transported to warehouses and packed in sawdust. The ice remained frozen and was delivered to residents' homes year-round.[1]

Two tragedies engulfed Ludington in 1881. For several months schools were closed as diphtheria raged through the city. It struck the rich and poor alike and was particularly devastating to children. The epidemic began in the winter when the ground was frozen, so a final burial for many had to wait until spring. In early June of 1881, the *Ludington Record* reported that as many as forty children were suffering from the disease at that time while the number of fatalities averaged "about one death per day." Families hit by the disease were quarantined and yellow flags identified the homes in which residents were infected. Doors draped in black streamers signified a family member had been lost. The June 16 edition of the *Ludington Record* noted the "deep sympathy in the community" for two families. The first was headed by Mr. and Mrs. William Allen, parents of Sarah, who was lost just one month shy of her fourth birthday. The second were members of the Loomis family who were tortured by the deaths of two sons in what the newspaper described as one of the "saddest cases" yet seen. Wallace, age three, died on a Sunday morning following a short, but severe, illness. The next day their oldest son Guy died at the age of nine after suffering for several weeks.[2]

As if residents of Ludington had not endured enough, the same edition of the newspaper described the aftermath of the most destructive fire ever to visit Ludington, on June 11, 1881. The Burr Robbins and Colvin Circus was in town that Saturday when the fire broke out near a bakery on West Loomis Street. It was discovered shortly before noon and the alarm was immediately given; however, many of the firefighters were watching the circus parade through town, so it took a few minutes to place their hand-drawn fire engine into position. Within minutes two structures were in flames, but it appeared the fire would be confined to this small area until one of the fire hoses broke. Before it could be repaired, a strong wind fanned the flames and the fire began to spread. In the space of the next few hours, nearly one hundred buildings were either damaged or destroyed, amounting to a property loss of about $200,000. The devastation was apparent the next day, as detailed in the *Ludington Record.*

> Every vacant lot in the vicinity of the fire for blocks around, was covered with remnants of some mercantile stock, or the household furniture of some unfortunate. Wearing apparel and cooking utensils were scattered in confusion, and groups of men, women, and children, who had been driven from their homes by the fire demon were guarding what little effects they had saved from their late homes. The walls of burned buildings were adding their might to the din of confusion, as one after another gave way and tumbled to the ground with a crash.[3]

The day following the fire, a meeting was held to discuss the city's future. Community members unanimously supported the reconstruction of the city, and "there wasn't a doomsayer among them."[4] Insurance adjusters arrived soon after the fire and policyholders received payouts within days. One of the first structures to be rebuilt was a saloon owned by John Fanon; the cost was about $3,000. Construction continued at a furious pace and, according to some observers, within six months the city looked better than it did prior to the fire.[5]

Luckily, the Stearns family emerged from the twin tragedies unscathed. As diphtheria and fire threatened Ludington in 1881, Justus, Paulina, and their nine-year-old son Robert L. Stearns were living in a section of town known as the Fourth Ward, where they established important social and business connections with family and friends. Ludington's Fourth Ward was located several blocks south of Ludington Avenue near Pere Marquette Lake. It contained the area near many sawmills, including those previously operated by Eber Ward. When Ludington originally was settled, numerous Scandinavian families lived in the area, which made it easy for them to work in the nearby mills. By the 1880s and 1890s the Fourth Ward boasted many Polish immigrants and included retail outlets, doctor and attorney offices, and a bank. One of the more important stores was the Double Brick Store located just south of the Washington Avenue Bridge; Stearns later would purchase the store.[6]

Justus Stearns was not the only individual closely tied to the Ward interests who lived in the Fourth Ward. One of the nicest homes was owned by John S.

The home of Justus and Paulina Stearns was built in 1881. Beginning in 1907, the building served as the region's first hospital. (Courtesy of David K. Petersen)

Woodruff, who moved to Ludington in 1871 to work in the lumber industry and successfully managed Eber Ward's operations for many years. His home was the site of numerous social events and later was moved to another location where the new owners transformed it into a funeral home. Lucius K. Baker was another Fourth Ward resident. Baker originally was from Ohio and followed Justus to Ludington to work for the Ward interests. In 1880 he worked as a clerk for Ward, which was similar to a position he previously held in Ohio. In a technical error, he was "double counted" in the 1880 census; he was listed as living in Ashtabula County, Ohio, and Mason County, Michigan, at the same time. By 1883 he was able to build his own spacious home just off Washington Avenue; he lived there with his family until he moved to Wisconsin to oversee Stearns's lumbering activities on Wisconsin's Bad River Reservation. Prior to his departure, Baker was involved actively with the local Republican Party, along with Stearns, in the 1880s and 1890s. Baker even served as Ludington's mayor in 1892. Even though he moved to Wisconsin, Baker maintained close ties to the Stearns family over the years and eventually would serve as a pallbearer at Paulina's funeral. He later was buried near Justus and Paulina Stearns in Ludington's Lakeview Cemetery.[7]

The brother of Paulina Stearns, T. R. Lyon, also lived in the Fourth Ward. Lyon had succeeded Woodruff as manager of the Ward businesses in the late 1870s and built an impressive two-story brick home on South Washington Avenue in 1881 at a cost of about $8,000. Shortly after Lyon completed his new home, Justus began construction of what was described as an "elegant residence" at an estimated cost of $6,000. His new residence also was located on South

Washington Avenue. It was no accident that Stearns would build his home in the Fourth Ward. In fact, in what could be seen as the importance he placed on his family connections, he lived next door to his brother-in-law T. R. Lyon for several years. Census records from 1880 listed Lyon's occupation as "Sawmill Proprietor" and showed there were four additional individuals living under his roof. These included his wife Hattie, his one-year-old daughter Emily, and two young women who worked as domestic servants. The same census identified Justus Stearns as a "Mill Owner" while Paulina was listed as "Keeping house," and young Robert was "at school." Census records do not indicate there were domestic servants living in the Stearns household at that time, demonstrating that while Stearns may have lived next door to his brother-in-law, he had yet to reach the same standard of living as others in his family.[8]

Justus and Paulina Stearns appeared to ease into their new community soon after their arrival. In September 1878 Justus became a charter member in Ludington's chapter of Royal Arcanum, one of the oldest fraternal organizations in North America. The group provided life insurance for members and was dedicated to community service and the protection of widows, orphans, and other dependents. Other members included several leading lumbermen such as Horace Butters, Antoine E. Cartier, and John S. Woodruff. Justus also became an active member in the local Republican Party and served as county chairman. Stearns's involvement in the party would continue for the remainder of his life.[9]

Paulina became a member of the Women's Christian Temperance Union (WCTU), which was one of the largest and most powerful women's organizations in the country. The WCTU fought alcohol abuse nationwide and boasted as many as 150,000 members in the late nineteenth century (Ludington's chapter was first organized in 1877). Paulina was elected second vice president of the local chapter in 1880 and participated in a concert to raise funds for the group in May of that year. The WCTU was very active in the community and constructed a temperance hall that accommodated many public events and even held a reading room; however, the building was destroyed in the great fire of 1881. The organization's efforts to fight alcohol abuse and drunkenness were partially successful in town; some of the city's saloons closed down shortly after it was formed. The WCTU also promoted women's suffrage. Susan B. Anthony visited in March 1879 and Elizabeth Cady Stanton followed in 1880. Each spoke passionately and helped to raise awareness of women's issues and raise funds for the local chapter. A letter to the editor sponsored by the WCTU in the *Ludington Record* from 1883 urged Ludington's women to support public education and the right to vote in their community. It is probable that the involvement of Justus and

Paulina in these civic organizations demonstrates the close relationship they had with the Woodruffs. John Woodruff was a member of the Republican Party and likely drafted Justus to join Royal Arcanum while his wife Helen was the founding president of Ludington's Women's Christian Temperance Union. Through personal relationships such as these Justus and Paulina developed a network of social and business contacts once they arrived in Ludington.[10]

Additional examples demonstrate the involvement of the Stearns family in Ludington's social scene. In November 1886 the *Ludington Record* noted Paulina celebrated her "birthday anniversary" in a special way with several friends and family, while at a later date Justus and Paulina were treated to a surprise party. About thirty friends surprised the couple at their own home, which led to an evening of social games. Everyone had a good time and prizes were awarded. Paulina won a bundle of red peppers and was named, "smarty come to the party." On another occasion Paulina entertained several members of her women's group, Boyssen Circle, at the Stearns home. For entertainment, each guest was given a list of twenty conundrums followed by a guessing contest. After the contest was complete, cake and ice cream were served. When the guests left that evening at 11:00 p.m., they commented on how pleasant the evening had been. By the early 1900s the social circle Justus and Paulina inhabited had extended to include Grand Rapids. For example, in 1902 the *Grand Rapids Press* reported that on successive afternoons, luncheons were held in honor of Paulina with numerous guests in attendance, while one hostess adorned tables with pink roses.[11]

Ludington's residents, and the Stearnses, entertained themselves in other pursuits as well. Progressive euchre struck the city in the mid-1880s. The game involved an evening with several couples playing at individual tables. The winners at each table moved to the higher table while the losing couple was relegated to the "booby" table, where they attempted to work their way up again. The pair who earned the most points for the evening won first prize. The couple spending the most time at the booby table was made the butt of the evening's jokes.[12]

The circus sometimes made a visit to town, but so too did traveling minstrel shows and groups of actors who staged Shakespeare's plays. In some cases the traveling troupes remained in town for one or two weeks and staged a different show each evening. Beginning in 1884 individuals interested in roller-skating could skate at the Ludington Roller Skating Park. When the arena opened in June of that year a Mr. Howard Bradley of Reed City put on an exhibit of "fancy skating." Other entertainments were offered at the facility, which could seat up to one thousand for special events or four hundred during a skating exhibition. On special occasions such as New Year's Day families often visited one another.

Women interested in "Receiving" guests would announce their intentions in the newspaper and the hours they would be "At Home." Refreshments often were served while men drove in sleighs from house to house leaving "Happy New Year" cards. The Fourth of July was another special occasion. An advertisement in the *Ludington Record* in early July 1885 for Sherman Bros. boasted they carried "the most complete stock of FIREWORKS in the city." Their inventory of goods included numerous "Flags, Firecrackers, Skyrockets, Roman Candles, Torpedoes, Colored Lights, Etc."[13] Shortly after the Fourth of July celebrations were complete that year, the newspaper reported on the festivities. Several races were staged. The first was a foot race, which Charley Wheeler won. Local firefighters next ran a "hose race," and the Fourth Ward Company emerged victorious. A yacht race to Lincoln and back completed the day's races. The primary entertainment during the afternoon was an exhibition given by the local life-saving crew in which the members capsized a lifeboat and demonstrated its self-righting capabilities. That evening the city swarmed with people eager to observe Ludington's display of fireworks. The show was described as, "a good one," and the city's residents had "a great time of it" celebrating the nation's birthday.[14]

Family and Travel

Undoubtedly, the Stearns family participated in many of these popular amusements common in Ludington; however, they also spent a great deal of time with members of their immediate family. A sample of the Ludington newspapers in the 1880s demonstrates that family interaction and travel was quite extensive. On September 2, 1880, the *Ludington Record* reported the return of Paulina Stearns from Conneaut, Ohio, from what must have been a visit to see her mother. About five weeks later the paper noted Paulina was planning a trip to Europe with her brother T. R. Lyon and two nieces. Their plan was to take the White Star Line to Liverpool and then spend much of the winter in Naples. Justus did not accompany her on this voyage as it was early on in the establishment of Stearns Siding. T. R. Lyon returned in December, but Paulina did not return until the following June. The next winter Justus went on a month-long European excursion with his brother-in-law T. R. Lyon and local lumberman George Roby. Their itinerary called for the trio to tour the principle cities of several European countries while abroad. On his way back to Michigan, he met Paulina, who had been visiting her mother in Conneaut. The couple returned home together that April. Mrs. Clarissa Lyon, Paulina's mother, spent Christmas in Ludington in both 1882 and 1884. The February 9 edition of the paper in 1888 indicated Paulina was planning another European trip with her brother, his wife, and her niece. It is likely these trips took place in the winter so as to avoid the bitter cold that shut down much of the city's activity. Additional visits with family involved several trips to and from Ohio, and excursions to Massachusetts and to Yellowstone National Park. These vacations also were indicative of the prosperity Stearns and members of his family experienced as early as the 1880s. Most American families in this era could not afford an extended vacation anywhere, much less in Europe, because they could not get away from work or a farm, and such trips were far too expensive. Nonetheless, Stearns family members embarked on multiple cross-Atlantic tours on what appeared to be a regular basis. The travel also invariably involved several family members; Paulina, Justus, or T. R. Lyon did not make these trips alone. A final trip of note involved sixteen-year-old Robert L. Stearns, who embarked on a European tour in June 1888 with his cousin Eber B. Ward. The two visited Rome, Paris, and the Swiss Alps before setting sail for home aboard the steamer *Alaska* in August 1888. This must have been an outstanding education, and adventure, for a young man coming of age in this era.[15]

Robert L. Stearns eventually would become his father's important business partner, but not before he first sought a career as an artist. Robert began his early education in a one-room country schoolhouse and then attended schools in the city of Ludington. His first job was tallying lumber in his father's lumber mill at Stearns Siding, just as Justus Stearns had done during his formative years in his own father's mill. After graduating from high school in 1889, Robert traveled to New York City where he studied at the Art Students League. While living in the city, he made several long-lasting friendships, including one with his studio partner Fletcher Ransom. In later years Ransom would help to complete some of Robert's work. Robert's goal was to become one of the nation's best illustrators, and he enjoyed life in the city's "bohemian" subculture. As he later recalled, "I thought surely that the editors would come battering down my doors to get my stuff. Instead I lived on rusks and water. Oh! Yes, I did sell some stuff to the *Life Magazine* of the day and to *Judge*, even some illustrations for books."[16] The *Ludington Record* recognized Robert's success and noted he was "getting into the front rank of artists in New York." He worked for a New York paper as a special artist and even produced a painting that sold. Paulina Stearns quietly bought back the piece and placed it in his room so he could see it upon his return for Christmas that year.[17]

It is probable that Robert would have embarked on a lifelong career as an illustrator if it had not been for his father. Justus Stearns was not supportive of his son's choice of career, and Robert recalled, "father wasn't sympathetic with would-be artists." Justus pressed his son to change his profession and declared,

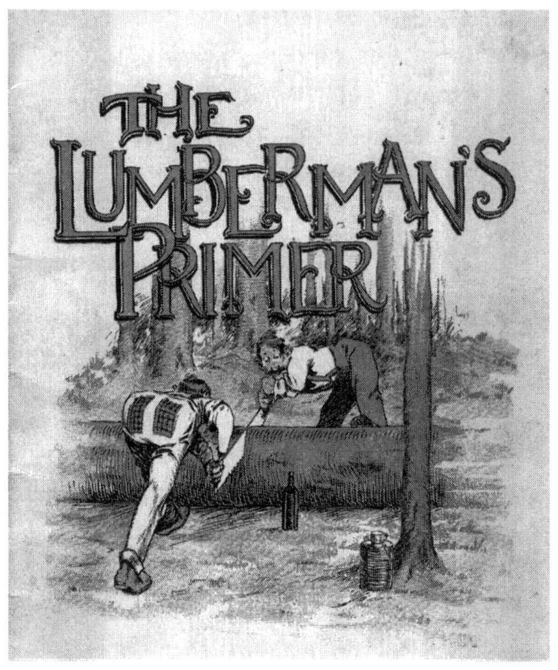

Robert L. Stearns produced the *Lumberman's Primer* as an advertisement of sorts for Stearns's lumber operations. (Courtesy of Robert E. Gable)

"Son, if you're going to inherit my business [lumber and mines] you've got to come home and learn it."[18] Robert returned to Michigan and worked for his father. His business travel led him to spend time in Tennessee, and before long he met and became engaged to Laura Estelle Freeman. The wedding was set to take place the evening of Wednesday, February 2, 1898, in Nashville. Justus left Ludington days prior to the celebration in what he believed to be plenty of time to take part in his son's wedding. While en route to Nashville, a snowstorm hit and the train became stuck in the snow. Stearns walked some distance in the blinding snowstorm, demonstrating "where there's a will there's a way," and made his way to Milwaukee, where he boarded another train bound for Nashville so he could bless the marriage of the young couple.[19]

While Robert's career goal of working as an artist faded as his responsibilities increased in his father's businesses, his passion for art remained an important part of his life. In September 1900 his artwork appeared in the *American Lumberman.* He also authored a series of illustrated works including *The Lumberman's Primer* and *The Coalman's Primer.* He was a noted satirist who loved to make fun of language with phrases like the "President's American" as opposed to the "King's English." Possibly his most unique creation was the character Ossawald

Crumb, a mythological west Michigan lumberjack, similar to Paul Bunyan, whom Robert labeled, "the man with the axe."[20] Just as Bunyan had his Blue Ox named Maude, Ossawald tamed a panther and named it Horace. Crumb was Stearns's "lumberman hero" of Michigan's pioneer era who stood as a symbol of the many individuals who sacrificed so much on the American frontier and influenced the development of the nation. Crumb also was a philosopher who provided Robert L. Stearns with a mouthpiece to present his own commentary on politics and society. A fictional conversation that took place between Crumb and a government agent certainly reflected the author's views as Ossawald railed: "That just shows how little you people in Washington know about the pockets of the people you are trying to govern. Indians don't have pockets—they don't even have pants. And if you people down in Washington don't quit spending the people's money the way you have been doing, the coming generation of good American citizens won't have any pockets either and will lose their pants besides."[21]

When he was not working on his art, Robert was working for his father and raising a family. Life changed considerably for Robert and his wife Laura when their daughter Paulina was born in March 1900. Luckily, the young couple lived right next to (grandma and grandpa) Paulina and Justus Stearns. By 1900 Paulina's brother T. R. Lyon had moved to Chicago, but Robert Stearns continued the tradition of family members living in close proximity to one another. In fact, Robert purchased the home of Lucius K. Baker, who had left Ludington in 1896 and moved to Wisconsin. Census records also indicate the improved economic status of both Stearns families. Twenty years earlier, there had been no servants living in the Stearns household. In 1900 two young women lived with Justus and Paulina who were listed as "servants" in that year's census. They were eighteen and nineteen years old, and each was born in Sweden. Two domestic servants also lived with Robert and Laura; they undoubtedly were a pair of sisters from Denmark.[22]

Changes in Ludington

Members of the Stearns family observed several changes that took place in Ludington in the last two decades of the nineteenth century. Possibly the most dramatic were the establishment of a water system and electricity for residents of the city in the 1880s. The water system was under construction, but not complete, when the fire hit in 1881. Pumping machinery was housed in a brick building located near Lake Michigan on the corner of West Ludington Avenue and Park Street. The intake and sewage disposal pipes were both connected to the channel leading to the lake. The city paid $80 each for forty hydrants placed throughout

Ludington, which brought a level of comfort to residents who had just experienced the devastation of a fire while living in a lumbering community with many homes, roads, and sidewalks constructed of wood. The waterworks later was expanded in 1891 after voters approved borrowing money to allow the city to purchase the Ludington Water Supply Company. Home construction reflected the popularity of new technology as indoor bathrooms replaced outhouses. Local hardware stores had a difficult time keeping tin bathtubs in stock. Even prior to the 1890s, Ludington's aesthetic appearance began to transform, as the *Ludington Record* observed in the spring of 1883. "Grading and sodding of lots in all parts of the city has been carried on for the past two weeks to the great improvement of the city's general appearance. Scores of shade trees have been planted during the same time and will add much in beauty in due time."[23] To protect the newly planted lawns, the city passed an ordinance prohibiting livestock from running loose. Most of the sand hills were cleared and swamps were drained by 1890, thereby reducing the number of mosquitoes and sand flies, which had been a nuisance to local residents for years.[24]

In April 1888, about twelve years following Stearns's arrival, Ludington celebrated the installation of ninety electric streetlights. After the lights were first turned on, a parade, which included the fire department, a marching band, and over one hundred citizens riding in carriages, followed the illuminated route to the wonderment of those in attendance. Local businesses lured patrons with their new lighting, but it took some time for residential customers to accept the new technology. The electric company allowed homeowners the option to test a porch light at the cost of fifty cents a month.[25]

Notwithstanding these civic improvements, Ludington continued to be a city dominated by the timber industry in the 1880s, but salt production also soon was added. It was advantageous for lumber companies to engage in the industry because once a well had been drilled, waste lumber could be used to fuel the evaporation of brine, which then produced salt. Years earlier, salt wells had been drilled successfully in the Saginaw Valley, the state's leading lumber-producing region. The town of Manistee, just thirty miles north of Ludington, began producing salt in 1881. In late 1882, Ludington's Pere Marquette Lumber Company contracted with a company to take charge of the drilling. The actual drilling did not commence until June 1883, as operations were delayed and weather did not permit work to be conducted during the winter. Work started and stopped several times over the next few months, but by October the company was boring for salt "day and night" and had reached a depth of about 330 feet. Throughout 1884 there were numerous troubles as the drilling continued intermittently, which led many residents to be discouraged, but when conditions allowed, crews worked on. By March 26, 1885, the *Ludington Record* described the operations as being "entirely satisfactory" when it was hoped a depth of two thousand feet would be reached later that week. Unfortunately for the promoters, they were required to pay a higher rate for each day's drilling below that depth, but the work continued. Finally, after two years, on May 21, the jubilation felt by many residents was reflected in a news headline that declared, "An Inexhaustible Supply of the Purest Rock-Salt Yet Discovered." By December of that year salt production began in earnest. It would continue to be an important industry in the area for several decades as Justus Stearns, and numerous other Ludington sawmill owners, drilled their own wells and began to manufacture salt along with lumber.[26]

Although Stearns operated his sawmill at Stearns Siding until the late 1890s, he continued to reside in Ludington where lumber production peaked in 1891. In that year, the city's mills collectively manufactured 146 million feet of lumber, and residents prospered. At the time, there were fourteen mills in the Ludington area, including those engaged in the manufacture of lumber, shingles, and lath. The lumbering industry also gave rise to subsidiary businesses manufacturing bowls, baskets, and clothespins. The mills operated six days a week, ten hours a day (prior to 1887 they ran for twelve hours), for eight or nine months out of the year, depending on the weather and the supply of logs. Unskilled workers could earn about $1.00 to $1.50 per day manufacturing salt or lumber, while skilled workers, such as filers (who sharpened the saw blades) and sawyers, might earn $3.00 per day. Bridger "Billie" Kolberg worked in the city's lumber industry, and in many ways his experiences can be seen as typical. At times he was employed in the lumber camps felling trees, but he also worked in town at the mills. He remembered working: "at the Danaher mills, Stearns and Butters mills . . . I always got $1.00 a day at camp with board and 1.75 in the mills on the carriage [the apparatus that carried the log to the saw blade]." Working in the lumber camps was difficult, but he recalled, "one thing we had [was] very good food and plenty of it. In those days even the women helped work in the camps. The men did most of the cooking but the women served it to the many men."[27]

The experiences of Frances Lemire also reflected the work patterns of the lumber industry and how boys could be lured to earn wages at a very young age. Lemire began to work at the age of ten when he was employed at "Danaher's mill tieing lath for fifty cents a day." He continued, "mill work was in the summer. In the winter I went into the woods to saw lumber trees for these mills."[28] Nels Johnson worked for Stearns at several locations, including Stearns Siding, Ludington, and Wisconsin. He also worked in lumber camps and the mills for several other

This group of Stearns employees working near Fountain had their photo taken on Christmas Eve. (Courtesy of William M. Anderson)

individuals. His experiences illustrated how it could be very frustrating to gain the talent necessary to become a skilled employee. As he described it, one year he:

> Got in with a filer in Brocker Mill and learnt the filing trade. I gave him $50.00 for learning me the trade. I worked all summer for nothing. He gave me [a] saw to practice on and believe me that was a very hard job for a young man. I hammered and hammered and thought that I would never learn it. I took that saw and threw it in a corner and told him that I could never learn it and I walked out of town but always came back. I was bound to make good and I have hammered lots of saws since. The filer's name was John Johnson and he was a good filer, he came from Freesoil.[29]

The hard work and money he invested in the additional training paid off for Johnson, as he continued to work in the lumber industry for many years.

Unfortunately, much of the progress Ludington's residents experienced was threatened in the 1890s. Lumber production steadily declined following its peak in 1891, and the first blow was experienced when the mill owned by Pardee, Cook, and Company was destroyed by fire in 1890. The owners chose not to rebuild. Danaher and Melendy had operated a mill in Ludington for years, but they moved their headquarters to Dollarville in Michigan's Upper Peninsula in 1897. The Pere Marquette Lumber Company closed their mill the same year. These manufacturers moved their operations to northern Michigan, Wisconsin, or other areas in search of greater tracts of virgin timber. The unthinkable had happened; much of Michigan's vast timber reserves were becoming depleted. A city like Ludington would be forced to diversify its economy or it might perish. These events also occurred within the context of a nationwide economic depression, referred to as the Panic of 1893.[30]

In an attempt to promote the diversity of the region's economy, in 1892 Justus Stearns joined a group of civic-minded Ludington citizens, led by Charles G. Wing, who organized the Citizen's Development Company. The organization's goal was to attract new manufacturing companies to the area. The group raised $50,000 and purchased two thousand acres of land immediately north of the city limits. The land was divided into several lots in what was referred to as the Manufacturer's Addition. Water and sewer lines were installed by the city while the Flint and Pere Marquette Railroad built a spur that connected their main line to the development. Lots were sold and the investment attracted four manufacturing companies. Unfortunately, each went out of business within a few years. This attempt by Ludington's business community was similar to one undertaken in Muskegon, Michigan, in the same era. Muskegon was another lumber town, located about sixty miles south of Ludington, attempting to prepare its future in a postlumber economy. Lumbermen, such as Charles Hackley, worked with other business leaders to encourage new industries to relocate to their city. In some cases, businesses received a bonus (or subsidy) from Muskegon's Board of Trade to locate their operations in Muskegon. While some firms were successful, results were mixed; many closed down in the 1890s or the first decade of the twentieth century.[31]

Possibly the low point for the city of Ludington came in the fall of 1895 when Ward's old South Mill, which had been owned by Justus's brother-in-law T. R. Lyon for nearly two decades, went up in flames. It was built originally in 1871, but had not run for about two years. Due to the lack of timber supply and decreased demand for finished lumber in the aftermath of the nation's economic downturn in the 1890s, Lyon needed to operate only the North Mill, while using parts and machinery from the South Mill. The *Ludington Record* noted that just a few years prior to the fire, the area had been the site of great activity; however, the loss of the mill demonstrated the "rapid decay and near extinction of the pine lumbering industry in Ludington."[32] There simply was not enough timber available in the area, or demand, for fourteen mills to operate in the city. Within a year there was talk of closing the high school due to lack of enrollment. On the eve of the July school board election, a letter to the editor written by local resident, J. H. Conrad, argued taxes already were too high and questioned whether the city should "continue to make the debt larger and run longer, and continue paying more interest until the lumbering interest is all out of here." He continued by questioning whether it was, "right and just to compel the people in the district school to pay for making doctors of the students and hire teachers to teach other than the English language, and hire teachers to teach singing." He ended by declaring that if parents wanted to further their child's education, they should pay for it themselves by sending their children to college. In the end, residents voted in favor of maintaining the high school, but over four hundred residents voted to close it down.[33]

In this time of discouragement, Ludington's residents searched for a benefactor who could help to bring the local economy out of its malaise. As early as 1896, the *Ludington Record* speculated that Justus Stearns might be that man. Initially, the newspaper reported that Stearns was interested in the Pere Marquette Lumber Company, and his purchase of the company was very near. The company's mill and salt block occupied valuable land on Pere Marquette Lake, and its extensive timber holdings in Hamlin Township could provide enough timber to supply the mills for several years; however, that deal never was consummated, and by August 1896 the *Ludington Record* began to focus its reporting on the possibility that Stearns might relocate his operations from Stearns Siding to Ludington. At the time, Stearns employed between two hundred and three hundred men each season at Stearns Siding, and the city's residents hoped he would bring those jobs to Ludington.[34]

Over the next several weeks that August, Stearns met with the Board of Trade to investigate the possibility of moving to the city. His plan was to purchase the North Mill and surrounding properties, enabling him to command control over water and rail lines, as well as the extensive salt production facilities. Stearns declared he wanted others to understand that "he would not seek a bonus under any circumstances but as a matter of business he should be protected from loss by reason of preferring Ludington."[35] His claim that he did not want a bonus was misleading. Like any good businessman, he knew an opportunity when he saw one and realized the city would benefit if he moved his base of operations. So instead of a bonus he sought "protection from loss" in the form of a reduction in his property taxes for a few years if he was to relocate to the city. He was in a position to bargain for this tax break as it clearly was recognized that if he did come to the city, it would lead to increased employment for hundreds and prosperity for Ludington. Editors of the local newspaper wrote, "it is hoped that a mutual understanding may be reached and that the Stearns manufacturing plant will become and continue to be a leading industry of this city."[36]

Apparently, Stearns was in no hurry to move forward until the matter of taxation was settled. He had invested a great deal in his Stearns Sidings operations and would be forced to desert several buildings, tramway tracks, and real estate if he was to relocate. He wanted the tax break to offset these costs, but it was controversial because he wanted the property assessed at a value of no more than $30,000 to $35,000. This led to considerable discussion among community leaders because the property had been assessed at a value of as much as $60,000 at the height of the lumber era. Everyone recognized the property value had dropped considerably over the course of the 1890s, but to what level was uncertain. Two years later, in May 1898, the *Ludington Record* reported that Stearns had purchased the North Mill, salt block, and surrounding property from T. R. Lyon for $20,000, and within one year he would move his business operations to Ludington. Within a short period of time, Stearns Siding became a ghost town. In direct contrast, the positive impact of Stearns's investment in the city of Ludington was demonstrated almost immediately when plans were put into place to extend a spur from the main track of the Flint and Pere Marquette Railroad to Stearns's North Mill. In addition to allowing Stearns greater rail access, another local business, the Phoenix Basket Company, also stood to benefit by this project.[37]

The *Ludington Appeal* rejoiced at the news that Stearns had purchased the property in the city. Prior to the sale, many feared Lyon would operate the mill for only one or two more years, because he had moved to Chicago and attended to his affairs more closely in that city than in Ludington. For two decades his plant had been recognized as the single largest employer in Ludington. Stearns's purchase came with the promise of an injection of new capital, ensuring the mill would operate for several years to come. Residents recognized the local timber reserves would not last forever, but once they were exhausted, it was conceivable that with the new owner's resources, logs and rough lumber could be imported from Wisconsin, or another location, allowing the North Mill to operate with raw materials from distant areas for many years to come. The paper predicted, "our city will take on new life and there will be fresh hope for the future."[38] As events progressed over the next two decades, the paper's prediction proved to be correct; Stearns eventually would transport logs from many locations, such as Kalkaska, Michigan, and the mill would operate until 1917.

Expansion in Ludington

Shortly after he made the purchase from T. R. Lyon in 1898, Stearns started to expand his business activities. The initial development began with two additional

Stearns Salt and Lumber Company letterhead. (Courtesy of Jim Fay)

deals involving Lyon. Stearns, who just had been elected Michigan's secretary of state, had to travel home to complete the first transaction, which involved a land purchase. Once the paperwork had been finalized, Stearns became the new owner of about thirty-five million board feet of standing pine. Then, in March 1899, Stearns's acquisition of the Double Brick Store was complete. T. R. Lyon had built and operated the store, which opened originally in 1882. Its inventory included a variety of general items such as shoes, boots, clothing, and hardware. Stearns planned to limit the inventory as opposed to what previously had been maintained, but hoped to stock items popular among his mill employees and local farmers. Advertisements over the next year included several articles of clothing, such as men's and ladies' work and dress shoes, hosiery and underwear, neckwear, and a wide range of work clothes. Grocery items included canned corn and peas, tomatoes, succotash, coffee, and tea. Pillsbury's Best flour was touted as the finest in stock, but the store did carry other brands. Items such as ladies' denim skirts, white pique skirts, and corded gingham novelties were advertised in the summer, while an expanded line of fall footwear was available in August. Several "Thanksgiving Necessities" were advertised in November, including oranges, lemons, cranberries, oysters, sweet potatoes, stuffed olives, and prepared pumpkin.[39]

Stearns's lumber operations also saw a great deal of activity. Extensive work was undertaken to upgrade the North Mill in 1898 and 1899. New piles were driven to repair the waterfront docks, new batteries of boilers were installed, new railroad tracks were run to the mill and warehouse, and new tramways were added to the lumberyard. In September 1899 Stearns signed a deal involving the sale of thirty-five million feet of lumber to the John Schroeder Lumber Company of Milwaukee. This transaction, which would keep the mills busy for quite some time, stood to earn Stearns a great deal of money and was described as "one of the most profitable lumber deals that has been negotiated here in late years."[40]

The same day the lumber deal was announced, Stearns negotiated an agreement with the Danaher and Melendy Company to lease their mill through December 1 of that year. Danaher had tried to sell the plant for $10,000, but received no offers, even though the mill's two band saws and circular saw were in good condition. There were plenty of logs waiting to be cut in Pere Marquette Lake with more arriving each day by rail. Stearns hoped to begin filling his recent order by leasing the additional mill. The project was expected to employ at least seventy additional men until December as Stearns hoped to run at full capacity. The town's residents understood the expanded operations would not last forever, but they were determined to earn as much as possible while the lumber industry still boomed. Stearns ultimately operated the mill until December 21. In the four months the Danaher mill was leased, the mill produced over four million feet of lumber. The *Ludington Record* noted the change that had taken place in the city in the previous year and credited Stearns. "The revival of business since Mr. Stearns moved to Ludington has been marked and these institutions will tide us through what would otherwise prove a trying period."[41]

In addition to delivering logs by rail to Ludington, Stearns also hired salesmen who sometimes employed innovative methods to purchase new timber holdings. Much of the forested land in Mason County had disappeared by the late 1890s, but there were still several isolated tracts that remained and a few large ones. In December 1899 a modest timber holding owned by Louie Olsen became available in Victory Township. A buyer from the Phoenix Basket Company drove out to review the land one morning. Upon hearing the timber was available, Charlie Brewster, a buyer for Stearns, set off as quickly as he could to head off his rival who had a thirty-minute head start. The timber under consideration was back from the road and Olsen was working near it that day. Brewster sprang from his rig when he arrived at his destination and without even hitching his horses, ran across the fields and scrambled over a barbed wire fence in hopes of closing a deal with Olsen prior to his competitor's arrival. In less than two minutes, a deal was struck for $500. The opposing timber purchaser arrived by a more leisurely route a few minutes later, only to find Brewster smiling as he left the property.[42]

It was about this time, in 1899, that Stearns became the largest manufacturer of lumber in Michigan. A new planing mill was erected in Ludington that fall and the whistle at Stearns's North Mill was used to sound weather signals for people in the area and stood as a beacon for the community. When he was interviewed in October 1899, Stearns flatly declared, "I will manufacture 150,000,000 feet of lumber this year."[43] This figure included lumber produced at his Ludington mills and his operations on two Wisconsin Indian reservations. He noted there

The mill in Ludington was the anchor of Stearns's Michigan holdings for several decades, beginning in 1898. (Archives of the Mason County Historical Society)

was a tremendous demand for lumber at that time and planned to cut a full supply of logs that winter to keep his mills running at full capacity. That November he purchased large tracts of pinelands in Wisconsin's Vilas and Oneida Counties from Frederick Weyerhaeuser, the famous lumberman. This would ensure his continued presence as Michigan's preeminent lumber baron. The deal cost Stearns $800,000 and was considered the largest transaction ever in that area. After the numbers were tallied for 1899, it turned out that while Stearns did not produce 150 million feet of lumber, he did produce about 125 million. One article claimed he was the largest manufacturer of pine in the world. Other Ludington mills had to shut down that year by the middle of December, but Stearns was so busy that his was the only mill operating the following January.[44]

Additional changes took place for Stearns's office employees and in his salt production facilities. In October 1901 a remodel of the offices changed the atmosphere for employees working there. Seven new oak desks were installed and rearranged to allow more privacy for the heads of several office departments. After experimenting with a new device for lifting salt from the grainers using a conveyor, a plan was adopted to implement it throughout the entire salt block. Additional improvements also were planned. A new well was to be drilled that winter. They expected to reach salt at a depth of about 2,400 feet. Once complete, this would provide the plant with three working wells. Plans also were developed to rebuild the old salt block. This had to be done about every seven years due to the steam from the vats and the overall dampness of the work, which could wreak havoc on the roof. New equipment would be added once the work on the salt block was complete.[45]

An article that originally appeared in Chicago's *American Lumberman,* and reprinted in the *Ludington Record,* summarized Stearns's overall accomplishments by 1901. He was described as having an "immense plant at Ludington."[46] His double mill in the city had a capacity of forty million to fifty million feet per year, and he also had a planing mill working 70 percent of the sawmill product. His salt block produced about 300,000 barrels of salt per year. Additionally, he had his own cooper shop to produce the barrels, two large lumber camps, and 40,000 acres of land, about 70 percent of which was still forested. By January 1902 Stearns reorganized his Ludington holdings under the official name Stearns Salt and Lumber Company. At the time, the company's capital assets were valued at $250,000. Outside of Ludington, he also operated the J. S. Stearns Lumber Company and Flambeau Lumber Company in Wisconsin where he expected to cut a total of twenty million feet of pine that year. Stearns had undertaken a risk by purchasing his brother-in-law's holdings in 1898, but it clearly had paid off within a short period of time.[47]

A sample of data from Stearns's Ludington plant between April and December 1900 demonstrated just how busy his operations became over the course of nine months. Two shifts (one day and one night) worked six days a week to run the mill, although operations did shut down for holidays on July 4 and December 25. Employees working the day shift received an extra day off on Labor Day (September 3) that year, but those working at night completed their shift as usual.[48] Additionally, New Year's Day was a work day, not a holiday, in 1901. Beginning in October, things began to slow down at the mill as crews likely began to travel to the forests to cut timber. That month, the night shift at the sawmill operated for only two weeks; in November it was one week; by December there was no night shift. Overall, more than twenty-seven million feet of lumber was manufactured in those nine months. August was the most productive month at the mill when over 3.8 million feet of lumber was produced, while December saw less than half of that at about 1.7 million. Levels of salt production were tied to the mills because burning the scrap lumber was needed as fuel to evaporate the brine, so the greatest manufacture of salt took place in July and August when over 41,000 and 39,000 barrels were produced each month respectively. Nearly 250,000 barrels of salt were manufactured over the course of

Table 1. Ludington mill reports, 1900

Month	Sawmill; Feet of Lumber Produced	Shingles Manufactured	Barrels of Salt Produced	Barrels of Salt Shipped	Cooper Shop; Barrels Made[a]
April	2,934,384	1,337,750	26,302	23,187	20,200
May	3,705,696	1,615,000	27,560	29,462	27,445
June	3,757,302	1,408,000	36,223	22,141	35,000
July	3,460,916	1,280,000	41,251	32,918	27,200
August	3,814,810	1,349,500	39,415	30,448	31,500
September	3,662,029	620,000	35,907	26,439	27,000
October	2,270,833	1,588,250	27,458	18,217	18,050
November	2,328,100	995,000	9,306	4,612	0
December	1,736,018	No data	4,694	10	No data
Nine Month Totals	27,670,088	10,193,500	248,116	187,434	186,395

Source: Mill Reports, 1900, Bentley Historical Library, Ann Arbor, Michigan.

a. Two factors might explain why it appeared the cooper shop did not make enough barrels to transport the amount of salt produced. First, there may have been an inventory of barrels on hand from previous months, which meant fewer needed to be assembled. However, a more likely factor was that at times a great deal of salt was shipped in bulk rather than packed in individual barrels. Therefore, there was no need to manufacture as many barrels. While it was possible Stearns maintained some inventory of salt at the plant, it was unlikely there would have been much.

those nine months. Perhaps in anticipation of the increased demand, the cooper shop produced 35,000 barrels (its highest total) in June with a grand total of more than 185,000 assembled between July and December. While no data are available for the number of shingles manufactured for December, between April and November, over ten million shingles were made. See table 1 for exact figures.

In general, the figures above demonstrate just how busy things had become at the Stearns plant in Ludington shortly after Stearns assumed control of the operations.

Early Philanthropy

With this expanded financial success Stearns began to increase his charitable activities. While Stearns's philanthropy was quite extensive in the years after 1902, and that era will be discussed later, some examples can be identified at this time to illustrate his charitable giving in the 1890s and early 1900s. One early example of his charity was seen during the Christmas season in 1896. That December Stearns "made about a hundred hearts glad" when he met with a group of young girls living in the Fourth Ward and presented each one with a "Sure Enough" doll that came with real hair and kid boots.[49] Stearns also offered significant donations to larger causes a few years later. In 1900 he contributed $1,000 to Olivet College, a small religious school with a liberal arts focus, located in Olivet, Michigan, in the south-central portion of the state. The following year he pledged to donate $25,000 to the school's endowment fund, and he later would serve on the college board as a trustee. Stearns also continued to contribute to causes in Ludington. One project involved the establishment of a free reading room in the city's Fourth Ward set to open in the fall of 1901. The following year a meeting was held to consider an Odd Fellows Home project. Stearns could not make the meeting, but pledged $1,000 to support the proposal, as he believed, "we must make a special effort to secure everything that will add to the attractiveness of our city. Every citizen should aid in this work so far as he is able."[50]

Beginning in the spring of 1901 Stearns contributed money to what would become an ongoing beautification project in the city of Ludington open to employees of the Stearns Salt and Lumber Company. A total of twelve prizes were awarded in a variety of classifications, such as best general appearance for a premise that had never been previously improved, best and most artistic display of annuals, the home with the best kept lawn, and the home with the best newly seeded or sodded lawn. First- and second-place winners received cash prizes and anyone wishing to have their yard considered could fill out an application. The newspaper dutifully reported the winners in September.[51]

One final example of Stearns's generosity was a Labor Day celebration in 1901. While there was no general observance of Labor Day in Ludington, all the Stearns plants recognized it as an extra holiday that year to be celebrated in a special manner. Stearns offered free transportation for a day's outing to Lake Hamlin for all employees and their families. Crowded trains began transporting passengers early in the morning and continued to run every half hour throughout the day. About 1,900 people received free tickets that provided transportation to the lake, a picnic lunch, and a ride on a floating palace specially chartered for the occasion. Family and friends ate lunch in small and large groups while sitting at picnic tables the Stearns Salt and Lumber Company provided. A new well was driven to provide cold water, and a band played music to entertain guests. It was a beautiful day without a cloud in the sky and it appeared as if everyone had a wonderful time. The entire event was planned by Robert L. Stearns, then age twenty-nine, who demonstrated his ability to organize a large celebration to ensure a crowd so large could have a great time. This had a very positive impact on the overall morale of the Stearns employees, as the *Ludington Record* noted, "There is not a man in those hundreds of his guests Monday who does not feel bound to Mr. Stearns by a new tie. Through all this coming year the memory of Labor Day will serve to lighten labor at the mill and in the yards."[52]

Conclusion

Ludington residents experienced a great deal in the final two decades of the nineteenth century. The city survived a diphtheria outbreak, a devastating fire, the closure of several manufacturing businesses, and the threatened closure of the high school; however, just as the city of Muskegon found a benefactor in Charles Hackley, Ludington did the same when its patron, Justus Stearns, purchased the former Ward holdings. By November 1901, there was no talk of closing the high school, and in fact concerns were raised regarding the overcrowding in the Fourth Ward's schools due to the expansion of Stearns's activities in the city. After the peak of lumber production in the early 1890s, the city simply could not support fourteen sawmills. An individual like Stearns also was needed to provide the capital necessary to upgrade the mills and invest in available forested lands and the rails necessary to transport the timber to Ludington. A news article from the *Ludington Record* in December 1901 put it best when it reflected that "Within the past year or two Ludington has felt a throb of life that has come from the injection of the elixir of life from the hand of J. S. Stearns."[53]

3

The Making of a Politician

The best men of the country are now conscious of the evil that threatens our institutions, and a movement has been started with which I am in full accord, and to which I am willing to devote my energy, and means when necessary, to abolish the political convention and substitute for it a direct vote of the people. I believe the voters of the different parties should name the candidates by direct vote; that the candidates should make the platform upon which they wish to stand, both in the state and in the legislative districts, and that caucuses and conventions with all their evils should be abolished.

Justus S. Stearns, "Candidate Stearns Discusses State Affairs," Stearns Salt and Lumber Company Records, 1881–1923, Bentley Historical Library, Ann Arbor, Michigan

When he was nearly eighty-five years old, Justus Stearns wrote a private letter in which he described himself as being "foolish enough" to enter politics in 1898, at the age of fifty-three, when he served one term as Michigan's secretary of state. He continued by writing that his political career ended in 1900 with a failed bid for the Republican nomination for Michigan's governor. Actually, Stearns became involved with politics at the local level long before 1898 and continued to be active politically throughout the remainder of his lifetime, including more than one additional run for governor. He was a lifelong Republican who may have been drawn to the Grand Old Party from an early age when he saw Abraham Lincoln in person at the age of fifteen and witnessed Lincoln's interaction with Grace Bedell at New York's Westfield train station in 1861. His devotion to Lincoln's memory was demonstrated further after the president's assassination when Justus made a special trip to Cleveland to pay respect to the slain leader as Lincoln's casket was transported from Washington, DC, to Illinois for his burial. Later, the letter Stearns wrote to Grace Bedell, recalling her encounter with President Lincoln, reinforced Stearns's devotion. Stearns also showed his admiration for another Republican president in a letter to Woodrow Wilson sent in 1913, in which he declared his support of the "Roosevelt Progressive wing of the [Republican] party."[1]

Stearns's allegiance to the Republican Party was not unique among Michigan lumber barons who, as a group, overwhelmingly supported the Republican Party and its policy to maintain protective tariffs for American businesses. Prior to Stearns's foray into the political arena, several Michigan lumbermen became involved in politics. Among others, these included governors Henry Crapo, David Jerome, and Russell Alger. Charles Hackley, whose mill in Muskegon was located sixty miles directly south of Ludington, and Henry Sage were other fellow Republican lumber barons. While Sage was an absentee owner who resided in New York, he founded a large sawmill in the Bay City area of Michigan and operated there for nearly three decades. Sage originally identified with the Whig Party, but then joined the newly formed Republicans due to his opposition to slavery, and from that time on he remained a staunch supporter of the Grand Old Party. Unfortunately, Stearns did not leave behind any written record identifying his views concerning slavery, but it is likely that Stearns agreed with Sage, given his admiration for Lincoln and his longtime affiliation with the Republican Party.[2]

The loyalty Stearns maintained toward the Republican Party was strong, although his stance on issues of political reform made him somewhat of a maverick within his own party and even prompted Democrats to reach out to him in 1904. He used the word "foolish" to describe his political career, but throughout his lifetime, he earned a reputation as a well-respected political figure and continued to receive honorary accolades as a statesman within the Republican Party. As a candidate for governor, Stearns demonstrated an enlightened sense of civic duty as he championed causes to expand democracy, such as the political primary and direct election of senators. He also supported empowering nominees with the ability to shape their party's platform for each election, as opposed to political cronies at party conventions. While he never served as governor, his advocacy for these Progressive causes demonstrated his greatest contribution as a politician and illustrated that his legacy went beyond the realm of business and industry. His efforts paved the way for others, such as Fred Warner and Chase Osborn, to implement reforms that ultimately improved the political process in the state of Michigan.

Political Beginnings

Stearns's political activities began in the 1880s when he was living in Michigan, where he found many ways to serve the community through his civic involvement. In more than one instance, his actions were noted, especially when he worked to improve voter turnout for his party in statewide elections. His name was put forward as a possible state senate candidate in 1884, when he was thirty-nine years old. Although supporters admitted he did not have legislative experience, they described him as "a gentleman of education and fine business capacity." At the Republican Party's senatorial convention that September, he fell one vote short of becoming the nominee. In later years he became a vocal proponent of the direct primary to replace the party convention. It is possible his negative view of party conventions began with this loss. Toward the end of the 1880s he was elected to the Ludington School Board; however, his business interests forced him to leave this office in 1890 and not seek reelection. One position he held for many years was chairman of the Mason County Republican Party. He must have been proud when he was chosen to serve as a presidential elector in 1888 at the age of forty-three. To complete his duties, he traveled to the state capital in Lansing to cast his ballot for Benjamin Harrison, the Republican nominee for president. Just as Stearns grew in stature as a prominent Michigan lumberman in the 1890s, his ambition to expand his political career grew during the decade. By 1898 he positioned himself to run for the office of secretary of state, which would place him within the administration of Republican governor Hazen Pingree.[3]

Governor Pingree was born in Maine and received training as a cobbler while growing up in Massachusetts. When the Civil War broke out, he enlisted in the First Massachusetts Heavy Artillery and served for the duration of the war. He even spent seven months as a prisoner of war at the notorious Andersonville prison in Georgia. Following the war, he moved to Detroit and became very successful after he and a partner founded a shoe factory. Supporters "drafted" him to run as a Republican candidate for mayor in 1889 as a leading businessman in the city. He was successful in his first campaign and won two additional terms as mayor of Detroit. While initially he was encouraged to run by influential business leaders, he remained popular with the people because of his willingness to fight on their behalf. He did so by challenging utility companies to lower their high rates and eventually supported municipal ownership of utilities as a way to protect average consumers. When the city and nation faced an economic downturn with the Panic of 1893, he allowed the unemployed to use public land in the city of Detroit to plant their own gardens. Supporters labeled them "Pingree's Potato Patches," demonstrating his popularity among the masses. Pingree's reputation as a reform-minded mayor allowed him to win the governor's mansion in 1896, where he continued to remain popular with the people, even if it put him at odds with leaders within his own party at times. This was best illustrated with his support of what commonly became known as the Atkinson bill. This proposal called for greater regulation and more equal taxation of railroads. The issue involved taxing all the railroad companies' assets, such as land and equipment, as opposed to simply taxing gross earnings. He fought in favor of this legislation during both terms as governor, much to the consternation of his fellow Republicans. Overall, Pingree's support of an expanded role for the government to protect consumers foreshadowed many of the reforms put forth by leaders of the Progressive movement in the early 1900s.[4]

It was not surprising, given Stearns's later support for political reform, that he would want to serve in the Pingree administration. Stearns's announcement to run for secretary of state in January 1898 was met with great enthusiasm in his hometown. The *Ludington Record* emphasized that his successful business career and personal popularity would ensure his victory as a candidate. Within a short time he had supporters from Cadillac, Manistee, Lake County, and Sault Sainte Marie. His primary rival for the Republican nomination was Fred Warner, a two-term veteran of the state senate from Oakland County. Stearns and Warner carried on a friendly battle for the nomination. Each had a campaign headquarters in the Russell House in Grand Rapids. Warner often entertained large crowds of followers in his room, while Stearns preferred the openness of the hotel lobby to greet supporters. Governor Pingree did not endorse either candidate prior to the convention because he was friendly with both men. In the end, Stearns won the nomination of the Republican Party for secretary of state, while Pingree was renominated for another term as governor. There was no ill will between Stearns and Warner; the latter campaigned for both Stearns and Pingree in the general election. Warner later would serve two terms as secretary of state, under Governor Aaron Bliss. In 1904 Stearns and Warner would face one another again as each sought the Republican nomination for governor.[5]

Once Stearns won the nomination of his party, his election as secretary of state virtually was assured as the Republican Party so dominated Michigan politics in the years following the Civil War, winning the party's nomination for a statewide office usually foreshadowed victory in the general election. This dominance by the Republican Party began when it was founded in 1854 and continued for several decades. Between 1865 and 1912 Republican candidates won twenty-two of twenty-four elections for governor, and no Democrat was sent to represent Michigan in the United States Senate between 1860 and 1922. As the 1898 election drew near, Stearns's hometown paper, the *Ludington Record,* which was staunchly Republican, heralded their favorite son and the entire slate of Republican candidates on the ballot. Stearns's opponent in the November election was Le Roy E. Lockwood. He represented the Democratic People's Union Party, which included members of the Democratic Party and supporters of the

"Free Silver" movement. When the election results were tallied, Stearns won an overwhelming majority as he defeated Lockwood by a vote of 236,576 to 170,119. With this victory, the lumber baron from Ludington was catapulted into the upper echelons of the Republican Party in the state of Michigan.[6]

As the newly elected secretary of state, Justus Stearns was charged with a wide range of responsibilities. The secretary served as the custodian of the state seal and was charged with affixing the seal to all proclamations the governor made. When Governor Pingree issued a proclamation recognizing Thursday, November 30, as Thanksgiving Day in 1899, and called on Michigan's residents to be thankful for their successful harvests and prosperity, the name of Justus S. Stearns, secretary of state, appeared at the bottom of this proclamation. The state seal also had to be affixed to commissions, warrants, pardons, and extradition requests from other states. Stearns's office maintained and published the laws, resolutions, and records of the state and amendments to the state constitution. Every ten years the secretary was responsible for conducting a census and annually supervised the printing of many reports pertaining to agriculture, state officers and boards, and business activities. By default the secretary of state also served on a range of boards such as the state board of auditors, state board of canvassers, the bureau of labor and industrial statistics, and many others. In return for this work, Stearns earned an annual salary of $800, which was set by the state constitution. By way of comparison, the governor served as the state's chief executive officer and earned a salary of $4,000. Stearns was assisted in his duties by the deputy secretary of state who was paid $2,000 each year. This disparity in compensation was drawn from the fact that Stearns's position was not considered full-time. It was the deputy secretary of state who oversaw the day-to-day duties of the office. While his second in command had a salary higher than his own, Stearns's personal income did not suffer. Because the deputy lived in Lansing year-round, Stearns was able to continue the oversight of his lumbering operations, which, as previously noted, were quite extensive. During his tenure as secretary of state he remained the largest manufacturer of lumber in the state of Michigan.[7]

One of the routine responsibilities of the secretary of state's office was to prepare for elections and compile election returns. Stearns was responsible for processing hundreds, if not thousands, of letters and forms sent to his office from party officials and candidates, identifying those properly nominated so their name could be placed on the ballot for upcoming elections. One example would be a letter dated October 22, 1900, in which the Prohibition Party of Michigan put forward the name of Nathan Norton Clark as their candidate for

Michigan's Sixth Congressional District in the upcoming election; he lost the subsequent election. Another example included a letter from the Republican Party chairman from Michigan's Fifth Congressional District, which renominated incumbent William Alden Smith as their candidate for Congress that year. Smith would go on to win his election and in later years served with distinction in the United States Senate. Taken collectively, there were numerous duties to be fulfilled and records to be maintained by the secretary of state's office, all of which were overseen by Justus Stearns during his two-year tenure as the head of this department.[8]

The Run for Governor

Not long after assuming his position as secretary of state, some began to consider Stearns as a possible candidate for the governor's race in 1900. He officially announced his candidacy late in 1899. When he did announce, he declared he had "considered the matter carefully," and argued there was no reason why the next governor should not come from western Michigan.[9] In his hometown of Ludington, reaction was strongly supportive. His advocates reasoned he would make an excellent governor due to his success in business, but aspects of his character also were stressed. He was described as being honest, considerate, truthful, and courteous. He acted in a genuine manner with an ability to put visitors at ease with a genial smile and handshake. When interacting with voters, Stearns demonstrated a true interest in what others had to say. The *Detroit Free Press* highlighted his views on taxation and experience in state government during his tenure as secretary of state. The *Grand Rapids Press* noted his announcement, but thought his candidacy might be handicapped due to his ties to Governor Hazen Pingree, whose actions remained popular with voters yet sometimes conflicted

While it looks like a campaign button, this pocket mirror promoted Stearns's candidacy for governor in 1900. Notice Stearns's lack of hair. (Courtesy of Robert E. Gable)

with the views of leaders within the Republican Party. These party leaders often had the most influence to determine which individual became the nominee.[10]

In early March 1900 Stearns issued his boldest statement concerning the platform he would promote in the upcoming campaign. This announcement could be broken down into three primary themes: equalization of taxes, leadership, and political reform. Stearns's support of equalization of taxes was possibly the strongest stance he took in the upcoming race at that time. If equalization of taxes was adopted, property owned by businesses and individuals would be taxed more fairly. He agreed with critics of the tax code in place at the time who were concerned that railroads "owned 38 per cent of the total valuation of taxable property in Michigan," yet they paid only "3.5 per cent of the state income from taxation." To rectify this, Stearns called for the immediate repeal of taxes on the gross earnings of companies to be replaced by a tax on their true value; this would include any land and other capital assets businesses held. A state board would be empowered to determine the full value of all properties owned by companies in industries such as railroad, telegraph, and telephone, among others. He pointed out that several Michigan governors, going back to the 1870s, had called for changes in the way businesses were taxed. His support of this proposal associated him with Governor Pingree and the Atkinson bill. Any additional revenues generated under the new tax code would be placed in a primary school fund to help generate revenue for education programs throughout the state. Stearns recognized that not all members of the Michigan Republican Party were united in support of this issue, but he argued this change in tax law was necessary to make the tax burden more equitable for all of Michigan's residents. He also noted that over 100,000 voters in Michigan supported an overhaul in the state's tax code, demonstrating it remained a popular proposal for many in the state.[11]

The second plank in his platform addressed the leadership approach he would take as governor. He did not believe in attacking those with whom he disagreed. Instead, he looked at issues from a business perspective. If there was a difference of opinion, the various problems and possible solutions should be studied using a bipartisan approach. He had a reputation as a problem solver and would bring the management skills that had served him well in the lumber industry and as secretary of state to the governor's office. Multiple parties, he believed, could best serve the public by working in an impartial and unselfish manner to settle all questions. In other words, he saw himself as someone who could work as a consensus builder to find real solutions to the problems facing citizens of Michigan.[12]

Furthermore, Stearns demonstrated his support for political reform by advocating for the direct election of United States senators. At the time, voters did not directly elect senators; instead, they were chosen by each state's legislature. For many years reformers had called for a change in the system with the goal of involving more people in the democratic process. Stearns supported these efforts and argued the state legislature should "devote its undivided attention to the task of legislating in the interest of the state and its citizens," rather than face distractions with disputes over which individuals should serve in the nation's capital as senators. He, and other reformers, supported amending the United States Constitution to allow voters to elect senators directly. Stearns emphatically declared, "I unqualifiedly favor the election of United States Senators by a direct vote of the people."[13]

Stearns's position on each of these issues put him more in line with Governor Pingree and the reform wing of Michigan's Republican Party, along with other politicians known as Progressives. The Progressive movement began in the 1890s and extended to about 1917 and American involvement in the First World War. Robert La Follette was a Republican Progressive leader from the nearby state of Wisconsin who first was elected governor and later served in the United States Senate. While in office, he argued in favor of the Wisconsin Idea, which, among other goals, called for an income tax on corporations and personal incomes and the direct election of United States Senators. Presidents Theodore Roosevelt (1901–9), William H. Taft (1909–13), and Woodrow Wilson (1913–21) were considered Progressives. During their tenure in the White House greater regulations were placed on big businesses. The constitution also was amended granting Congress the authority to impose an income tax (Sixteenth Amendment in 1913) and allowing for the direct election of United States Senators (Seventeenth Amendment in 1917). Stearns was proud of his connection with the Progressive movement and later wrote about it in a letter to Woodrow Wilson. He started his letter by confiding he had always been a Republican (Wilson was a Democrat), but he was, "a supporter of the Roosevelt Progressive wing of the party," and "a great admirer of the splendid reforms and results that you and your party leaders are bringing about."[14] Stearns's advocacy of Progressive reforms demonstrated he was a bit ahead of his time in his home state, as most holding leadership positions within the Michigan Republican Party in 1900 did not support those Progressive proposals. Adopting these stances meant Stearns would face an uphill climb to win his party's nomination that summer.

It would be a wide-open race for the Republican nomination for governor in 1900; there was no incumbent candidate and six individuals were interested in running. In reality Stearns would face three main opponents for the Republican nomination that year in what some labeled the "Battle of the Millionaires"; each of the top candidates (including Stearns) was incredibly wealthy. The first of Stearns's rivals was Aaron Bliss, a fellow lumber baron from Saginaw. Bliss was born in New York, grew up on a farm, and was transformed by his service on behalf of the Union Army during the Civil War. He enlisted in a New York cavalry unit and eventually rose to the rank of captain. He was captured, spent time as a prisoner of war, and on his second attempt to escape, was successful. His military service helped his candidacy, as it did for many other Republican veterans, in the years after the Civil War. Following his discharge, he became involved in the timber industry and later amassed a fortune while living in Saginaw. Prior to the campaign in 1900 he had been elected to the Michigan state senate, worked in the administration of Governor Russell Alger (another lumberman turned politician), and served one term in the United States House of Representatives.[15]

Dexter Ferry, a businessman from Detroit, also hoped to gain the Republican nomination for governor. He was born in New York and moved to Michigan in 1852. He had voted the Republican ticket since the party was formed in the 1850s. While he worked on a farm for a time as a young man, he made his fortune as a seed merchant, eventually organizing the firm of D. M. Ferry & Co. Their products were sold throughout the nation and were well known in Europe. He had served as chair of the Republican State Central Committee and was involved in party politics for some time, but only rarely had stood for elective office.[16]

The third major opponent Stearns faced was Chase Osborn, a newspaperman from Michigan's Upper Peninsula. As a young man, Osborn held a number of jobs, but became involved in journalism following his graduation from Purdue University in Indiana. He was well known in Michigan as the owner of the *Sault Ste. Marie News* and had traveled extensively in and outside of North America. He previously had been the state game and fish warden and was serving as the state commissioner of railroads in 1900. His biggest obstacle for the nomination lay in the fact he was from the Upper Peninsula. Michigan never had elected a governor from the Upper Peninsula, although in later years Osborn would become the state's first governor from the region.[17]

Throughout the spring of 1900 the candidates worked to gain support from different groups in Michigan. The party convention was to be held in Grand Rapids at the end of June. There was a great deal of speculation as journalists wondered if any alliances might be made between candidates to secure additional support in the race. Among others, one rumor involved Stearns; it appeared as if Ferry and Bliss might have been working together to undermine support for him in Detroit. Stearns had a great number of followers in several areas of the state, such as Grand Rapids, Ottawa County, Port Huron, and his home county of Mason. He also received recognition for renting space for his campaign headquarters in Lansing, rather than simply using his office as secretary of state to conduct work on his campaign.[18] On the eve of the convention, each candidate planned to stage an exciting entry to the meeting. Ferry's supporters intended to arrive on a special train with a brass band, thousands of cigars, and a large portrait of their candidate. Stearns's campaign organized a great parade involving marching bands and several men, each wearing a white fedora hat, similar to the hat Stearns favored. In the end, about 2,500 marched on behalf of Stearns, so many there were not enough hats for each marcher.[19]

The Republican state convention in Grand Rapids that year was one of the most exciting in state history. The head of the state Republican Party, Gerrit Diekema of the city of Holland, chaired the convention. The hall was decorated artistically for the occasion, and it was filled to capacity with spectators as well as delegates, most of whom seemed to be dressed in their best Sunday clothes. The total number of votes available was 841, and a majority of 421 was needed to win the nomination for governor. Because there were so many candidates and no single individual was seen as a frontrunner, political observers predicted more than one ballot would be needed for a candidate to win a majority. Following the standard protocol, the name of each candidate for governor was placed into nomination early in the proceedings. Each nominee had a supporter offer a tribute in his favor. Ludington's leading orator, Judge James B. McMahon, who was then a member of the circuit court, gave an enthusiastic speech on behalf of Justus Stearns, and Stearns's supporters responded with a resounding ovation. At the end of the first ballot, Bliss garnered 259 votes to Ferry's 251. Stearns received 215 votes, while no other candidate received more than 61. Stearns's forces believed Bliss would be unable to maintain his support if the balloting continued for long. Several more ballots were taken over the course of that day and the next. Stearns's supporters held out hope for his candidacy, and he was able to maintain a minimum of at least 203 votes until the fifteenth ballot was taken. However, after two days of voting, and nineteen ballots, Aaron Bliss secured a landslide victory and captured the Republican nomination for governor.[20]

A variety of factors led to Stearns's defeat at the convention. One was his association with former governor Hazen Pingree. As previously stated, the governor had a stormy relationship with some members of his party throughout his two terms in office. Stearns served in the Pingree administration and both men supported the Atkinson bill, which did not have widespread support in the Republican base. The fact that Stearns came out so strongly in favor of revising the tax code and regulation of businesses probably hurt his chances the most. Not only did this put him at odds with mainstream members of his own party, but also business interests, particularly the railroads, did not want greater regulation, so they undoubtedly pressured delegates to support candidates other than Stearns. Bliss certainly was helped by his status as a Civil War veteran, while the fact that Stearns was from the west side of the state also played a role. The majority of the state's population lay to the east, and Michigan voters never had chosen a candidate from western Michigan to serve as governor.[21]

Stearns and his followers clearly were disappointed with their loss at the convention, yet Stearns supported the Republican ticket that year. Loyalty to his political party was demonstrated when Stearns even went so far as to sponsor "Republican Day" at Epworth Heights in Ludington, about one month following his loss to Bliss at the convention. Aaron Bliss and several prominent Republicans visited Ludington in August to generate support for that year's election. Bliss would go on to defeat William C. Maybury, the Democratic nominee for governor, in the fall.[22]

A Second Run for Governor

While Stearns supported Bliss as the Republican nominee in 1900, he broke from Bliss and others within his own party when the governor came up for reelection in 1902. Stearns's tone in this campaign was much more combative as he and his supporters criticized other Republicans and rallied around the issue of primary reform, which reinforced his connection to the Progressive movement and its support of expanded democracy. Primary reform would be his top issue for the next two years. Stearns outlined his views on the direct primary using simple terms in January 1902, and he hoped the state legislature would consider the issue in a special session. In an interview Stearns declared, "A bill should be so drafted that each citizen would have an equal right to vote for the man of his choice and to have his vote honestly counted."[23] Under the system in place at the time, voters were encouraged to attend local caucus meetings where candidates could be nominated and delegates were chosen to attend the state conventions. Citizens were called to attend a caucus to consider members for local offices, another to choose candidates for the state legislature, and still another to select their favorites for state offices. Stearns argued local party bosses often dominated these caucuses and created a cumbersome process that required additional effort on the part of interested citizens to complete their civic duty. Delegates then were sent to party conventions, but sometimes they betrayed the wishes of their local communities when offered cash or a chance to obtain a high profile job. Direct primary reform offered the best solution, according to Stearns, to eliminate the corruption he saw as rampant at the state level by eliminating the middleman and allowing voters to directly choose the candidate they supported. Additionally, Stearns had personal reasons to replace the party conventions with a direct primary because he had been "stung" by losses at party conventions twice. The first was in 1884, when he lost his campaign for the state senate at a nominating convention. Then, in 1900 he had been denied his party's nomination for governor on the nineteenth ballot at the state convention. Stearns even complained privately that the railroads "controlled, all the state offices" and that Bliss had "bought the nomination through money furnished by the railroads." Given this history, and his support for other democratic reforms, it should have come as no surprise that Stearns would become a staunch advocate of replacing the nominating convention with the primary system.[24]

Stearns continued his attack and angered others in his party in January 1902 by charging that a handful of corporations had "for years sent their hired men out to eighteen or twenty senatorial districts, selected their man for senator, and then sent money to secure his nomination and election. It has become so bad now that it isn't necessary to maintain the third house or lobby, so effectively has the money been expended along this line that the lobby is made up of members of the legislature."[25] The fact he used the numbers "eighteen to twenty" was significant; this seemed to be an indirect reference to a group of Republican senators referred to as the "Immortal Nineteen" who continually had opposed reforms on the railroad industry and the direct primary. Even though he was not a declared candidate for governor at the time, this charge made by Stearns in the beginning of an election year helped to set the negative tone that may have hurt him in the long run. Immediately, the press began to wonder if Stearns had gone too far in his criticism. The *Grand Rapids Press* reported that Republicans in Lansing believed Stearns's combative statements would hurt his ability to gain the support of elements in his party who might otherwise be likely to favor his candidacy that year, and in the future. Additionally, there had been a long tradition within the state Republican Party that a sitting governor would not face a challenge if he sought reelection after one term. It appeared as if Stearns would break with this tradition, which further put him at odds with his party. Earlier in the month an article in the *Detroit Free Press* noted that support for Bliss had been soft among some of Michigan's residents, and Stearns or Dexter Ferry might pose a challenge to Bliss. When Stearns left for Washington, DC, and met with several members of Michigan's congressional delegation, there was a great deal of speculation, which probably was false, that Michigan senator James

McMillan tried to pressure Stearns to opt out of a race for the nomination. Even if it was untrue, the meeting with McMillan was significant, as he was considered to be a "Republican boss" who controlled the actions of his political party from his senate seat in Washington.[26]

For some time it was unclear as to when, or whether, Stearns would announce his candidacy officially. He did so on April 12, 1902. His announcement came in the form of a letter in which he outlined the program he would support. This included a plan to cut state spending so as to allow for a general tax cut for citizens. He called for a final adjustment in the tax code so that all property, whether owned by individuals or corporations, would be taxed fairly. Most importantly, Stearns promoted the passage of a comprehensive primary election law to ensure the people would have more direct influence over the political process. While others also challenged Bliss for the party's nomination, no other candidates outside of the governor and Stearns had much of a chance.[27]

As the date for that year's convention came closer, tension between the two candidates grew. In a scathing attack that May, Stearns accused Bliss of allowing executives from the Michigan Central Railroad to handpick a new member of the state tax commission empowered to regulate the railroad industry. Stearns called for a grand jury to investigate the charges. He even offered to pay for half the cost of the investigation. In a similar vein, when Bliss claimed to support primary reform, Stearns challenged the governor to call the legislature into a special session to consider the issue. When opponents of primary reform balked at the idea of the special session, since it would cost the taxpayers additional money, Stearns countered by offering to pay for half the cost of any such session if Bliss paid the other half. Governor Bliss never called for the special session.[28]

Stearns did not have as much widespread support for his candidacy in 1902 as he did in 1900, but he still gathered endorsements from organizations and individuals. One example was the Kent County Republican Party, which held strong in its support of the primary election law and other reforms. Prior to the convention, the county organization issued a statement in support of Stearns and declared, "we heartily endorse his candidacy and commend him to the favorable consideration of the republicans throughout the state."[29] In early June of that year, Edward Cahill announced his support of Stearns. Cahill was a well-known Republican throughout the state and a former justice of the Michigan State Supreme Court. He also had a prominent law practice in Lansing and even had served as a special counsel to Governor Pingree. In an open letter meant to serve as an endorsement of Stearns, Cahill declared he was concerned for the future of democracy due to corruption and believed the best method to protect the "body politic" was the elimination of the party conventions. He wanted a statewide direct primary election to replace the conventions. Cahill argued that Justus Stearns was the man best able to use his influence within the Republican Party to bring about the necessary changes to the state and called on "all friends of good government in the republican party" to support Stearns's candidacy.[30]

The Republican convention that year was to be held in Detroit. Unfortunately for Stearns, Bliss, as the sitting governor, had a great deal of control over the proceedings as well as the support of conservatives within the party. Stearns's negative attacks on Bliss undoubtedly angered some potential supporters. Despite the support of individuals such as Edward Cahill, there would be only one ballot necessary to determine the party's nominee for governor in 1902. Aaron Bliss won the first ballot with 811 votes to 214 for Justus Stearns. It was a bitter defeat for Stearns. Custom dictated that candidates for governor should present themselves at the convention, even if they lose. When he was called to the stage, he could not be found, creating considerable comment among the delegates. Some of Stearns's supporters, including former Republican congressman Henry F. Thomas, called upon him to bolt the Republican Party and run as an independent; he rejected the idea. Throughout the course of the general election campaign that fall, he remained relatively quiet but did declare his support for Bliss; the governor was reelected for a second term.[31]

A Third Run for Governor

The battle for the nomination in 1904 would involve the final attempt for Stearns to win the governor's seat. He showed that while he was a Republican, he was foremost a political reformer determined to stand true to his principles. In February 1904 Justus Stearns announced his intention to seek the Republican nomination for governor a third time. According to the *Ludington Chronicle*, his announcement came as a surprise to no one who knew him well. His platform was very familiar. His top priority was the passage of true primary reform. As before, he also supported equal taxation of corporate and private property as well as municipal ownership of utilities. One additional issue he supported in this campaign included a constitutional limitation on the governor's pardon power so it could not be abused. This probably was due to pardons Governor Pingree handed out near the end of his administration to three of his personal aides who were convicted of financial wrongdoing. The overall theme of Stearns's announcement was to return power to Michigan's citizens while taking it away from unscrupulous corporations and legislators.[32]

PRIMARY REFORM BALLOT

PROPOSED AND ADVOCATED BY

Justus S. Stearns

STATE TICKET.

JUDICIARY.

CONGRESSIONAL.

LEGISLATIVE.

COUNTY.

This sample ballot appeared in the *Grand Rapids Press* April 27, 1904, as Stearns worked to promote the primary system as a replacement for party conventions. (Courtesy of NewsBank)

Stearns hoped to promote a greater understanding of the direct primary with a unique advertising campaign. A full-page ad appeared in several newspapers featuring an image of Stearns, along with highlights of his platform, and an example of the primary reform ballot. Critics previously had charged the primary ballot would be too large and confusing to voters. As shown in the advertisement, it was only nine by ten inches in size and the primary ballot simplified things. Stearns argued the adoption of the primary system would replace seven precinct caucuses and eleven conventions and remove the delegate from the equation, allowing voters to directly choose the candidate they supported for nomination.[33]

The advertising campaign for the election was undertaken in late April and the campaign appeared to be gaining some momentum, but then tragedy struck the Stearns's household. Paulina Stearns, Justus's wife of over thirty-six years, was dying. The *Ludington Chronicle* reported May 4 she was "very near death" with members of the family maintaining a vigil at her bedside; she was "not expected to live over a few days, and perhaps not more than a few hours."[34] She passed away the evening of May 5 from acute kidney problems, having become ill while traveling about one month prior to her death. The couple had sought treatment from Chicago's most prominent doctors; they could only inform Paulina that her case was very serious. She then came home to Ludington. Her funeral was conducted shortly thereafter and it was largely a private affair; the *Ludington Chronicle* noted that Mrs. Stearns was one who did not seek personal notoriety. The Stearns family received numerous notes of sympathy, including one sponsored by Congressman Roswell P. Bishop and passed by Michigan's congressional delegation in Washington, DC, which recognized Paulina's heroism during her illness. John Grant, president of Epworth Heights where she spent a great deal of time during the summer, described her as "an ideal Christian wife and mother. Her life was filled with numberless acts of kindness and gentle ministrations."[35] The *Grand Rapids Press* declared that Stearns neglected his campaign for the nomination once Paulina became sick and remained at her side at all times during her illness. Thereafter, following a brief pause, Stearns continued his campaign for the Republican nomination. While it is unclear what effect the death of his wife of so many years had on Stearns's candidacy, the loss of his spouse surely was devastating.[36]

Stearns's primary rival for the Republican nomination that year was Fred M. Warner. The two previously had sought the office of secretary of state in 1898, the

This political cartoon appeared in the *Grand Rapids Press* June 10, 1904. Stearns was not afraid to criticize his fellow Republicans who stood in the way of his goal to implement the political primary in Michigan. (Courtesy of NewsBank)

year Stearns was elected to that office. Warner actually followed Stearns into this position and was elected secretary of state for two terms. Prior to that, he had served as a state senator. In the 1904 campaign, Warner was the "Machine" candidate for governor and had the backing of most party leaders. On the leading issue of primary reform, Warner offered support for some changes but was not as committed as Stearns. He advocated an end to the improper use of money to "buy" votes at caucus meetings or party conventions and hoped to see a primary law pass the legislature; however, he supported a limited primary, allowing it for local officials, but did not advocate its use for statewide offices such as governor. Stearns was popular in many regions of the state, but with the support of the Republican "Machine" it appeared by late June as if Warner easily would win the nomination.[37]

That year, the convention was again held in Detroit and began June 30. When it became clear the party platform would not endorse comprehensive primary reform, Stearns withdrew his name from consideration. Warner then was nominated on the first ballot. In Stearns's hometown, he was described as a hero who alone fought on behalf of reforming the political system. Within days of the convention, the *Detroit Free Press* issued an editorial in which it praised Stearns for placing his principle in support of reform above those of his political party, which they believed was the correct stance. He was congratulated for his conduct.[38]

Immediately following the convention, there was speculation that Stearns might run on an independent ticket, yet he refused to do so; however, in July Stearns began to receive overtures from Democrats as some hoped he might cross party lines and run as their candidate for governor. The Michigan Democratic Party had supported issues of political reform for years, and had been denied a role in state government for so long, they saw in Stearns an opportunity to gain the governor's mansion. Support for his candidacy as a Democrat was seen in various parts of the state, and when he arrived at his Grand Rapids office he discovered more than two thousand letters urging him to run as either a Democrat or Independent. Many Republicans even offered to vote for Stearns if he ran as a Democrat. For some time, Stearns refused to comment, but many Republican friends indicated he would accept the nomination if it was offered. When Stearns continued to maintain his silence, the *Grand Rapids Press* commented on the situation by publishing an intriguing political cartoon on July 27 that portrayed Justus Stearns as the Sphinx with hopeful Democrats and reformers surrounding him under the caption, "If The Sphinx Would Speak."[39]

Stearns finally issued a statement a few days later. He would not specifically commit to seeking the Democratic nomination, but he did not say he would

IF THE SPHINX WOULD SPEAK.
STEARNS

This political cartoon appeared in the *Grand Rapids Press* July 27, 1904. Following his failure to win the Republican nomination for governor in 1904, many Democrats and other reformers hoped Stearns would continue his bid for the governor's mansion as either a Democrat or Independent. He remained silent to their overtures for some time. (Courtesy of NewsBank)

refuse it either. He then declared, "if the Democrats will nominate a man of high standing who will stand for primary reform and equal taxation, and who will go into the fight to win I will not only support him, but will make a liberal contribution to his campaign fund." He continued, "I am a loyal Republican and feel that the best thing I can do for the Republican Party in Michigan will be to assist in getting it out of the hands of those now controlling it."[40] Mentioning his affiliation with the Republican Party at this time surely did not improve his prospects if his only goal was to become the Democratic nominee for governor; however, as this and other actions seemed to demonstrate, he was more interested in achieving reform in state government than winning a political office for himself. The statement played into the hands of Democrats who did not support Stearns's candidacy. Democrats opposed to his presence on the ticket continually referred to the fact he was a lifelong Republican and wondered if longtime Democrats might refuse to vote for him, or vote at all, if he appeared on the Democratic ticket.[41]

On the eve of the Democratic Convention, Grand Rapids mayor Edwin Sweet, one of the contenders for the nomination, withdrew his name for consideration as the party's nominee for governor. It appeared as if the momentum in support of Stearns's candidacy would make his nomination a reality. Several newspapers predicted Stearns would win the nomination without difficulty. Then, in a surprising turn of events at the last minute, the candidacy of Woodbridge Ferris, an educator from Big Rapids and founder of the Ferris Institute, was put forward. Following a series of contentious speeches in favor of both Stearns and Ferris, a spokesman for Stearns withdrew the Ludington man's name from consideration and declared Stearns's support for the candidacy of Ferris. The rise of Ferris and Stearns's concession came as a complete surprise, but Stearns did not seem bothered. When called up to the stage later in the convention, Stearns received a resounding ovation and pledged his support for Ferris and the Democratic ticket.[42]

Once again the lumberman from Ludington was denied a chance to serve as the state's governor. The *Grand Rapids Press* responded by criticizing the Democrats and declaring they had lost an opportunity. They described Ferris as a worthy and capable candidate, yet Stearns was more charismatic and stood for an issue voters could rally behind. The *Detroit Free Press,* which previously had described Stearns as courageous, was highly critical of his decision to so easily switch his party affiliation and seek the Democratic nomination. They argued Stearns's personal ambition for higher office allowed him to abandon his

SOMEBODY MOVED THE BRIDGE.
PRIMARY REFORM PLANK
STEARNS
After getting everything arranged the machine men threw Mr. Stearns.

Somebody Moved the Bridge. This political cartoon appeared in the *Grand Rapids Press* August 4, 1904. The Democrats considered nominating Stearns as their candidate for governor, but surprisingly chose Woodbridge Ferris instead. (Courtesy of NewsBank)

principles and demonstrated his "political stupidity." They concluded by declaring, "Justus S. Stearns has passed as a factor in the political life of the state."[43] The editors of the *Detroit Free Press* were correct in their assessment that Stearns no longer would be a political factor in state of Michigan. But, had he abandoned his principles? A close examination of his political philosophy indicated he had not. Ever since he had emerged as a candidate for secretary of state he had campaigned on the platform of political reform. Stearns had become a champion for numerous causes first advocated by Republican governor Hazen Pingree and fought on behalf of those principles even while others in his party did not. He always maintained he was a loyal Republican, and while his argument that he never actively sought the Democratic nomination seemed self-serving, members of his political party came closer to his own views in subsequent years.

Stearns remained out of the spotlight during summer and fall of 1904 until about one week prior to the general election when he issued a public letter. In it he proclaimed his support for Ferris and the state Democratic ticket, while urging Democrats and Republicans who supported honest government to vote for Woodbridge Ferris. It was to no avail. Fred Warner defeated Ferris by a vote of 283,799 to 223,527. Warner subsequently went on to serve three terms as Michigan governor, from 1905 to 1911. Ironically, while in office, Governor Warner pushed the state legislature to enact several pieces of Progressive legislation originally advocated by Stearns. Among other accomplishments, this included greater regulation of railroads and new taxes on the telephone and telegraph industry with revenues to go toward education. By 1909 a comprehensive primary election law was put into place.[44]

After 1904 Stearns did not seek election to statewide office, although his name appeared upon occasion as a possible candidate for various positions. These included US senator and congressman as well as mayor of Ludington. In some cases it was supposed that he would run as a Republican while in others either a Democrat or an Independent. He never sought any of these offices. When he was interviewed in 1912 he declared he was "pleased . . . to be out of politics" but remained focused on his expanding business interests; however, he never remained completely out of politics.[45] By the mid-1910s it was clear that not only had he returned to the Republican Party, but he also maintained a respected leadership role. He was unanimously chosen to serve as a presidential elector for Michigan's Ninth Congressional District at the state convention in 1916. Later, in 1925, he was named by President Calvin Coolidge to serve as a member of Michigan's Advisory Commission for the nation's Sesquicentennial Exhibition Association. He even was chosen to serve as a delegate to the Republican

National Convention in 1928 that nominated Herbert Hoover for president. His selection for these positions demonstrated accolades awarded to someone who must have been a well-respected member of his party. When Stearns died in 1933 there was an outpouring of messages in support of his achievements. One message came from Wescott H. Read, the chairman of the Mason County Republican Party where Stearns had lived and had served as chairman himself. The county party passed a resolution in honor of Mr. Stearns. It noted his "loyalty to the Party is unquestioned and in him, the Republican Party found one who throughout the years by his generous and active support and by his acceptance of the responsibilities of good citizenship set an example of Party loyalty which we here today would do well to follow."[46]

Conclusion

One might wonder how best to evaluate the political career of Justus S. Stearns. As with most political figures, his actions and accomplishments met with mixed results. But it seems much too harsh to use the word "foolish" (as he put it in his eighties) to describe it, or "stupid" (as the *Detroit Free Press* had in 1904). He served admirably as secretary of state from 1899 to 1900 and was a candidate for governor on three (one could argue four) occasions. Furthermore, each time he failed to receive the Republican nomination, the man who would become the next governor had defeated him. Stearns might have been embarrassed by his flirtation with the Democratic Party in 1904 and wanted to deny his actions of that year. He once wrote, "I am glad to say [the election of 1900], ended my political career as far as aspiration to office was concerned."[47] One might recall that he nearly received the Democratic Party's nomination the same year in which Paulina, his wife of thirty-six years, died. If he did want to deny his actions in this race, there was no need to do so. He momentarily left the Republican Party in 1904 in a very public manner due to his position on the issue of political reform. He also resumed his allegiance to the party, as illustrated in 1916, when he was named a presidential elector at the Republican convention. He never would have been chosen to serve as an elector if his loyalty to the party had been in question. In subsequent years, Republican governors Fred Warner and Chase Osborn adopted many of the same issues Stearns first had championed; in some cases he fought for these programs a decade prior to their actions. Historians have labeled Warner, Osborn, and even Woodbridge Ferris, Progressive reformers. Stearns should be placed into this category as well, but he never was able to put all the necessary pieces of a campaign together to win statewide office after 1900. His rhetoric at times could be harsh toward members of his own party, as seen with his accusations concerning Governor Bliss and the "Immortal Nineteen." He also may have demonstrated a naïveté as a politician with the tactics by which he sought the Democratic nomination for governor in 1904. When considering Stearns's career in politics, maybe the *Detroit Free Press* offered the most insightful analysis immediately following his defeat at the Republican convention in 1904. They congratulated Stearns for placing his principles above the cause of his party, even though his stubborn support of primary reform may have cost him the nomination. As their editorial staff concluded, "in losing he has won, and in winning his opponents have not gained."[48]

4

Lumbering on Wisconsin Indian Reservations

I had an Indian friend named Cushaway. He told me that the government was about to sell some timber up in northwestern Wisconsin. I went to Washington, D.C. and with the help of a one-armed congressman named Bishop, succeeded in buying considerable stumpage. . . . At this time I took J. S. Stearns as a partner. Stearns put in $35,000 and took out $1,600,000.

Fred Herrick as quoted by J. M. Pond, "Fred Herrick: The Story of One of the Most Colorful Careers in the Lumber Industry of This Country," *Four L Lumber News* 12, no. 23 (1930): 18, 42.

Justus Stearns expanded his lumbering activities beyond the borders of Michigan and into Wisconsin beginning in the 1890s. He described his activities in a letter to his cousin by explaining, "In 1892 I purchased all the timber on two Indian Reservations over in Wisconsin. . . . I, with a couple of associates whom I had taken in with me, built a sawmill on each reservation and manufactured lumber there for 25 years, paying the Indians during this time over $10,000,000."[1] This was part of a trend that included many Michigan lumber barons as they sought to expand their timber empires when the state's once-bountiful forested lands began to disappear. Contemporaries, such as Charles Hackley and Henry Sage, invested their capital in land and companies in Wisconsin, Minnesota, the South, and even the far West in the 1880s. Stearns and his partners secured exclusive contracts to log timber on two Wisconsin Indian reservations beginning in the early 1890s. These operations, which extended to 1922, were quite profitable. Their success allowed Stearns to accumulate capital that he later invested in the timber industry and other business enterprises in his hometown of Ludington as well as in Kentucky and Tennessee. His activities in Wisconsin led to a short-term economic boom for individual Indians because it provided employment. This boom also provided much-needed funds for internal improvements such as roads and clean drinking water, but the boom was followed by a long-term bust in which many of those who continued to live on the reservation were destitute.[2]

In many ways, Stearns's activities in Wisconsin can be seen as an example of the failed Indian policies the United States government adopted in the late nineteenth and early twentieth centuries. The government's attitude toward Native Americans was shortsighted and paternalistic. In the short run officials hoped that timber operations could provide income to people who were impoverished, while the long-term goal was to force Indians to assimilate into American society and establish farms. This chapter also will demonstrate Stearns's actions as an absentee timber baron. The entrepreneurial leadership and charitable contributions he made in Stearns Siding and Ludington characterized his previous investments in the communities. By contrast, once his Wisconsin operations were underway, he efficiently cut the timber, took in the profits, and when the timber started to disappear, sought new locations to expand his business empire without having established the same level of commitment to the community as he had in Michigan.

Partnership with Fred Herrick, Joseph Cushway, and Roswell Bishop

Stearns became involved in the lumbering operations on these Wisconsin Indian reservations through a partnership with lumberman Fred Herrick. Herrick had a long and successful, albeit controversial, career in the lumber industry. He was born in Wisconsin in 1854, but his family moved to Benton Harbor, in southwest Michigan, when he was just a year and a half. As a boy he became "hooked" on the timber trade when he purchased an oak tree for about $20. He cut the tree into logs and hauled them to a nearby mill where he sold them for $80. His quick profit of $60 made him determined to become a lumberman. As he grew older, he worked for logging companies that cut Michigan timber and sold it to mills in the Chicago area. In this way, he joined the industry at the ground level and learned to establish effective and efficient operations. Later in life he had timber holdings in Alabama, Mississippi, and Wisconsin, with major interests in Idaho and Oregon. He was a rugged outdoorsman who once boasted, "I do my loggin' in the woods, not in the Davenport hotel" (located in Spokane, Washington).[3] While he had a reputation for being gruff and demanded a full day's work from each of his employees, he paid slightly above the average wage. He also inspired loyalty in his workforce; many remained with him for twenty-five to thirty years. At one time he employed three thousand men and amassed a fortune estimated to be as much as $12 million. His downfall began in 1923 when he began investing heavily in operations in Oregon. By 1927 the price of lumber plummeted and he was left with one hundred million feet of finished lumber that had lost more than half its value. Herrick tried to sell off holdings and raise capital, but in 1929 he was forced to declare bankruptcy as he faced more than one hundred creditors and his empire came crashing down.[4]

Earlier, Herrick had moved to Ludington, and by the 1890s he was cutting elm and basswood logs on his own. Part of his business involved sending hemlock bark to tanneries in Milwaukee. As he later described it, he then caught a break. "I had an Indian friend name Cushaway. He told me that the government was about to sell some Indian timber up in northwestern Wisconsin. I went to Washington, D.C., and with the help of a one-armed congressman named Bishop, succeeded in buying considerable stumpage."[5]

Joseph Cushway was the "Indian friend" to whom Herrick referred. Cushway was born in Paw Paw, Michigan, in 1850 to parents of French and Native American ancestry. He was educated in the area's public schools, but retained his knowledge of the Potawatomie language and traditions. His language skills were so advanced that at the age of sixteen he served as an assistant interpreter at a series of treaty negotiations between the United States government and the Pohegan band of Potawatomie Indians. Following this success, he often traveled to Washington, DC, to conduct business for the tribe, and at one time he was recognized as the leader of the Potawatomie in Michigan. Cushway eventually settled in Mason County in 1882, about eight miles south of Custer, in Eden Township, on four hundred acres of prime farmland. He was known for his hospitality and earned a reputation as a successful farmer with large crop yields and fine-looking fields. Through his contacts in the nation's capital he heard of the pending sale of timber on Wisconsin's Indian reservations.[6]

Roswell P. Bishop was the "one-armed congressman" Herrick mentioned who eventually developed a friendship with Stearns. Bishop, who originally hailed from New York, enlisted in Company C, Forty-Third New York Infantry Volunteers, following the outbreak of hostilities in the Civil War. At the Battle of Lee's Mill in April 1862, he was shot through the arm, which was shattered so badly it had to be amputated above the elbow. After the war, Bishop traveled to Michigan, enrolled at the University of Michigan, and eventually studied law. He later moved to Mason County where he soon established a successful law practice and in 1876 was elected the county's prosecuting attorney. He served several terms in the state legislature and then in 1894 became the only resident in Ludington's history to be elected to the US House of Representatives. While in Congress he sponsored a series of appropriations that funded new break walls along the entrance to Ludington's harbor, earning him the title "Father of the Million Dollar Harbor."[7]

The quartet of Herrick, Cushway, Stearns, and Bishop worked together to establish and maintain lumbering interests in Wisconsin. Stearns and Herrick formed a logging company in the 1890s to cut timber on one Indian reservation. Their exclusive contract became a model for other logging companies. Stearns later formed his own business to operate independently on another reservation. Cushway's responsibility was to negotiate contracts with local Indian leaders and landowners, authorizing the company to cut timber on land allotted to individual tribal members. Bishop supported the initial contract negotiated in 1892. In 1895 he entered Congress, and in subsequent years he looked after the group's interests in Washington, DC, and eventually protected their contracts. Congressman Bishop and Stearns also became friends; at one time, the two had neighboring cottages located in Ludington's Epworth Heights community.[8]

Chippewa

The logging and lumber operations Stearns established in Wisconsin were located on Chippewa reservation land. The Chippewa were the largest group of American Indians to occupy Wisconsin prior to the 1700s. It is believed they originally lived near the mouth of the Saint Lawrence River in Quebec and migrated westward in the late 1500s or early 1600s. The Chippewa used another name to refer to themselves: Anishinabe. This name could be translated as "first or original man." Neighboring tribes called them Ojibwa, which probably derived from the word *o-jib-i-weg*, which meant "those who make pictographs."[9] The Chippewa earned this designation due to their use of birch bark rolls to maintain special tribal records. This unique characteristic of Chippewa engraving may be the best example of written documents maintained by Native Americans living north of Mexico prior to European contact. English traders later corrupted the word Ojibwa into Chippewa. The United States government and modern ethnologists and historians have used the term *Chippewa* to refer to the Anishinabe people.[10]

The goal of the federal government's Indian policies changed many times throughout the nineteenth century. Within the context of these varying policies Stearns and others took advantage of the opportunity to conduct business on Native American land. In the first half of the century the government's objective was to concentrate Indians onto reservations. This generally was implemented by negotiating treaties, sometimes conducted in the aftermath of armed conflict, between the two groups. Toward the middle and latter half of the 1800s, the government attempted to assimilate Native Americans into white society. This approach often involved the allotment of reservation land (usually in increments of 160 or 80 acres) to specific Indians. The ultimate goal was to sever the tie between an individual Indian and a tribe, replacing it with a connection to the nation as a whole. Once individuals received their allotted lands, it was hoped Native Americans would become farmers, like many of their white neighbors. Taken collectively, these policies failed Indian people miserably.[11]

Three sets of treaties were negotiated between 1837 and 1854 involving the Chippewa of Wisconsin and officials from the United States. In return for their land cessions and agreement to live on reservations, the Chippewa received annuities and other forms of government assistance. The Chippewa treaty of 1854 marked a turning point for the affected Indian people. Among other provisions, this treaty established four permanent reservations in Wisconsin, including Red Cliff, Bad River, Lac Courte Oreilles, and Lac du Flambeau. Stearns later operated on both the Bad River and Lac du Flambeau reservations.[12]

The Bad River Reservation was located along the southern shore of Lake Superior in Ashland County, about ten miles outside of Ashland, Wisconsin. The reserve covered six townships including 124,333 acres of land with a population of 655 residents in 1897. It was densely covered with both pine and hardwood forests and was known among the Indians as *Kie-gig-ga-ning,* or "Agricultural Paradise," due to the fertility of the soil and abundance of berries and wild rice. The Chippewa originally labeled the river that gave the reservation its name "Swamp River" or *Mashki Sibling,* because it flowed through swampy lands. Whites later became confused and labeled it "Bad River" instead of "Swamp River." Another explanation for the river's name was accepted after the arrival of whites who came to log timber. During the spring floods, the Bad River could be treacherous, and many whites perished in its waters.[13]

The Lac du Flambeau Reservation was located in northeast Wisconsin as well, east and south of the Bad River lands. Its territory was more isolated and encompassed parts of Vilas, Iron, and Oneida Counties. The reservation had a population of 785 and included 69,824 acres in 1897. Spruce and cedar trees remained abundant and were surrounded by more than 126 spring-fed lakes. A tradition of spearing fish by torchlight led the Chippewa to name the region *Waus-wag-im-ing,* or "Lake of the Torches." French explorers adopted the equivalent of this Indian name and called the area Lac du Flambeau.[14]

One factor that led the United States government to negotiate treaties with the Chippewa was the desire to exploit Wisconsin's extensive forests. Additionally, lumbermen supported the steps the government took as they "viewed with envious eyes the timber on Indian reservations." According to some estimates,

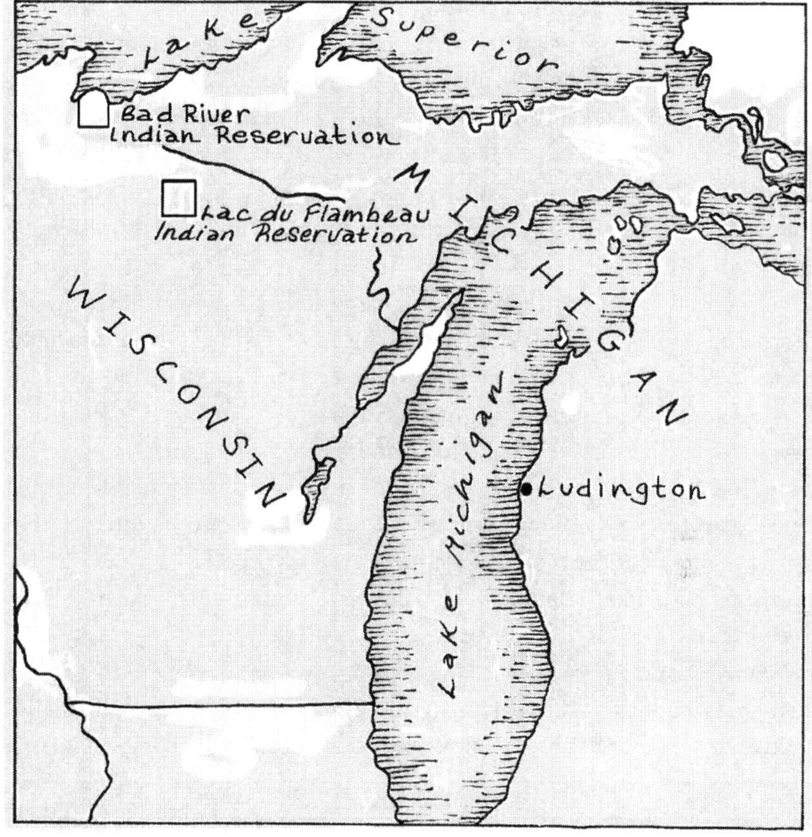

Stearns operated on both the Lac du Flambeau and Bad River Reservations. (Courtesy of Rebecca Mott)

the state's vast forest reserves amounted to 129 billion feet of lumber. There was a tremendous market for finished lumber as the nation's population spread westward in the nineteenth century. The first sawmill in the Bad River area was established in 1846, and lumbering operations continued intermittently until the late 1880s. Numerous Indians who had received their allotted lands contracted with local companies to sell the timber on their land. In this way, several million feet of lumber was sold for profit and provided a small income; however, this economic boom was short-lived, and it became clear that multiple problems developed with the manner in which the logging was conducted. First, due to a lack of oversight, some contractors illegally cut timber from unallotted as well as allotted property. Second, numerous allotments were "selectively" cut with only the most valuable timber being logged. This created a fire hazard due to the waste and remaining timber. Finally, there was an inequity in the contracting system, the results of which led many Indians to be cheated by corrupt contractors who paid less than market value for their timber and forced Indian allottees, rather than contractors, to accept additional risk from fire or other damages associated with the logging operations. The problems in Wisconsin drew the attention of Congress in the late 1880s. In the short run this resulted in a halt on the cutting and felling of trees on reservations, while in the long run it led to greater governmental regulation.[15]

The temporary moratorium on logging led many Chippewa to a state of destitution, and blow downs and forest fires threatened the future of the timber on the reservation land. Conditions at Lac du Flambeau appeared to be the worst. With a lack of logging, unemployment was rampant. Some families cultivated two or three acres of land for corn and vegetables, but there were no large farms. Many lived exclusively in wigwams, but in some cases multiple families shared one of fifty framed houses near the lake. A Department of Interior report based on data from the census of 1890 described the Lac du Flambeau Indians as living in a "destitute condition. Dire poverty is raging among them."[16] While several families on the Bad River reservation lived on productive farms, they still had several requests. They asked that a physician be appointed to attend to their needs, but their most urgent requests were "that a sawmill and gristmill be erected on the reservation," and that they receive their land allotments as soon as possible. They wanted permission to cut their timber to counter whites who trespassed on their land and cut timber without authorization.[17]

It was within this context that in July 1892 Thomas Morgan, the Commissioner of Indian Affairs in Washington, DC, received a handwritten letter from Wa-se-gwan-ne-bi, the head chief of the Lac du Flambeau band. In it, the chief outlined an offer made by the Joseph H. Cushway & Co. to establish a sawmill on the Lac du Flambeau reservation. Justus Stearns, Fred Herrick, and Joseph Cushway were involved with the company. The letter explained that at an open council meeting, the proposal offered by the J. H. Cushway Company had been "thoroughly explained and interpreted" by tribal member Edward Poupart. The members present "unanimously agreed" to move forward and accept the company's proposal in part due to the involvement of Joseph Cushway, "because he is an Indian, he understands and speaks our Language." The head chief requested the government move quickly because "much of our timber is now going to waste and depreciating in value owing to its age and severe forest fires which has killed large portions."[18]

Along with this request came a petition, signed by thirty-five members of the Chippewa tribe, asking for approval of the proposal. Most members made their mark with an *X*, but three members signed their names and indicated the proposal had been interpreted and explained. Less than two months later Wa-se-gwan-ne-bi sent another letter, signed by five additional chiefs and headmen declaring they were, "extremely anxious" the government look favorably upon the petition made by Cushway & Co. "and grant the prayer of the same." A note of desperation was apparent in the letter; the tribal leaders wrote, "We and our people are in need of the money to be derived from this sale to furnish us the necessaries of life and to make us comfortable. There seems to us to be no good reason for allowing this timber to rot and go to waste, benefitting neither the Government or ourselves when the opportunity is offered to get a fair price out of it and the money obtained can be of so much benefit. We again urge that you give this matter attention and grant our petition."[19] Following the clarification of the company's initial offer, President Benjamin Harrison approved the plan September 28, 1892.[20]

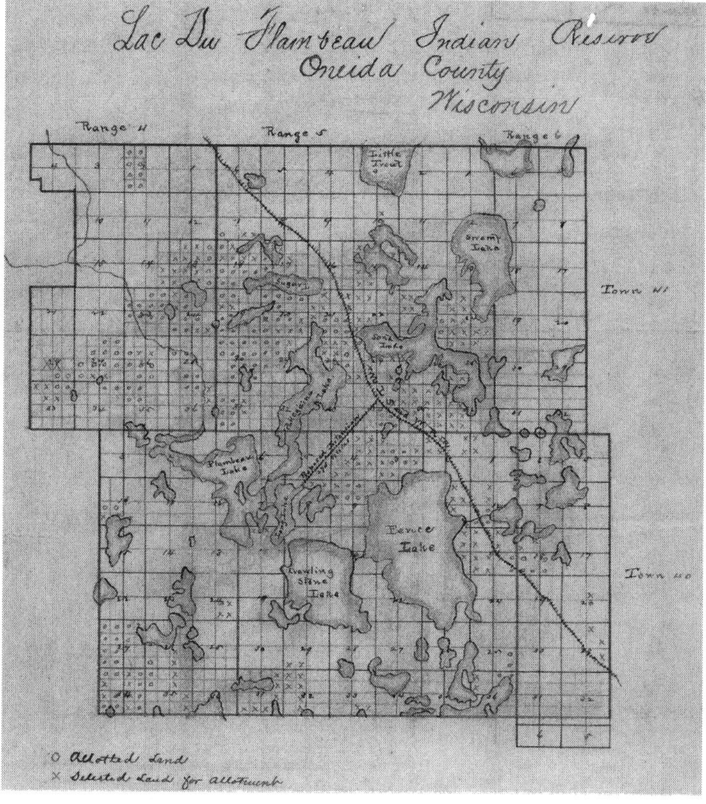

Lac du Flambeau Indian Reservation. (Courtesy of the National Archives, Washington, DC)

The contract for Cushway & Co. to operate on the Lac du Flambeau was seen as an experiment, but it eventually evolved into a model for logging on many other reservations. A few primary provisions were at the heart of this plan. The company was required to establish a lumber mill on the reservation property to ensure all manufacturing of the lumber and shingles took place on Chippewa land. The mill had to have a daily capacity of 50,000 board feet, and the shingle mill needed to produce at least 200,000 shingles a day. Non-Indians could be hired to work on the reservation, but Indians were to be given preference for employment. All the timber was to be clear-cut; no conservation methods were employed at the time because the goal was to provide the Indians with as much value, and employment, as quickly as possible. Finally, the company agreed to offer contracts at a fixed rate for a minimum of seven years or more. See table 2 for timber prices.

The Indian Service supported the proposal for humanitarian and paternalistic reasons. The timber prices included in the contracts were substantially higher than offers previously received, which created an opportunity to lessen the suffering and tremendous poverty on the reservation. Officials also grew concerned that if the dead and down timber wasn't quickly harvested, it would be lost to fire or rot. Finally, in an example of the government's paternalism, members of the Indian Service "believed that the Lac du Flambeau Indians could learn the work ethic from this type of arrangement."[21] The following year the Lake Shore Lumber Company, which operated their own sawmill far from the reservation, offered to negotiate contracts with the Lac du Flambeau Indians under the same conditions, but would pay an additional $1 per thousand feet for green merchantable white pine. The Indian Service rejected their offer because the company had no plans to operate a mill on the reservation. In later years accusations were

Table 2. Price for timber on Lac du Flambeau Reservation

Lac du Flambeau Timber	Price per thousand foot (1892)
Green merchantable white pine	$4.00
Dead and down merchantable pine	$2.00
Merchantable green Norway pine	$2.00
Merchantable birch	$1.00
Merchantable hemlock	$0.50
Pine shingle timber	$0.65

Sources: Kinney, *Indian Forest and Range*, 30–32; Godfrey, *A Forestry History*, 74.

made concerning the exclusive contract held by J. H. Cushway & Co., and there were many complaints from Indians concerning the prices they received. However, the practice of requiring operators to locate their mills on the reservation land in return for a monopoly to contract with Native Americans for their timber became an accepted practice by 1894.[22]

In theory, the arrangement that emerged had the potential to serve both the Indians and the lumber companies. Requiring the sawmills to be located on the reservation ensured employment for Native Americans, particularly when members of the Lac du Flambeau tribe were given preference in hiring. Problems developed, however, in many areas. These initial contracts maintained the same price structure for as many as ten years, without taking into account changes in market conditions. This would prove to benefit Stearns and his partners, to the detriment of the Indians, because the price of lumber rose sharply over the course of the decade, yet the Indians continued to be compensated at the low rates negotiated in 1892. Oversight by government officials was lacking while Stearns and his colleagues repeatedly were accused of abuses such as logging timber on unauthorized lands and not honoring the contracts that had been negotiated. Finally, for the majority of the time Stearns operated in Wisconsin, no efforts were made to conserve forested lands for future sustainability; to maintain compliance with regulations the United States government established, most land was clear-cut with a long-term goal to encourage Indians to assimilate into American society and become farmers. This would lead to disastrous results by the 1920s for Indians living on the reservations.[23]

Table 3. Lac du Flambeau Reservation timber statistics (1893–1903)

Season	W. Pine	N. Pine	Hemlock	Shingle	Elm	Bass-Wood	Dead and Down
1893–94	1,893,300	406,440	28,970	2,720,830	-	-	1,167,370
1894–95	3,835,110	539,330	119,970	2,222,560	-	-	548,230
1895–96	8,245,280	5,337,260	1,335,810	2,104,930	-	-	1,706,480
1896–97	3,427,010	3,037,350	1,270,520	2,270,050	-	-	2,576,260
1897–98	9,392,920	2,545,760	4,149,660	1,819,600	-	-	1,970,070
1898–99	4,637,840	2,475,460	2,222,220	855,040	-	-	398,220
1899–1900	4,414,290	4,078,740	1,827,580	438,280	-	9,100	676,970
1900–1901	4,645,690	2,758,710	1,243,530	102,480	15,210	-	325,500
1901–2	4,199,030	1,321,690	2,174,420	128,960	-	42,440	516,500
1902–3	1,240,920	464,580	116,680	8,000	-	-	96,610

Source: Godfrey, *A Forestry History*, 76.

Following the acceptance of the proposal, and the negotiation of several contracts with individual Indian allottees, Stearns and his partners went to work building their mill. A site was chosen on unallotted reservation land with a right of way to connect the mill to several railroad lines. Native American labor was used to build a large double-band sawmill, and track was laid to the other railroads. The overall cost of construction was about $40,000, and when it was complete, it offered year-round employment on the Lac du Flambeau Reservation, where lumber molding, flooring, shingles, and lath were made. The commercial success of the project was demonstrated in its first year of operations when Cushway & Co. logged over six million board feet of timber. By the 1895–96 season, nearly triple that amount was cut and removed. Logging continued at a steady pace for several years and the Lac du Flambeau Indians made up the bulk of the workforce in the operations.[24] See table 3 for the exact figures for timber processed.

Table 3 provides detailed data that chronicle the success of Stearns and his partners logging timber on the reservation; however, their prosperity permanently transformed the land. While it did create a short-term economic boom, a long-term bust followed once the forests were gone.

Bad River

Stearns partnered with Herrick and Cushway to establish the operations on the Lac du Flambeau Reservation; however, he operated primarily on his own on the Bad River Reservation's far more extensive forest reserves from 1894 to 1922. Timber on the Bad River Reservation was particularly vulnerable to forest fires due to previous logging practices in the area. As early as September 1893 nearly 150 members of the Bad River band of Chippewa signed a petition calling for the sale of burned timber on their reservation to Justus Stearns.[25] Correspondence from the fall of 1893 sent by Commissioner of Indian Affairs D. M. Browning to Secretary of Interior John Noble indicated the factors that shaped the provisions of the contract eventually awarded to Stearns. First, W. A. Mercer, the Indian agent in charge of the La Pointe Agency, solicited bids from numerous logging companies in the vicinity of the Bad River Reservation. Several companies submitted proposals, but their offers were not nearly as high as those Stearns offered. A second consideration involved the need to move quickly. Mercer noted, "the Indians on the reservation are practically without work and very few of them have anything in the way of provisions to carry them through the winter." He also observed much of the timber was in a "precarious condition" and could be lost due to the "ravages of worms," if not quickly harvested.[26] A final factor that shaped the agreement involved the success of the lumbering contract negotiated by the Lac du Flambeau Indians on their reservation land. The agreement had been in place for only one season, but due to its initial success, the Commissioner of Indian Affairs wanted Stearns's contract to be "upon the same plan as that adopted in September, 1892, for the disposition of the timber on the Lac du Flambeau reservation, of the same [La Pointe Indian] Agency, to J. H. Cushway & Company."[27]

Stearns must have had several thoughts going through his mind when he made his proposal. He already had achieved success as a lumberman when he moved beyond his family connections in Ludington and founded Stearns Siding. His partnership with Herrick had proved he could operate outside of Michigan, but the bid to log timber on the Bad River Reservation was his own. It did not involve the safety of the experienced Herrick as a partner. Furthermore, the nation was in the midst of an economic depression: the Panic of 1893. Back in the 1870s when the United States experienced another economic downturn, he had been forced into bankruptcy. Prior to that, his own father had failed when he and a partner tried to establish an oil refining operation in Erie, Pennsylvania. In the end Stearns must have believed it was worth the investment because his offer was twice the amount paid for first class white pine purchased in other parts of Wisconsin and Minnesota. He likely assumed that whoever secured the original contract during the hard economic times of the early 1890s would benefit in the long run, when the nation's economy recovered, and the price of finished lumber was sure to rise. It proved to be a fruitful gamble for Stearns; by 1900 the price of lumber rose significantly, and he was able to secure significant profits based upon the conditions of the contract.[28]

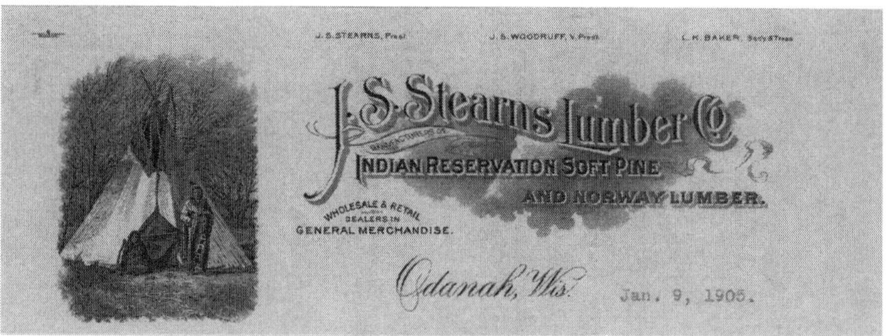

J. S. Stearns Lumber Company letterhead. This letterhead was used by Stearns's lumber company, which operated on the Bad River Indian reservation. (Courtesy of Wisconsin Historical Society, Image ID# 88849)

President Grover Cleveland ultimately approved Stearns's proposal in March 1894. Very soon afterward, the J. S. Stearns Lumber Company entered into contracts to harvest fifty million feet of burned timber and to purchase timber from Bad River Indians who had received their individual allotments. Once this contract on the Bad River Reservation was executed, Stearns controlled a great deal of the lumbering interests in northern Wisconsin, since he was also part owner of J. H. Cushway & Co. The timber rates were the same as those negotiated with the Lac du Flambeau except for increased prices for hemlock and birch and additional prices on basswood, elm, maple, and oak. See table 4 for specific timber prices.

Stearns hired Lucius K. Baker to oversee operations on the reservation. Baker and Stearns first met in Ashtabula County, Ohio, and when Stearns moved to Ludington in 1876, Baker accompanied him. When the J. S. Stearns Lumber Company was formed, Baker officially served as secretary, treasurer, and general manager. Stearns made several trips to Wisconsin to visit his operations; his wife Paulina sometimes accompanied him. His keen interest in the Bad River logging operations was demonstrated by a trip he made to the reservation in July 1898. At the time Stearns was in the middle of an election campaign as he ran for the position of Michigan secretary of state. He took time away from campaigning to meet the new Indian agent in charge of enforcing the timber contracts on the reservations. While Stearns often visited his holdings in Wisconsin, Baker supervised the day-to-day operations, demonstrating that Stearns was an absentee owner.[29]

Logging on the Bad River Reservation began in 1894 when about two million board feet of timber was cut. The following year saw an increase to nearly

Table 4. Price for timber on Bad River Reservation

Bad River Timber	Price per thousand foot (1893)
Green merchantable white pine	$4.00
Dead and down merchantable pine	$2.00
Merchantable green Norway pine	$2.00
Merchantable birch	$2.00 (an increase of $1.00)
Merchantable hemlock	$2.00 (an increase of $1.50)
Pine shingle timber	$0.65
Oak	$4.00
Basswood	$2.00
Elm	$2.00
Maple	$2.00

Source: Godfrey, *A Forestry History*, 65; Kinney, *Indian Forest and Range*, 34.

Table 5. Bad River Reservation timber statistics (1893–1903)

Season	W. Pine	N. Pine	Hemlock	Shingle	Elm	Bass-Wood	Dead and Down
1893–94	1,072,580	644,790	123,880	213,560	2,590	6,860	99,650
1894–95	4,959,040	3,392,710	103,300	1,007,230	40,620	6,150	433,290
1895–96	4,883,970	3,011,460	36,510	2,195,160	39,000	14,980	3,718,130
1896–97	9,166,500	1,990,990	3,610	1,137,970	320	2,330	6,759,600
1897–98	12,308,060	3,483,840	55,270	1,705,920	22,780	4,660	12,058,080
1898–99	12,923,320	12,923,320	34,660	2,545,330	4,000	2,360	5,773,360
1899–1900	17,645,540	8,567,850	155,860	927,620	317,980	61,390	405,470
1900–1901	22,536,870	10,637,540	80,020	768,670	127,250	3,710	267,440
1901–2	26,102,760	10,244,080	100,210	610,000	7,760	1,830	148,380
1902–3	21,229,780	10,755,470	2,299,820	353,230	84,640	29,030	776,320

Source: Godfrey, *A Forestry History*, 67.

ten million board feet. Operations increased over the winter of 1895/96 when over thirteen million board feet of timber was cut.[30] See table 5 for exact figures.

A quick comparison of the Bad River Reservation statistics to those of the Lac du Flambeau Reservation demonstrates how extensive the timber reserves were at Bad River. The amount of timber cut at Bad River far surpassed that of Lac du Flambeau, and the sawmill operated on the reservation into the early 1920s.

Unfortunately, forest fires consumed much of the timber on the Bad River Reservation, often devastating unallotted lands. In response, the Bad River Tribal Council acted to approve a special contract to cut the burned timber as quickly as possible. The goal was to harvest the merchantable timber before pine worms could destroy it. The special contract was approved and Stearns was able to increase his activities and, as shown in table 5, cut 12,058,080 board feet of dead and down timber during the 1897–98 season. Because so much of this damaged timber was cut from unallotted land, payments from the J. S. Stearns Lumber Company went to the Bad River band rather than to individual members of the tribe.[31] As the payments increased, a large fund accrued that allowed for much-needed internal improvements to be made on the reservation. Among other projects, these included the construction of over twenty miles of roads and several miles of sidewalks. Five new wells were dug, which greatly improved the health of many families who had been using swamp and river water. Streets were improved and straightened and a new cemetery was fenced and seeded with grass. The new roads facilitated the marketing and transportation of crops outside the reservation and made it easier to obtain supplies from the city. These public works projects also lowered the unemployment rate because all the work was completed by Indian labor.[32]

Lawsuit

Stearns's successful operations in Wisconsin were threatened by a lawsuit filed in 1897 that also provided insight into the relationship among Stearns, Herrick, and Cushway. The lawsuit was brought by Richard A. Seymour and John Seymour, brothers living in Manistee, Michigan, and Antoine Cartier of Ludington, Michigan. The plaintiffs alleged they made an oral agreement with Joseph H. Cushway and Fred Herrick to form a partnership to purchase the right to cut timber on the Lac du Flambeau Reservation. However, they argued that Herrick and Cushway then committed fraud by substituting Stearns in their place. They sued in the Supreme Court of the state of Wisconsin to recover profits in the amount of $250,000.[33]

The stage for the lawsuit was set back in the summer of 1892 when Herrick and Cushway negotiated with the Lac du Flambeau band and government officials to secure the initial contracts to conduct logging operations on the reservation. Herrick was asked to demonstrate he had the capital to establish a large timber company, so he traveled to Ludington where he made a pitch to the Seymour brothers and Antoine Cartier to partner with him in his business venture. The men were interested in Herrick's proposal, and a verbal agreement appeared to have been reached. Richard and John Seymour were born in Montreal, Canada, and later relocated to Manistee where the brothers established a transportation enterprise. Their business evolved into the Northern Michigan Transportation Company, which boasted a payroll of one thousand employees and the use of seven steamships. Antoine Cartier also was a native of Quebec who traced his family lineage back to the explorer Jacques Cartier, made famous for exploring the Saint Lawrence River. Antoine Cartier lived in Manistee for a time, but then settled in Ludington in 1877, where he was engaged in the lumber business. He served as the city's mayor from 1880 to 1888, while two of his sons later served in the same capacity. He held extensive lumbering operations in Michigan, under the firm name Cartier Lumber Company. In subsequent years, Antoine Cartier and his son Warren carried on what appeared to have been a somewhat friendly rivalry with Stearns as the most important business leaders in the city of Ludington. It is probable this lawsuit explains why there was tension at times in the relationship between the city's two leading citizens.[34]

The apparent agreement between the Seymour brothers, Cartier, Herrick, and Cushway proved to be very interesting. Cushway, who was described in court documents as a "half-breed Indian," planned to serve as an agent and interpreter to negotiate contracts with individual Indians to cut timber on their land allotments. It was Herrick's responsibility to supply the capital necessary to purchase the rights to cut timber and manufacture lumber. The agreement called for Cushway to receive "one-fourth of the net profits of such undertaking, and said Fred Herrick the three-fourths of the net profits, to be shared with his associates in such undertaking."[35] Herrick proposed the Seymour brothers would supply one-third of the capital, while Cartier and Herrick would each supply the same portions. All parties appeared to verbally accept the conditions of the agreement. Due to the complexity of the negotiations with the Lac du Flambeau, Herrick traveled more than once to Washington, DC, to ensure all conditions met with the approval of the government. Throughout the summer of 1892 Herrick updated his partners as to the status of the negotiations.[36]

By the fall, Herrick met with Justus Stearns and the situation had changed. Herrick agreed to enter into a partnership with Stearns because he was able to secure better terms for himself than were in place with his other would-be partners. Herrick sent a letter to the Seymour brothers dated November 22, 1892, in which he wrote, "The talk we have had as to making a deal between you, Mr. Cartier, and myself as to my timber at Lac du Flambeau, will not materialize."[37] The men then traveled to the reservation in Wisconsin for an explanation from Herrick. When confronted, Herrick denied they had a deal and challenged them to file a lawsuit if they were unhappy. The new partners of Herrick, Cushway, and Stearns then entered into a new contract which was *written* and dated December 2, 1892, under the firm name of J. H. Cushway & Co. Shortly after the agreements were finalized on the Lac du Flambeau Reservation, Stearns and Herrick bought out Cushway's interests in the company, yet it continued to operate under the name J. H. Cushway & Co. Stearns's family connections once again helped as Herrick was later quoted as saying, "I did borrow $200,000 from a man named Lyons, to start the operation."[38] Undoubtedly, the man referred to as Lyons was T. R. Lyon, the brother-in-law of Justus S. Stearns.

The key issue to be decided by the court in the original trial was whether or not a contract had been made. While it was clear there had been general agreement by both parties on several terms, both Herrick and Stearns denied that a formal contract had been reached. The trial judge concluded, "I am clearly of the opinion, although I come to that conclusion reluctantly, that this partnership was absolutely void . . . that it left Mr. Herrick as much at liberty to obtain this timber, or to take in other partners, or to deal for himself alone or with others, as though no such agreement had ever been made."[39] Stearns and Herrick won their case, but their accusers appealed. The appeal focused on two concerns. The first dealt with whether or not Stearns, and particularly Herrick, had been guilty of fraud, as their accusers charged they had violated the original contract. The appeals court determined there had been no fraud because there had never been any written agreement; it was only verbal. The second issue addressed whether or not the original partners had begun to conduct business operations and therefore act like a business. The court again found they had not when it determined, "the plaintiffs [Richard and John Seymour and Antoine Cartier] paid no consideration for the timber in question, and contributed nothing whatever, either of time, labor, or money to the business of the said Cushway & Co."[40] Once again, the complaint was dismissed as the decision in the initial trial was affirmed. The victory in the trial was important for Justus Stearns. The publishers of the *Ludington Record* must have agreed and included an article describing a telegram Paulina Stearns received from her husband announcing "that the important lawsuit between Messrs Seymour and others, and himself had been decided in his favor."[41]

Continuing Operations in Wisconsin

Stearns's logging operations on the Lac du Flambeau and Bad River Reservations proved to be quite successful throughout the 1890s, but his exclusive contracts to cut timber were set to expire in 1902 and 1903. Between the time the initial contracts were negotiated in the 1890s and 1902, the market for lumber had changed and its price had increased significantly. In the meantime, due to the nature of the contracts, Stearns was able to purchase timber for as little as one-third the going rate, while the Indians received less compensation than what the market dictated. Many Indians argued this was unfair and that any new contracts should reflect the change in market conditions. Following procedures adopted in previous years to ensure Native Americans received a fair price for their timber, an advertisement for sealed bids was released by the Indian Service January 20, 1903, requiring a minimum bid per thousand feet of $6 for white pine and $4 for Norway pine. The minimum requirements reflected the increased value of the timber, indicating the Indians would receive more under these new contracts than they had in the past, while Stearns would have to pay more for the authority to continue his logging operations in Wisconsin.[42]

A total of five bids, including one submitted by Justus Stearns, were received by noon February 21, 1903. It was difficult to compare them due to the various prices offered for white and Norway pine as opposed to other, less desirable,

Justus S. Stearns holding a pen. Stearns was in his late thirties or early forties when this photo was taken. (Courtesy of Robert E. Gable)

species. After careful consideration the secretary of interior rejected all five proposals. Soon thereafter, negotiations commenced between Stearns and Interior Department officials to enter into an agreement fair to both Stearns and the Indians. Stearns received preferential treatment according to government officials, "by reason of his former purchase of timber from other allottees of this reservation and of the informal understanding at the time."[43] Furthermore, Stearns believed he was morally entitled to the new contract as long as he was willing to pay a fair price. He already had invested $80,000 in his sawmill on the reservation, spent $15,000 to build dams on the river to float the logs to his mill, and was in the process of constructing a railroad to reach additional stretches of less accessible timber in the interior. Interior Department officials spoke highly of Stearns and at the time declared there was no "fault found with his treatment of the department or of the Indians." A final agreement was reached and approved by President Theodore Roosevelt June 11, 1903.[44]

Stearns was fortunate to secure the contract providing him with the exclusive right to log timber on the two Indian reservations; however, he paid significantly more for this right under conditions outlined in the new contracts. In fact, the bidding process, and negotiations with Stearns, resulted in a pricing rate that was advantageous to the Indians and was even higher than government officials thought the timber was worth at that time. Based on the contract originally negotiated in 1893 on the Bad River Reservation, Stearns had paid $4 for white pine and $2 for Norway pine per thousand board feet; under the new agreement reached in 1903, he would pay $8 for each. Officials predicted the total cost over the next several years to cut timber on the reservations would be about $3 million. If the new pricing scheme had not been adopted, Stearns probably would have paid about $1 million less. Believing he could still turn a handsome profit, Stearns traveled to Washington, DC, in 1903 to sign several contracts with individual Indians granting him the right to log their property. The initial number of contracts to be finalized amounted to more than four hundred, each of which had to be made in quadruplicates, thereby requiring Stearns to sign his name about 1,700 times. Terms of the new contracts, and Stearns's willingness to pay considerably more for the right to continue operating, indicate prices in the initial contracts had been very favorable for him.[45] See table 6 for full price comparisons between the contracts originally adopted in the 1890s and 1903.

Logging operations also were subject to additional regulations under terms set forth in the new contracts. An escalator clause allowed the president of the United States the ability to increase the prices for certain species if market conditions warranted a change. More specific regulations concerning piling and burning of waste were outlined in an effort to prevent forest fires. For the first time, logging restrictions with an effort toward reforestation were included in the new agreement. In previous years, Stearns had been encouraged, even required, to clear-cut forested lands as the government's long-term goal always

Table 6. Price for timber on Bad River and Lac du Flambeau Reservations

Timber	Price per Thousand Foot			
	Bad River		Lac du Flambeau	
	1893	1903	1892	1903
Green merchantable white pine	$4.00	$8.00	$4.00	$7.00
Dead and down merchantable pine	$2.00		$2.00	
Merchantable green Norway pine	$2.00	$8.00	$2.00	$7.00
Merchantable birch	$2.00	$3.50	$1.00	$2.50
Merchantable hemlock	$2.00	$1.50	$0.50	$1.50
Pine shingle timber	$0.65		$0.65	
Basswood	$2.00	$4.00		$4.00
Elm	$2.00	$2.00		$2.00
Maple	$2.00	$3.00		$3.00
Oak	$4.00	$6.00		$6.00

Source: Kinney, *Indian Forest and Range*, 30, 34, 54–55, 62. Additional information is found in Godfrey, *A Forestry History*, 68; "Stearns Long Job," *Grand Rapids Press*, May 22, 1903, 1.

had been for Native Americans to receive the most amount of money for their timber and to become farmers once the forested lands had been cleared. The new restrictions required Stearns's logging crews to leave groups of between two to four mature pines in place about every four hundred feet. The hope was that by adopting this policy, the trees that remained standing would serve as seed trees for the cutover areas and the forest could be regenerated for the future. Problems dealing with the regulation of leaving seed trees emerged soon after they were implemented. By 1908 Joseph Farr, general superintendent of logging for the Indian Service, observed that about one-third of the seed trees left standing had either blown down or died and that most Indians complained about the new regulations. In other areas it was reported that 60 to 75 percent of the trees had blown down. At the same time, officials determined that allowing a handful of trees to remain standing led to an estimated loss of nearly $140 in timber revenue for each Indian holding eighty acres of land. By the fall of 1908, government employees abandoned the requirement to leave seed trees because it did not appear to be working, and it led to financial losses for Native Americans. This meant that once again it would become government policy to clear-cut forested lands as the short-term economic gain of selling more timber was adopted over a more long-term goal of managing forested lands for sustainability.[46]

J. S. Stearns Odanah. This postcard shows a crew of Stearns men working on the Bad River reservation with an extraordinarily large load of logs from 1909. (Courtesy of Dale Peterson)

Once the new set of contracts was completed, Stearns continued his timber operations by removing significant amounts of hardwood at a steady pace. His crews also were able to gain access to remote stands of the more valuable white and Norway pine once construction was complete for new rail lines. Logging on the Lac du Flambeau reservation lands continued steadily until the timber gave out in 1914. Up until that time, tribal members earned good wages working in lumber camps or in the lumber mill. After 1914, many left the reservation to work in the lumbering industry in different areas, or sustained themselves by hunting, fishing, trapping, guiding tourists, gathering berries, making maple sugar, or other methods as the region became popular among white tourists. Unfortunately, very few were able to successfully engage in self-sustaining farms because the soil proved to be of poor quality.[47]

In contrast to conditions on the Lac du Flambeau Reservation, logging on the Bad River Reservation would continue until the 1920s. According to a Wisconsin state forester, by 1906 "the Bad River reservation still contained the largest body of timber on any reservation in Wisconsin with the exception of the Menominee Reservation." At times, Stearns was encouraged to increase the pace of his activities and was granted special short-term contracts, due to devastation caused by forest fires. In the fall of 1908 the J. S. Stearns Lumber Company prepared for the most extensive logging operations in its history to prevent fire-damaged timber from being lost to rot and disease. Over the course of the winter of 1908/9 Stearns logged close to 200 million feet of timber while employing as many as three thousand men—more than twice the number typically on the payroll each winter. While this appeared to be a windfall for Stearns, it nearly resulted in financial disaster for his company. Contractors demanded abnormally high wages that winter, and once the timber was cut, the price of lumber plummeted. Stearns complained his company was in a dire condition and attempted to negotiate a lower price, but the Indian Service would not relent. Fortunately, by 1911 the demand for lumber increased and the company's financial position stabilized. The next year the price of lumber rose so high it triggered the escalator clause written into the contract, and Stearns was required to increase his payments to Indians or forfeit his contracts. The most significant increase in cost involved the price paid for white pine, which was raised from $8 to $10.[48]

Wisconsin's Timber Industry

Indian allottees and laborers, as well as Stearns, received benefits from the lumbering activity on the reservation lands in this era. The J. S. Stearns Lumber Company was the largest employer operating in northern Wisconsin's timber industry. In the mid- to late 1890s Stearns's operations routinely employed well over one hundred Indians in the winter logging camps, while over seventy-five worked in the summer in various capacities at the sawmills. The annual payroll for the J. S. Stearns Lumber Company included wages of over $32,000 paid to Indians by the early 1900s with an average of nearly $3,000 added to the local economy each month. By 1914 his company employed 1,500 men on the Bad River Reservation, about one-third of whom were Chippewa Indians. Common laborers earned between $1.15 and $4.00 per day, while sawyers, inspectors, and foremen easily might earn $5.00 or more a day. Steady employment was available through the era of the First World War, and by 1920 the company had 1,200 men on the payroll, including 150–200 Native Americans; others could obtain jobs if they wanted them. One Bad River band member, who went by the English name of Edward Haskins, contracted with Stearns to cut timber in the woods. He employed over one hundred men one season and expected to provide between seven and eight million feet of logs to be cut into lumber. Non-Indians also worked on the reservation lands, as Stearns often hired workers from Ludington to work in the forests and sawmills in Wisconsin, but Native Americans always made up a significant portion of the labor force. Over the course of its lumbering operations on the Bad River Reservation between 1893 and 1922, the Stearns Lumber Company cut over 1.2 billion board feet of timber, for which members of the Bad River nation received about $7 million. Indian laborers earned about $2 million in compensation over the same period of time. According to J. P. Kinney, who worked as a forester for the Indian Service for many years and studied conditions on the Bad River Reservation in detail, "From this income of approximately $9,000,000, over a period of 29 years, the Indians must have realized great material benefits."[49] While the figure of $9 million represents a significant amount of money, it provides only a partial understanding of the situation on the reservations.

Despite the economic boom the lumbering operations provided, there were many complaints from residents living on both the Bad River and Lac du Flambeau Reservations due to transgressions Stearns's company committed. One dealt with a provision referred to as the 65-cent clause. This allowed the company to purchase all "defective" timber at a rate of 65 cents per thousand. If a log had even the slightest defect, it would be purchased at this lower price. Indians complained that far too much timber had been identified improperly as "defective." Another problem involved dead and down timber with a minimum set price of $2 per thousand. A committee made of up Indians provided oversight and was empowered to examine timber to determine if it had been spoiled by fire. The committee was accused of condemning hundreds of acres of timber that never had been damaged. Members of the Indian Service and the Indians themselves also complained that at times Stearns's crews violated contracts by removing only the most valuable timber (pine) while leaving behind less valuable species. These actions, along with improper cleanup of slash and other debris, increased the threat of damaging fires. By far, the major complaint from the Indians was that Stearns's company had been allowed to log timber for too long at the low rates negotiated in 1892 and 1893. Over the course of the decade of the 1890s, the price of lumber had nearly tripled for some species, allowing Stearns to reap large profits, at the expense of the Indians. Forester J. P. Kinney investigated the situation and concluded that the Indians received "totally inadequate prices . . . for their timber because of provisions in previous contracts that allowed timber to be taken at old contract rates." While this situation was rectified by the new contracts signed in 1903, those who were paid under the old rates suffered and never could recoup their losses.[50]

Forest Service employees regularly praised the logging practices Stearns implemented, while Native Americans often held a different view. Approval of Stearns's activity was included in a report submitted by forester Edward Braniff, in which he commented, "I have never found a cleaner, better logging operation than the one on the Bad River Reservation." Braniff's observations were confirmed by other employees, including Dr. B. E. Fernow, the dean of American foresters. In contrast, Bad River residents declared that Stearns violated regulations to increase his own profits. In 1911 and 1912 Stearns was charged with violating contracts by logging healthy stands of trees while declaring they were damaged by fire, therefore reducing the price he had to pay for the timber. Stearns denied he did anything wrong, but offered as compensation a "gratuity" of $1,000. Following an investigation, it was determined that at least 30 percent of the timber logged in one area was green, or untouched by fire, at the time of the cutting, although it would have died within one or two years. The commissioner of Indian Affairs recommended a settlement of $2,000, which the Tribal Council rejected. Eventually, Stearns paid $8,125.60 to settle the matter because he was responsible for the actions of the men logging the green timber because they were working for his company.[51]

By the late 1920s, the United States Senate, under the leadership of Wisconsin's Robert La Follette Jr. conducted a series of hearings that investigated abuses that had taken place on Wisconsin's Indian reservations. Some of the violations described at these hearings were associated with the actions of Stearns's companies. According to testimony of Charles D. Armstrong, a Bad River resident who was employed by the J. S. Stearns Lumber Company, the abuses dated back to 1893. Armstrong observed that lumber company crews violated "their contract right from the start of their operations by removing timber from unallotted lands" and used it for the construction of the mill.[52] Additional testimony was provided by Daniel Grady, who was appointed to serve as special counsel by the Wisconsin state legislature to investigate claims made by Indians that Stearns and other operators never paid Indians for timber cut on their land. Over the course of his testimony, he declared, "I am satisfied from the investigation made that large quantities of timber have been removed from the reservation for which no compensation has been made to the Indians." Grady further identified the so-called Stearns Method of reporting as little as one-third of the amount of timber cut on some allotments. It was unclear how often this underreporting had taken place, but several scalers were acquainted with the Stearns Method and were available to testify if necessary.[53] Another investigator, Oliver M. Olson, reviewed the impact of violations on one specific tract of land and determined, "the Stearns Lumber Company . . . robbed the owner out of $10,885.28 of timber" with the cooperation of the Indian agent on the reservation.[54]

The Indians also protested about the company stores the J. S. Stearns Lumber Company operated. The company store located on the Bad River Reservation was a large establishment, and its shelves contained a wide range of items, but according to tribal members, they were available only at "exorbitant prices." Merchants from the nearby town of Ashland had been accustomed to selling groceries and meats on the reservation; however, according to a report filed by the Indian Rights Association, by 1902 this practice was prohibited, thereby enabling the company store to monopolize trade on the reservation to a great extent. Native American employees also were paid in coupons, rather than regular paychecks, which were only redeemable at the Stearns Company Store. White employees were paid in cash. Other establishments in Ashland would accept the coupons as payment, but usually at a reduced rate of 60 to 75 cents for every dollar. In addition to the company store, Stearns exerted a great deal of influence over the entire tribal economy; he owned a blacksmith shop, an icehouse, a barbershop, and several miles of railroad track on reservation land. Because the company operated so many businesses, and paid Indian employees with coupons, much of the wealth paid to the Indians simply cycled back to the J. S. Stearns Lumber Company. An editorial that appeared in the reservation newspaper seemed to summarize the frustration many tribal members held when it compared Stearns's control over the region to an octopus. "It seems to one as though the Indian Department in Washington D.C. is being operated not for the benefit of the Indian on this reservation, but for the express purpose of this octopus, this great timber and money grabbing monster, this 'sapper' of the Indian's vitality."[55]

Stearns was not alone among the many lumbermen of this era accused of wrongdoings; his company's actions were part of an overall pattern of misdeeds perpetrated by many in the industry. As one experienced logger described it, the competition to acquire pineland at the lowest cost possible involved "one of the greatest periods of graft and exploitation that this nation has ever gone through. The rule was to beat the other fellow before he beat you and it was followed with a conscientiousness born of greed and avarice." The phrase "Round Forties" was commonly known among those engaged in the timber industry and it was "the rule in many instances." A "Round Forty" was when a lumberman purchased a forty-acre plot of land and then, "Cut your own forty and all the forties around it," even when he did not own the additional adjacent properties.[56]

It is unclear exactly why Stearns treated his Native American employees differently from their white counterparts; however, as writer Patty Loew has argued, there was a great deal of "racial arrogance that whites exhibited toward Indians," and "scientific racism dominated discussions about Indians" in this era.[57] Stearns was just one of many of his contemporaries who likely held these beliefs. The hearings sponsored by Senator La Follette, which identified the Stearns Method, exposed the transgressions of other timber companies as well, including the Bekkedal Lumber Company that operated in parts of northwestern Wisconsin. On at least four occasions between 1916 and 1925 timber was cut on tribal land, yet the Indians never received payment. Another timber company, Signor, Crisler, and Company, was accused of trespassing on Indian land and cutting timber without permission on numerous occasions. The company paid little, if any, compensation to landowners. Indians who worked for Signor also were paid in coupons redeemable only at the company store, located on the Lac Courte Oreilles Reservation, while white employees were paid in cash. Father Chrysostom Verwyst, who served as a missionary to the Chippewa Indians for many years, described the lumber companies operating in Wisconsin as "thieving corporations, who will cheat him [Indians] whenever they can." The dishonest acts of the lumbermen in their dealings with Native Americans in this era were not confined to Wisconsin. In the 1870s, lumberman Henry Sage operated on Michigan's Isabella Reservation, where the Indians received only a fraction of the value for the timber located on their land. A subsequent investigation described a "tale of wholesale debauchery and intimidation of the Indians" Sage and other lumber barons perpetrated on the reservation.[58]

Lake Forest cottage. Stearns built his own cottage at Ludington's Epworth Heights community in 1901, shown here at the top of Sunset Bluff. His next door neighbor was Congressman Roswell Bishop. (Courtesy of Epworth Heights Museum)

Conflict also emerged between the government's appointed Indian agent, S. W. Campbell, and members of the Bad River band. Campbell maintained strict control over the timber money tribal members received. Once a band member sold his/her timber rights, he/she received 5 percent of the sale. The remainder was deposited into a personal account. Rather than offering cash, Campbell often distributed the 5 percent payments in the forms of coupons redeemable for goods at the Stearns Company Store. This angered residents as it furthered Stearns's profits and influence over the local economy. Additionally, individuals often were not allowed to withdraw more than $10 to $15 per month from their individual bank accounts without special authorization from Campbell. This was in contrast to the manner in which Campbell's predecessor, J. C. L. Scott, allowed for withdrawals of $25 to $30. Campbell defended his actions by arguing he was protecting the Indians from whites who wanted to cheat them out of their money. In subsequent years a federal audit revealed that Campbell maintained between $30,000 and $200,000 of Indian timber money in his own personal bank account. Campbell later was discharged due to misuse of funds.[59]

Three primary factors enabled Stearns to continue his transgressions on the Lac du Flambeau and Bad River Indian Reservations. First, Stearns's political connections undoubtedly were helpful. Roswell P. Bishop was one of his original partners in the Joseph H. Cushway Company, and the two owned neighboring cottages in Ludington's Epworth Heights community. By 1903, the same year Stearns was forced to renegotiate the lumber contracts on both reservations, Bishop was a four-term veteran of Congress. An article from the *Grand Rapids Press* published in 1906 commented on their friendship and declared, "Stearns and Bishop have been very close for many years. It is understood that Bishop as congressman looked after Stearns' Indian land timber interests." Having a member of Congress look after his interests surely benefited Stearns.[60]

A second factor involved the probable collusion between Stearns and S. W. Campbell, the Indian agent in charge of the La Pointe Indian Agency from 1898 to 1906. In the annual report to the secretary of interior filed in 1899, Campbell declared, "there have been no serious complaints made by either Indians or contractors, and the timber operations have been conducted strictly in accordance with the regulations of the Department." Similar observations were repeated in the annual reports submitted by Campbell over the next several years.[61] In reality, complaints of irregularities were lodged as early as 1899, when several chiefs petitioned the secretary of the interior concerning abuses in which pine timber was wasted on Bad River lands. The Indian Rights Association also identified the corruption that was widespread on the Bad River Reservation in a report filed in 1902 in which the Indian farmer admitted under oath to cheating an Indian allottee out of nearly $200. Several other charges of corruption were pending against him, with the full knowledge of Agent Campbell, who appeared to condone the actions. Charges of "official laxity" and "corruption" also were made by the Indian Rights Association concerning conditions on the Lac du Flambeau Reservation, where Campbell did nothing in regard to allegations that Stearns was guilty of "cutting timber on unallotted lands in violation of the law."[62] Furthermore, at a series of Senate hearings conducted in 1909, claims that "corruption was rampant, and lumber company abuse was commonplace" were made concerning conditions on the Bad River Reservation. Possibly the most damaging example of collusion was published by a Chicago newspaper following a federal audit that revealed that Campbell maintained timber money belonging to Indians in his own personal bank account. He then made low-interest loans from this account to Stearns. While the full extent of the collusion between Stearns and Campbell is unclear, the evidence shows that some did exist and that while Campbell and other Indian Service employees claimed "no serious complaints" were made by the Indians, several complaints were registered, yet were not included in the annual reports Campbell submitted.[63]

A final factor that enabled Stearns to continue operating in Wisconsin in apparent violation of the negotiated contracts dealt with the general policies established by the national government in this era. Initially, the government's goal was to provide short-term employment for Indians in the timber industry, to be followed by the assimilation of Native Americans into American society and their transformation into sedentary farmers. As long as progress appeared to be taking place in these areas, government oversight was lax and ineffectual. This attitude was apparent in a letter written in June 1895 by Secretary E. Whittlesey, of the Board of Indian Commissioners, who visited Stearns's operations on both the Lac du Flambeau and Bad River Reservations. He observed that each reservation contained "a large expensive lumber mill, with the best modern machinery." His analysis also reflected the government's paternalism when he wrote, "these Indians have made more progress in the last two years than in any ten previous years," as demonstrated by the "neat frame houses scattered over the reservations and in the increased acreage of land under cultivation." Whittlesey continued by arguing that Stearns's contracts offered fair prices and provided employment year-round at good wages.[64] This attitude was further illustrated in an article appearing in the *National Magazine* in March 1903 that argued the sawmills allowed for the advance of "progress" onto Indian reservations. The author noted that Stearns's lumbering operations provided employment to Indians, creating an opportunity for them "to work like white men, and thus actually earn their living." The author continued this line of commentary and observed, "The Indians are building real homes. They are painting these little homes like white people; they embellish them with pretty little dormers and bay windows."[65]

Conclusion

Stearns's operations on the Bad River Reservation continued until the early 1920s. By that time, the timber from reservation land had been cleared and Stearns planned to transport additional logs from his holdings in Michigan's Upper Peninsula. Native American workers protested changes in wages and labor conditions in the fall of 1921 and went on strike. In response, Stearns abruptly closed the mill on the reservation. While the mill ran on a limited basis until 1922, its closure signified an end to an era. As a result, non-Indian employees fled the community while the remaining Native Americans faced unemployment, economic uncertainty, and frustration at their situation. In the following years, numerous health problems also faced the reservation's residents; possibly the most dangerous was tuberculosis. A study of 629 Bad River Indians conducted in October 1923 discovered that 4.5 percent of the children under age eighteen were infected, while 16.5 percent of adults carried the disease. Other ailments included numerous cases of individuals who were underweight, had decaying teeth, tonsillitis, or diarrhea. In 1937, fifteen years after the mill was shut down, fewer than one dozen families had electricity and most homes did not have running water. By the early 1940s, about two hundred Indian families lived on the reservation; of these, 150 had an average income of less than $750. There was plenty of criticism to go around concerning the conditions Bad River residents faced, many of whom were quick to blame Stearns for their problems.[66]

A level of responsibility for the plight of the Indians must fall on the shoulders of the United States government. A lack of oversight and enforcement of negotiated contracts allowed timber company violations to continue for decades. Additionally, going back to the 1890s, the government's policy (other than a short window of time between 1904 and 1908) always had been to clear-cut the land so it eventually could be farmed. Once the forests had disappeared, some Native Americans were able to establish self-sufficient farms; most did not. The cost of clearing the land was simply too much and the soils were not always conducive for farming. Land on the Bad River Reservation was so badly damaged by the timber operations that government officials believed it might not recover for decades. Based on the policies the United States government implemented, it was only a matter of time before the "boom" caused by cutting down the forests would be followed by a "bust" in which Native Americans would suffer. The actions of the Indians themselves also contributed to their poor economic condition because the money they received was not always spent wisely. Prior to Stearns's departure, officials at the La Pointe Indian Agency observed Native Americans spending their money "foolishly and recklessly" due to their lack of experience handling such wealth. Many also struggled with alcoholism as they attempted to cope with decades of shifting policies the US government adopted and the realities of reservation life in the twentieth century. In 1914, Superintendent Philip S. Everest estimated that 90 percent of the Bad River Chippewa used alcohol, and it was not difficult for the Indians to purchase it. Unfortunately, for many residents of the Bad River and Lac du Flambeau Reservations, the legacy of Stearns's lumber operations between 1893 and 1922 was negative.[67]

The actions of Justus Stearns and other lumber barons contributed significantly to the plight Native Americans living in Wisconsin faced. Stearns was accused of violating contracts and underreporting the amount of timber cut by his company, which cheated the Indians out of money they deserved. The practice of doing so even was labeled the "Stearns Method" by Daniel Grady, the special counsel the state hired to investigate abuses on Indian land. By paying Indians in coupons redeemable only at company stores, while paying white laborers in cash, a two-tiered system was established whereby the wages of Indian laborers cycled back to his company, thereby increasing profits. Although Stearns's operations in Michigan and Kentucky often involved significant contributions to charitable causes, it does not appear as if he was involved in any such endeavors in Wisconsin. Stearns's actions demonstrate the complexity of business capitalism in this era. As an entrepreneur, Stearns took risks and became wealthy due to his activities on the two Indian reservations. He used this wealth not only to invest in new business endeavors, but he also contributed significantly to philanthropic enterprises. At the same time, Stearns was very much an absentee owner in Wisconsin who did not challenge commonly held racist beliefs concerning American Indians. Instead, like his fellow absentee lumber barons with similar racial attitudes, he felt little social responsibility for conditions on the Indian reservations once his timber operations had ceased and he moved his business endeavors elsewhere.[68]

5

Establishing Operations in Kentucky and Tennessee

One cold rainy day in the Spring of 1902, Mr. E. E. Barthell, an attorney of Nashville, Tennessee, got off at Pine Knot and was met by Mr. Stearns' representative. They rode horseback to the old Gum Tree Tie yard. Beneath the old Gum, sitting on a waste dump taken from the railroad cut nearby, with a portfolio as a desk upon which to write, proxies were produced, articles of incorporation were signed, officers were elected, and the Stearns Coal Company, the Stearns Lumber Company, and the Kentucky & Tennessee Railway were born.

W. A. Kinne, *The Gum Tree Story*

According to a long-standing tradition repeated on many occasions, including by members of the Stearns family and a United States senator, a bag of bologna sandwiches played a prominent role in the founding of Stearns's coal and timber operations in Kentucky and Tennessee. The story involved John Toomey, a resident of Scott County, Tennessee, who traveled to Michigan with the goal of securing a private meeting with Justus Stearns in 1898. His purpose was to interest Stearns in some Tennessee property. Toomey attempted to meet with Stearns in his Grand Rapids office one day, but was denied. He came the next day and again he was denied. When he arrived a third day, with a sack of bologna and several pieces of bread, Toomey informed the secretary he would remain in the lobby until he was granted an audience with Mr. Stearns. Eventually, a meeting was held. Following further investigation, Stearns's brother-in-law, T. R. Lyon, was engaged to act as agent for Stearns to purchase the property. The determination of Mr. Toomey, armed with a sack of bologna and bread, set in motion a series of events that would transform what was known as the Big South Fork region of Kentucky and Tennessee. The timing of Toomey's visit was fortuitous; by the late 1890s Michigan's timber industry was experiencing a decline. Lumber barons such as Stearns were looking to invest their capital in new regions of the country and in new industries. Stearns took advantage of this opportunity; his

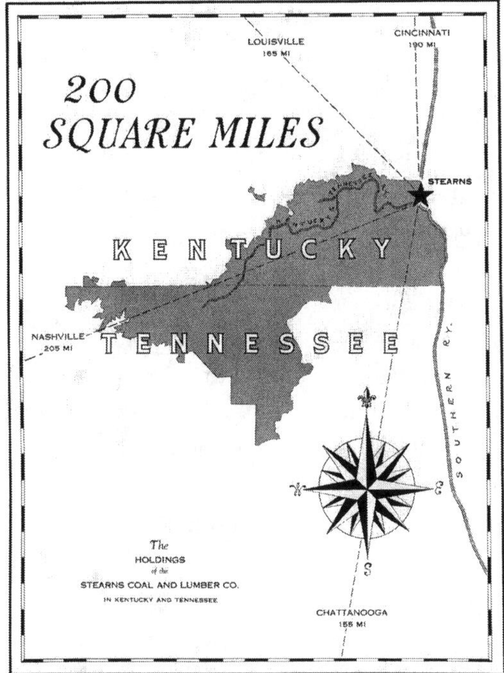

This map identifies the holdings of the Stearns Coal and Lumber Company in Kentucky and Tennessee. (Courtesy of Robert E. Gable)

original land purchase in the region encompassed about 30,000 acres. Eventually he would establish an empire of property two hundred square miles in size with mines and a sawmill that produced nearly one million tons of coal and eighteen million board feet of lumber in 1929.[1]

Mining and Timber in Kentucky and Tennessee

Much of the land originally owned by Stearns was sold later to the United States government in the 1930s and included a large portion of what became the Daniel Boone National Forest. This sale involved surface rights only; the company retained the valuable mineral rights. Additional land became part of the Big South Fork National River and Recreation Area created by Congress in 1974. The recreation area encompasses nearly 125,000 acres of property along the Big South Fork of the Cumberland River in Kentucky and Tennessee. It includes portions of Morgan, Scott, Fentress, and Picket Counties in Tennessee, and McCreary County in Kentucky. While in recent years it has emerged as a region with a strong tourism base, for nearly a century beginning in the 1880s it was the hub of extractive industries such as coal mining and timber operations. Today's tourists are drawn by the rugged terrain dominated by the

Cumberland River and its tributaries that carved steep gorges into the mountain ranges; however, the numerous hills and river valleys made the already difficult task of establishing coal and timber operations all the more challenging in the early 1900s.[2]

Stearns's mining and timber operations in Kentucky and Tennessee were unique as compared to mining communities in neighboring counties and states. The fact that the Stearns Coal and Lumber Company operated successfully for over seventy years demonstrated it could provide the steady leadership necessary in an uncertain industry. While mining and timber operations ended in the 1970s, the company continued a variety of real estate operations until it closed in 2012. When a major portion of the company was sold to Blue Diamond in 1975, Stearns stood as the oldest continuous mining operation in the history of Kentucky. Much of the reason for the company's success was due to the leadership provided by Justus Stearns, whose actions demonstrated he was a successful entrepreneur. Company officials took an interest in the lives of their employees and the surrounding community. They built homes, established schools, brought electricity and running water, and provided employment opportunities that raised the standard of living for people in a region known for its poverty. These actions also brought the region's residents into the industrial age, which would leave a legacy for generations to come. Justus Stearns never permanently resided in Kentucky, and while he visited often and provided the vision for his business, he was an absentee owner. However, three subsequent generations of Stearns family members who strove to improve life in the community lived in Stearns, Kentucky, took an active role in the organization's operations, and became stakeholders in the town. No operation as extensive as Stearns's could continue in excess of seven decades without some level of controversy, but the company's investment in the community in the early years helped to avoid some of the divisiveness that characterized other coal company towns.[3]

According to historian Ronald Eller, Stearns entered the coal mining industry during the second major phase in the development of the coalfields of the Appalachian South. The first phase began in the 1870s and 1880s in southeastern West Virginia and southwestern Virginia. The majority of these early coal producers had previous experience in the industry and hailed from the older coal mining communities of Pennsylvania. These pioneers paved the way for others, but were small in number. A second phase, which included Stearns, began in the early 1900s and was much larger; these newcomers tended to be younger and better educated. Between 1890 and 1920 nearly five hundred company towns were founded in the region. The third phase began in the 1920s and was characterized by consolidation. Increased competition and mounting expenses led many independent coal companies to sell out to larger corporations.[4]

Additionally, Eller surveyed the profiles of 140 men who operated coal mines in southwestern Virginia, southern West Virginia, and eastern Kentucky between 1880 and 1930. His study also can be used to compare Stearns's background and experiences to the traits of other contemporary coal barons. Eller found that, in general, those who established mining operations in the region were "independent, well-educated, and predominantly upper middle class." Additionally, "most were not native mountaineers," as only 22 percent came from the region.[5] A significant number of men, 46 percent, came from the North, chiefly Pennsylvania, while 31 percent were from the nonmountain South. Stearns had spent a short time in Pennsylvania, but was born in New York, and by 1902 he had been a resident of Michigan for over twenty-five years. Although Stearns was raised in what could be considered a middle-class family, his marriage to Paulina Lyon, and subsequent activities as a lumberman in Michigan and Wisconsin, had increased his wealth and social status significantly. Contrary to the "well-educated" background common among other coal barons, Stearns attended only common schools, aside from one business course he took as a young man. Stearns's actions also "bucked the trend" of consolidation that characterized the industry in the 1920s. He established the Stearns Coal and Lumber Company in 1902, and the company continued to mine coal up to the 1970s. These figures show that Stearns's background and experiences were both typical and atypical compared to his peers in the coal industry.[6]

L. E. Bryant and W. A. Kinne

Stearns's family connections helped to influence his successful operations in Michigan, but his initial partner in Kentucky was local resident Louis Bryant. L. E. Bryant, as he was commonly known, was the son of James and Roberta Bryant who originally came from Boyle County, Kentucky. Beginning in the 1880s, James Bryant began to purchase large tracts of land in both Kentucky and Tennessee. In some cases the land was poorly surveyed and the title was in question. Nevertheless, when James Bryant died in 1884, he claimed to own tens of thousands of acres of property, which he left to his wife Roberta. It fell to their son, L. E. Bryant, to secure the proper title to this land and develop it. The younger Bryant was a well-educated and ambitious young man. He graduated from Princeton University and then traveled to Freiburg, Germany, where he received an engineering degree from the School of Mines. Bryant often approached squatters living on land he believed his father had purchased and declared they were trespassing on "Bryant Land." If they refused to move, he offered a "lease" allowing them to remain on the land for a short time. As long as the inhabitants signed a document recognizing Bryant as the legal owner of the land, he rarely asked them to move. If they refused to sign the lease, he threatened a lawsuit, but if his own claim was questionable, he often agreed to deed the surface rights to the squatter in return for the mineral rights to the land. Numerous individuals agreed to this because they believed they had received a good trade in return for securing a legal title to the property on which they lived. Through techniques such as these Bryant was able to properly secure the title, or at least the mineral rights, to thousands of acres of land. Over the years, his land surveys came to be respected and others regarded title work for property to be complete if Bryant had conducted it.[7]

Bryant was a visionary who understood the potential wealth that existed beneath the soil and established the first coal mining operations in the region following the arrival of the Cincinnati Southern Railroad to the Big South Fork area in 1880. Bryant worked hard to promote the region's resources to outsiders. In a bold move on the eve of the Chicago World's Fair in 1893, he mined a single block of coal that weighed one ton from his mine at Worley. He hauled it by oxen to the Southern Railway line where it continued the remainder of its journey to Chicago by rail. Bryant proudly exhibited this piece to the fair's visitors in hopes of demonstrating the potential for coal production in Kentucky and Tennessee. Unfortunately for Bryant, he failed to attract investors until Stearns became interested a few years later. Bryant was trained as a mining engineer; he understood coal mining and held the mineral rights to the land. What he lacked was the capital necessary to build a railroad linking the tremendous coal reserves located in the Big South Fork region to the larger markets where coal was in greater demand. Eventually Stearns would establish a mutually beneficial partnership with Bryant to exploit the vast coal reserves in the area; Stearns provided the wealth and built the required railroad network. He had experience mining for salt in Michigan, but conditions for mining coal were quite different. Bryant provided his coal mining expertise and access to mineral rights. The two worked together for about twenty years, until Stearns bought out his partner in the 1920s and continued on his own.[8]

Sometime after John Toomey's interview with Justus Stearns, William Alfred Kinne, who had been working for Stearns since 1892, was sent to Kentucky and Tennessee to review the area and negotiate the purchase of a large parcel of land later known as the "Big Survey" for Stearns. He would serve as the first of many Michigan men who helped to launch Stearns's operations in the

South. W. A. Kinne, as he was most often known, was a graduate of the University of Michigan with a degree in civil engineering. For several months he traversed the lower reaches of the Big South Fork and worked as an agent for Justus Stearns, offering to purchase land from numerous residents. He promised local residents that once Stearns was able to establish his own operations in the area, better working and living conditions would follow. Not everyone trusted Kinne when he first arrived, but over time, in his own low-key manner, he was able to gain the confidence of many. He traveled by horseback and became comfortable meeting with people at local gatherings such as a community pie supper, funeral, or even a small group of whittlers sitting under a shade tree. He ate simple meals of corn pone and hog meat and washed it down with spring water served in a dipping gourd. According to local historian Samuel Perry, within a short amount of time, "Kinne ceased to be a foreigner. He taught the mountaineers much about the world beyond the Cumberland. In return, he, himself, was taught."[9]

Kinne and Stearns would have to remain patient when seeking title to land because in some cases proper titles could be difficult to determine and sales could take days or months to complete; the decision to sell land sometimes divided families. Two examples can demonstrate the complications involved with the land purchases and shed light on the people living in rural Kentucky and Tennessee in that era. The first instance involved land controlled by William Hatfield's heirs. All members of the family agreed to sell the land, with the exception of his widow, who refused. It appeared the deal would fall through, but Mr. Hatfield's sons convinced their mother to approve the sale. Unfortunately, Kinne had left town by that time. So, Mrs. Hatfield, who was about sixty years old, traveled nineteen miles by mule to Helenwood, Tennessee, to sign the necessary paperwork. She successfully reached town in time and signed everything required to complete the sale, but when the train came through, she became upset and declared she "had heard of those things but had never ridden one of those contraptions or never would.[10] She later moved to Texas to live with her son, but returned to see the old family property when she was in her eighties.

Possibly the most complex case Kinne was required to unravel involved land originally purchased by James Coffey in the early 1800s. It involved five or six lines of descendants and was further complicated by the destruction of records by fire. Following his initial purchase, Coffey sold his property to Jacob Troxell, who then handed it down to his son George. George married a young woman named Patsy and the two led an unsavory and eventful life. Prior to their marriage, Patsy was said to be a beautiful girl with "firey red hair" and a "striking appearance." She also was a "woodscolt," or an illegitimate child, who, after being taken in by foster parents at the age of eight or nine, was accused of killing her half sister. Despite her past, George and Patsy married and the two carried on a stormy relationship. At times they lived together harmoniously, while on other occasions they became separated. According to one account, during the Civil War, Patsy joined the soldiers marching with General Ambrose Burnside and gave birth, only to destroy her newborn child by "dashing it against a tree."[11] Following this incident, she was ordered to leave the camp of soldiers and never to return. Patsy and George did have children who reached adulthood, and it was through the descendants of one son, "Cut Short" John Troxell, that Stearns came to purchase this tract of land. By unraveling complicated histories such as these, Kinne laid the groundwork so land could be transferred properly to the Stearns interests. Eventually Kinne successfully negotiated a large purchase of what came to be known as the "Big Survey" of about 30,000 acres of land in Tennessee. Due to his successful negotiations and actions over many decades, it was likely that Kinne contributed more to the success of the Stearns Coal and Lumber Company than any individual outside of Justus Stearns himself. While originally a "Michigan Man," Kinne demonstrated he truly became a man of the Cumberland by choosing Somerset, Kentucky, to be his final resting place.[12]

Coal, Timber, Railroad Operations, and the Town of Stearns

Once Kinne successfully negotiated the purchase of the "Big Survey," Stearns undertook a remarkable level of activity in the early years of the twentieth century as he oversaw the establishment of coal mining and timber operations, a railroad, and a community that would bear his name. According to company records, as early as February 1902 the foundation for Stearns's coal mining empire was laid when a lease covering coal deposits beneath about 22,000 acres of land was negotiated between the Bryant family and Stearns. Terms of the lease called for Stearns to pay Mrs. Roberta Bryant (the mother of L. E. Bryant) a royalty of 5 cents for every ton of coal mined from the Bryant property. Later that year, under an old gum tree, articles of incorporation were signed for the Stearns Coal Company. Justus Stearns, who turned fifty-seven in 1902, was chosen to serve as chairman. The secretary was W. T. Culver, who had served as Stearns's lieutenant in numerous endeavors ever since the establishment of Stearns Siding in the 1880s. Robert L. Stearns, Justus's son, became treasurer. The company's attorney, Edward E. Barthell, prepared all the paperwork. Barthell, who hailed from Nashville, initially was hired while practicing law in Tennessee. He later moved to Chicago where he headed Stearns's legal department for several years.

July 4th in Stearns, Kentucky. Residents gather to celebrate Independence Day about 1920. (Courtesy of McCreary County Museum)

Additionally, Barthell was the brother-in-law of Robert L. Stearns. Barthell's wife, Florence Eugenia Freeman, was the sister of Robert's wife, Laura.[13]

Work on what would become Mine #1 was undertaken immediately. The camp near the first mine was named Barthell, in honor of the company's attorney. The land encompassing the camp and mine was owned by the Bryant family, but was included in the lease signed in 1902 and demonstrated the close business ties between Bryant and Stearns at the time. On June 1, 1903, the first shipment of coal left the yards at Barthell and company employees had reason to be proud. For years, the check from this initial sale of coal was displayed prominently in the company offices. To honor their success Stearns arranged for a carnival to visit the town. This gesture demonstrated the benevolence the Stearns organization offered: company leaders recognized the hard work of their employees by sponsoring a celebration. For many years the company continued this tradition by hosting a community-wide party every Independence Day. The company even arranged for Edwin Morrow, who would soon be named city attorney of the nearby town of Somerset, to address the crowd. Morrow later served as the governor of Kentucky and would have a unique relationship with the company over the years, but on the day of the festivities, he spoke of the wonderful future the residents of Stearns surely would enjoy. The celebrations had an immediate and long-lasting impact that was "instrumental in cementing the new bonds

Stearns, Kentucky, sawmill. The sawmill established by Stearns was possibly the nation's first all-electric mill. (Courtesy of McCreary County Museum)

between the company and its workers . . . the carnival became a symbol of fellowship, trust, and pride."[14] Mine #1 continued to operate for the rest of the year and produced a total of 32,595 tons of coal. The next several years saw a steady increase in coal production, and within seven years the company had six mines in operation, which produced 272,837 tons in 1910.[15]

Another initial project Stearns undertook was the construction of a sawmill and its necessary accompaniments. Some believed Stearns initially came to Kentucky strictly in search of new sources of timber and only later discovered the importance of the coal deposits. It was more likely that Stearns invested capital in the Big South Fork area in hopes of extracting value from both the coal and timber resources that were plentiful in the region. Whereas Stearns required an experienced partner, such as Louis Bryant, to provide expertise with the mining of coal, the company already had technical experts who could establish a state-of-the-art sawmill operation. After all, at that time Stearns probably remained the largest producer of finished lumber in the state of Michigan. Several experienced Stearns employees were brought from Michigan to provide leadership to the new operations under construction in Kentucky. When it was complete, the lumber mill that was constructed was "unlike any other in the South," although it was no small task to get established.[16] At the time, there were no power utilities in the area, so Stearns was required to establish his own. Once again, he built upon his experience in Michigan, where he owned and operated a power plant in Ludington. Before long, the region's first electrical plant provided power for

commercial and domestic use, and what was possibly the nation's first all-electric sawmill began to operate. The company started out hiring its own loggers who worked in teams cutting timber using crosscut saws. Logging of pine timber was conducted along the Big South Fork River and logs were floated downstream where they were collected in a boom and towed to the railroad before being loaded onto railroad cars for transportation to the mill at Stearns. The mill operated successfully until 1909, and it was refurbished and operated again in the 1920s.[17]

The third major project undertaken by Stearns involved the planning and construction of a railroad to transport finished lumber and coal to outside markets. Documents creating the Kentucky and Tennessee (K&T) Railroad were developed and signed the same day the Stearns coal and lumber operations were created in the spring of 1902. A letter from J. R. Thompson, president of the Southern Construction and Building Company charged with overseeing the construction of the railroad, demonstrated the work was well underway by December of that year. The railroad eventually would serve as a lifeline for the Stearns Coal and Lumber Company. In the early days, Stearns employees took the railway to work in the various mines each morning and returned home by rail in the evening. Those riding to and from work were allowed to ride free of charge. The largest railroad revenue by far came from the transportation of coal from the Stearns mines and others located in the area. Construction of this "lifeline" was expensive. According to an article in the *Louisville Post* from 1922, "cost for the first 15 miles was $50,000 a mile."[18] Company records confirm this estimate and indicate the company invested $166,730.99 between 1902 and 1904 to

K&T train emerging from tunnel. (Courtesy of McCreary County Museum)

construct approximately 3.5 miles of rail from the town of Stearns to the mine at Barthell. Costs were expensive because the rail line dropped nearly five hundred feet over the course of the first four miles. Not only did this require additional costs to grade and construct the track, but also it meant the company had to invest in more powerful locomotives to haul heavy loads up the steep incline.[19]

When it was created originally, the Kentucky and Tennessee Railroad was organized as a Michigan corporation. In 1904 it was reorganized with a charter from the state of Kentucky under the slightly new name, Kentucky and Tennessee Railway. By 1906 construction had continued southward about 7.5 additional miles to Yamacraw. There the pace of work slowed; crews were required to build a bridge over the Big South Fork River. The bridge itself was quite a feat of engineering because it was about six hundred feet long, made entirely of concrete, and required five large arches to span the full width of the river. A company engineer from Michigan oversaw the bridge's construction. He also had supervised the design of the Stearns lumber mill. Shortly after the bridge was completed a large storm caused the river to rise twenty feet and break nearly a million feet of logs from their booms upstream. The logs piled up against the bridge, which threatened the newly finished structure; despite the threats the storm caused, the bridge held. Construction then continued to extend the rail line. By the 1920s the K&T was extended all the way from Stearns, across the Big South Fork, and up Rock Creek to Bell Farm, Kentucky, a distance of some twenty-one miles.[20]

In 1909 Stearns entered into an agreement with the Southern Railway that proved to be lucrative. In that era coal fueled the nation's powerful locomotives and Stearns won the bid to refuel trains between Cincinnati and Chattanooga. It required a heavy investment to construct the necessary coal chutes over the rail lines. Company records show that from September 1910 to January 1913 the Kentucky and Tennessee Railway spent over $130,000 to meet the conditions of the new contract. Once the coal chutes were completed, however, it guaranteed numerous trains would stop in Stearns to refuel with coal from the Stearns mines. This was seen particularly with the Southern Railway's "Sunshine Special" express train, which made only two stops (Lexington and Stearns) on its way from Cincinnati to Chattanooga. Clearly, this contract enhanced the company's business and allowed more opportunities for the people living in what had been a terribly isolated area.[21]

A final project demonstrating the company's development in its early years was the establishment of the town of Stearns and additional company towns at mine locations in the surrounding area. The city was strategically located and became an anchor for the organization as it was positioned right where the K&T

K&T bridge. When it was completed in 1907, the bridge was the largest reinforced concrete railroad bridge in the South. (Courtesy of McCreary County Museum)

connected with the main line of the Cincinnati Southern Railway. The property originally had been owned by John Mounce, who obtained it in 1819. It later became part of the old Sellar's farm, but then was acquired by Bryant. It encompassed about five hundred acres of land, and the property was purchased, rather than leased, by Stearns. The first building to be constructed was a general store, which came to be known as Store No. 1. Construction of a hotel began almost at the same time as the first store was being built. The completion of the new store, with its inventory of unique items, was of great interest to the local inhabitants as it meant a wider variety of items would be available for purchase. Over time, sixteen "Company Stores" supervised by R. W. Henderson dotted the company's lands where residents of Stearns and the various mining camps could purchase brand name items for the first time locally.[22]

A new school, 16 x 32 feet in dimension, was built at company expense and opened in 1903. This was the first of many schools the company built that provided educational opportunities for the local residents. J. E. Butler, who later was named general manager and eventually served as company president, was a former teacher and principal who had graduated from the University of Michigan with a degree in literature. Investment in the region's educational system emerged as another example of the company's goodwill as it became policy that school construction should be part of any expansion of the organization into new areas. This also made the company a magnet of sorts for ambitious young people, particularly those with families because there was a "pathetic eagerness [among parents] that their children should have the advantages of an education which had many times been denied" to them. In the company towns of Barthell, Worley, Yamacraw, Rock Creek, and elsewhere, a total of nine schools were completed by the 1920s. School construction reached its peak in 1919 when the company built a modern school for elementary and high school students, made of brick and concrete, in the town of Stearns. In 1927, when two additional rooms were added to the school, more than four hundred students were enrolled in the high school with a potential for about one hundred graduating seniors each year. This was something in which local residents could take pride; after all, Stearns was located in McCreary County, with a population of only 14,627 in 1930. These numbers could be contrasted to Harlan County; a much larger coal-dependent county in eastern Kentucky with a population of more than 35,000 in 1928, which produced fewer than one hundred high school graduates. Furthermore, a national study of mining communities undertaken by the US Coal Commission in 1923 also demonstrated the unique emphasis placed on education by the Stearns Company, when it showed that of the 167 towns included in the study, only seventy-eight had high schools. Access to education, and the potential for the next generation's economic advancement, had become more readily available at Stearns than in other similar, and even larger, communities.[23]

Even critics of the coal mining companies, such as the author and activist Harry M. Caudill, were forced to acknowledge that Justus Stearns built the town of Stearns and by 1910 provided it with "electric lights, running water, a sewerage system, a recreation building, and telephones."[24] Employees could opt to live in company housing or choose to maintain their traditional residences while working in the mines; however, company housing tended to offer a higher standard of living because eventually most were equipped with electric lights in each room. This can be compared to the rest of the state; it was not until the 1940s when a majority of Kentucky's residents would have access to electricity in their homes.[25] The water tank that provided the miners' washhouse at Barthell with running water, as early as 1906, was impressive. It could hold 15,000 gallons of water with a capacity of 8,000 gallons per hour and nearly 200,000 gallons a day. While the miners had access to running water at the washhouses, residents of the mining camps obtained water for their homes from wells shared by six or eight families living in company housing. The study from 1923 discovered that fewer than 14 percent of company houses nationwide came with access to running water.[26] By 1903 the company had constructed over twenty-five homes in the company town of Barthell, at an average cost of $550. An in-depth study of the Barthell community, undertaken by Kim McBride, showed that residents paid between $3 and $7 in monthly rent for their homes. This more than likely was deducted from their wages at that time, but definitely became the common practice in later years. Presumably, higher rents were paid for homes with four rooms, as opposed to those with only two.[27]

Over time, the town of Stearns and surrounding communities saw a great deal of growth. To facilitate communication, in the early years the company established a telephone system that eventually grew to include more than fifty miles of telephone lines. Running water and sewage systems were put into place. Following a fire that destroyed the Stearns Hotel in 1908, another was constructed the following year. In 1922, fifty rooms were added to the hotel, which became famous for the great food and hospitality it offered visitors. In 1920 the State Bank of Stearns opened; Justus served as bank president for many years. A swimming pool, recreation hall, golf course, and several baseball fields provided leisure opportunities that often were paid for in part, or entirely, by the company. In some cases, such as the new baseball field built in 1926, part of the funding for the project came from a subscription paid by employees, while the company funded the remaining balance. An opera house was built next to the company store about 1910, which doubled as the town's first movie theater beginning in 1919. The main road that ran through the community of Stearns was paved in 1921; the company funded the project, while the state oversaw its construction. Each of these advancements took place in the town of Stearns without the adoption of municipal taxes.[28]

While it was true the investments in the community the Stearns Coal and Lumber Company made were examples of the founder's benevolence, they also made good business sense. After all, contented employees often were more productive and tended not to go on strike. Additionally, the development of company towns with uniform housing and parallel streets became common in the industry as they helped laborers adapt to their new work environment. Many of Stearns's employees had grown up on farms and were familiar with a pace of work governed by the rhythms of the seasons. Company towns, with their rigid social order, facilitated the sometimes-difficult task of converting farm laborers into industrial workers and demonstrated one step in the transformation of the United States from an agrarian society into an industrial power in the early twentieth century. Spending money to help establish stronger schools and recreational facilities was considered by many in the industry as just another business expense. As another southern coal baron commented, "We don't mean to convey the idea that we are more altruistic or have more generosity than any other group of employers . . . we try to do everything possible to make our men contented and satisfied in order to keep them. A lot of this welfare work is done with that object in view. We think it is good business."[29]

One of the full-time residents of the Stearns community was Robert L. Stearns. While his father often visited the Kentucky operations, Robert oversaw the company's day-to-day activities beginning in 1905, when he reached the age of thirty-three. His three-story home overlooking the entire Stearns complex was nicknamed "Hillcrest Club" where he was known to entertain celebrities, well-known artists, and other prominent individuals. He maintained Stearns as his permanent residence for several years and became an active member of the community. Even after purchasing another home in Cincinnati when his children grew older, it appeared as if he spent at least half of his time each month in Stearns. Diary entries from the 1910s and 1920s chronicled his extensive travels between Stearns, Cincinnati, Ludington, and other cities where the Stearns Empire began to spread by opening retail coal-sale outlets. Commuting via train was the most efficient way to travel in this era, but trains could be crowded and uncomfortable, and sometimes did not run on time. To make his necessary connections, Robert might be required to rise incredibly early (such as 2:00 a.m. on several occasions), and often he endured long stretches of time when he spent only one or two consecutive nights at one location.[30]

A diary entry for April 11, 1912, demonstrated the active management and attention to detail Robert L. Stearns took as he described a typical day spent in Stearns conducting company business:

> Up at 6:15–Breakfast 6:30
> Then to stores 1 and 3 and depot
> To office and open and dist. mail
> Answer letters
> Talk with Birch lumber and coal sales
> " " " " Dyas about going Cent. Ky.
> " " " " Patrick about taking lumber from yard
> " " " " Stevens dead hogs
> " " " " Braunne " "
> " " " " Henderson as to some bills
> Worked on prospectus of coal lands
> Signed vouchers
> Talked with Blevins, time keeper
> Out over proposed county seat site with Kinne
> Went over blue prints for Ross track river curve
> Talk with Seaton about motors
> To dinner 12 to 12:45
> More work on prospectus
> Opened mail and distributed
> Answered letters
> Out around property where fire was threatening
> Backfired
> Supper 6 to 7
> Talked new county with Kinne
> " " " " Petersen about $9,000,000.00 plant
> " " " " Butler increased mining rate
> " " " " Burch coal matters
> Wrote letters and home 9:45[31]

Justus Stearns was an absentee owner of his Kentucky operations, yet his actions were not typical compared to other absentee owners of his era. The fact that his own son lived at the company headquarters and took such personal charge of its operations was unique. Absentee ownership was an industry norm and often created resentment in other mining communities where employees shared feelings of futility, believing their destiny was strictly controlled by the mining companies. In contrast to the extensive investment in the town of Stearns by officials of the Stearns Coal and Lumber Company, managers of other organizations often "failed to develop a sense of identification with the community" and discouraged top employees from becoming involved with the local community. "Thus, mining management was essentially unrelated to and unconcerned with the town's problems and development."[32] For Stearns miners and their families, the opposite was true in their case as top company officials lived locally, had a personal stake in their community, and therefore became active members who contributed to its welfare on a regular basis.

One of Robert L. Stearns's diary entries (above) can be seen as an example of his interest in community affairs. Two entries, "Out over proposed county seat site with Kinne," and "Talked new county with Kinne," referred to the creation of McCreary County by the state legislature in 1912. The newly formed county was created from portions of Pulaski, Wayne, and Whitley Counties and was named for Governor James B. McCreary, a Confederate war hero and politician. The establishment of the new county would help residents living in outlying areas because in the past the distances to their respective county seats were too far for their needs to be met. Many believed the city of Stearns would be the logical site for the new county's seat given the Stearns Coal and Lumber Company was the dominant force in the region. However, while company officials supported the creation of the new county in hopes that it could bring more law and order to an area where violence could be commonplace, they believed the residents of the county should determine the new seat of government and did not pressure voters to choose Stearns over another city. A battle then emerged between Whitley City and Pine Knot, with most employees of the company in support of Whitley City. As shown by the entries in Stearns's diary, company officials were very aware of public opinion as the decision to choose the county's new seat of government drew near. In the end, Whitley City was chosen over Pine Knot.[33]

Another program that revealed the Stearns's operations to be unique was the implementation of a company-sponsored demonstration farm in McCreary County. C. W. Broyles, an agronomist from the University of Michigan, operated the farm. Broyles also owned the first steam-powered tractor in the area. The farm's purpose was to help residents improve their farming techniques. Company officials actually encouraged employees and their families to supplement their diets by establishing small-scale farms and raising animals. Whereas residents of coal company towns in eastern Kentucky and West Virginia were subject entirely to the boom or bust nature of the industry, many Stearns miners were able to supplement their incomes and provide for their own economic welfare during hard times by maintaining family farms. Company stores were stocked with shelves of durable goods but rarely contained fresh produce. Residents living in Stearns could have small gardens, while those in outlying communities with more space cultivated large cornfields. Canning could preserve produce, but food storage could be a problem because most homes were cramped and did not contain cellars. Many families kept chickens, a cow, some pigs, even rabbits or a goat. At one family's home, the chickens were allowed to roost in the trees, because they had no chicken coop. Families raising a cow or chickens could supplement their income by selling milk or eggs to neighbors and coworkers.[34]

Encouraging its employees to establish small-scale farms could be a double-edged sword for the company. It clearly enhanced morale and granted workers access to a more balanced diet. Healthier workers also were more productive. Additionally, due to market conditions, the mines did not always operate at full capacity. If orders for coal were down, as they often fluctuated, there could be a great deal of inventory and the mines might run only two or three days each week. If the "down time" occurred in the summer months (as it often did when demand for heating coal was lower) employees could maintain their economic independence, even if income from their wages was lower than expected. On the other hand, entries from the diary of Robert L. Stearns, such as, "Shortage of miners, in consequence of making their farms," from May 1911 or, "Men at mines dropping out rapidly to go to farms," from April 1913 reflected his frustration when employees chose to prepare their land for spring planting rather than work in the mines. By 1917 a bonus system was implemented providing an incentive for men to continue working in the mines, rather than on their farms, when coal sales were strong, to maintain mine production at full capacity.[35]

Stearns officials also brought in the first medical professionals to practice in the area. The first doctor the company employed to provide health care for its workers was George R. Tubbs. He began his study of medicine at the Hospital College of Medicine located in Louisville, Kentucky, in 1896 and graduated four years later. He eventually found his way to Stearns in 1902 and described his initial experiences in a letter written many years later. "There were only three or four houses when I arrived. I was the first doctor there and delivered the first baby to be born in Stearns. The baby was named George, for me. I think the family name was Haynes."[36] When the doctor arrived, the Kentucky and

Tennessee Railroad had not been completed and there were no suitable roads, even for horses, so he often was required to walk five miles to reach his patients. The company employed him to provide health care for all the employees, including those constructing the K&T Railroad, mill workers, and men working in the mines. It remains unclear exactly how much these initial employees were charged for their health care plan, but by 1922 single men had $1.00 per month, while men with families had $1.50 per month, deducted from their paychecks to be members of the Stearns Sick and Accident Association. As late as 1938, and possibly beyond this date, the same amount was deducted from their paychecks. This can be contrasted to the more common $2.00 deduction most Kentucky miners paid. Stearns miners paying the family rate received coverage for all members of their family. Company records for November 1903 also indicate that for his services Dr. Tubbs received $154.75 while the following month he received $169.60.[37]

Dr. Tubbs worked for the company for only two years, and it appears he left abruptly due to a disagreement with J. E. Butler concerning smallpox vaccinations. In 1904 smallpox appeared in the community and Tubbs feared an epidemic. When the vaccine arrived, Tubbs went with Butler to meet the mine workers preparing for the morning shift at Barthell, but men seemed reluctant to accept the vaccine. Butler was concerned a general outbreak would lead to a quarantine and bring all work on the railroad and coal mines to a standstill. Consequently, Butler rolled up his sleeves and had the doctor vaccinate him first, in full view of the men, to show he was not afraid. Tubbs thought this was odd because Butler had informed him in a private conversation he already had survived smallpox and his vaccination would be unnecessary. Nevertheless, the doctor did as he was told. Butler also ordered Tubbs not to report the handful of cases that had emerged, but the doctor did so anyway, fearing he might lose his medical license if he did not. In the meantime, Butler's arm became irritated and turned red and began to swell. When he learned that Tubbs had reported the smallpox cases to the authorities, Butler declared his "employment would be ended as soon as he could find a doctor who would follow his orders." Tubbs decided not to wait and left Stearns within a few days. Other doctors followed Tubbs, and most lasted longer than two years. Additional medical practitioners from the early years include J. H. Murphy, Robert Sievers, P. Hogue, and Lemuel J. Godbey.[38]

According to the US Coal Commission, "dental service was in practicable reach of only a small minority," of American coal mining communities in 1923.[39] Prior to 1913 there were no licensed dentists practicing in McCreary County. Area residents in the company's early years received care from itinerant dentists who set up temporary offices in grocery stores or other convenient locations. Early drills were foot-powered. It was not until the arrival of Dr. Mitchell Thomas in 1913 that a licensed dentist became available for members of the community. He was not an employee of the company, but after practicing in Stearns for about three years, he decided to move to a new location, which he hoped would be more lucrative. When Robert L. Stearns learned Thomas might be leaving, he urged the dentist to remain in town and worked out an arrangement beneficial to both parties. Robert and Justus agreed to build a house for Dr. Thomas and his family in 1916. It was a nice home that, in later years, included eight rooms, two baths, a garage, and a barn with a large yard. Members of the family lived in the house until 1973 and at that time were paying rent of $31 per month. Dr. Mitchell Thomas's son, Frank Thomas, grew up in that house, was trained as a dentist, and practiced dentistry in Stearns for many years. He later served as president of the Stearns Coal and Lumber Company, saying, about the change in his profession, that he "was still in an extractive industry."[40]

Conclusion

Taken as a whole, Justus Stearns's commitment to have his company invest in the community's schools, allowing, and even encouraging, employees to engage in small-scale farming, and providing health care professionals to care for sick and injured employees and their family members, laid a positive foundation for his company's relationship with rank and file employees. These programs were distinctly progressive compared to the national standards of the day. While tension existed between labor and management in later years, it was tempered due to the actions of officials in the company's formative years. Prior to the arrival of the Stearns operations, the community of Stearns did not even exist. Much of the surrounding area remained isolated with poor schools, widespread poverty, and a lack of opportunity for advancement. Beginning in 1902 and continuing for many years after Justus Stearns's death, the Stearns Coal and Lumber Company served as the dominant force that positively shaped the economic development and social life for families living in the northern portions of the Big South Fork area of Kentucky and Tennessee.[41]

6

Mining Coal in Kentucky

There was an art and a science to coal mining, even in the early days.

Personal interview, William "Doc" Coffey

I'd rather live in a coal mine than anyplace I'd ever lived. . . . There was something, buddy, that was just enticing. You had your own store, commissary they called it. And everybody knew everybody. If you needed help, boys, you could get it immediately. The whole camp would nearly turn out to help you. And that's why I really like it. And I just really loved to go around to the drift mouth, when I lived there, and just stand there and inhale that air coming out of there.

Donald Whalen: McBride, Barthell Coal Camp, 244, University of Kentucky Libraries

After operating for nearly ten years in Kentucky and Tennessee, Stearns's activities in the area were reorganized with a new focus. The coal and lumber operations were consolidated into one business in 1910, while the K&T Railway remained separate. The sawmill shut down temporarily following the reorganization, while the new company placed a renewed emphasis on coal production, rather than lumber. Over the course of the next several years, output at the Stearns mines steadily increased. The labor force working in the mines was drawn largely from the states of Kentucky and Tennessee, as opposed to other mining operations in the country that often relied heavily on the labor of immigrants. Mining coal was a difficult occupation that left men dirty and calloused. Stearns employed modern mining techniques and established high standards for safety at his mines. Yet accidents, some of which ended in fatalities, did occur.[1]

The Mines

All of the early Stearns company mines were drift mines, rather than shaft or slope mines. Drift mines could be opened on the side of a mountain after the coal seam outcrop was exposed. Slope mines were employed if the coal seam was

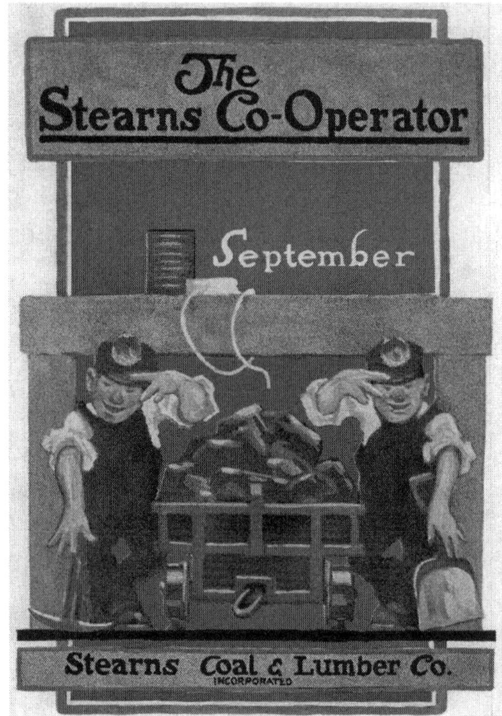

The Stearns *Co-Operator* was published monthly to highlight various businesses in the Stearns Empire. This edition highlights Stearns Coal and Lumber Company operations. The cover art was drawn by Robert L. Stearns. (Courtesy of Robert E. Gable)

near enough to the surface that a slope from the surface could reach it, yet the coal remained unexposed. If coal was deep underground, shaft mines were necessary, requiring a vertical elevator to move men back and forth to their workstations and to bring coal from the mine to the surface. While the initial cost of establishing a drift mine was much less than a shaft mine, dangerous gases and water still could accumulate, so this type of mining had its own complications.[2]

The coal located in Kentucky's coalfields was bituminous, which has a higher degree of impurities, but could be mined less expensively compared to the anthracite fields of denser, low-sulfur coal common to Pennsylvania. Stearns coal seams, averaging about 4.5 feet of coal in thickness, lay in relatively horizontal beds through the mountains, but all could be reached from the side of the mountains, where the coal was exposed. A drift mine required the creation of a flat working area by "facing up" a high wall above the base of the seam. Then, one or more parallel tunnels were started. In the early years, a two-entry system generally was used. A pair of tunnels that ran side by side, each about 12 to 14 feet wide, extended from the drift mouth into the side of a mountain. These

A group of miners is shown here sitting on a mine locomotive. (Courtesy of McCreary County Museum)

served as "main streets" and might continue 70 feet until the main entries were joined with cross tunnels. After the first crosscut tunnels were some distance into the mine, a fan was installed to "suck" the air out from one entry (normally the left-hand entry), which pulled fresh air into the mine from the main entry. Miners would enter the mine through the "drift mouth" following fresh air as they walked through a series of tunnels to reach their workstations. The mines were organized and mapped, similar to the layout of a city. Farther in, secondary tunnels ran perpendicular to the main entries, which continued directly from the drift mouth. As work progressed underground, they were connected to other tunnels, so the mines often extended under the mountain for several miles. Miners generally were assigned a "room," extending an entry or cross-entry, in which to work. There, they loaded coal into cars, which then were transported back out of the mine through the drift mouth. One veteran miner, who later served as general mine superintendent, William "Doc" Coffey, described it this way: "The way to explain what a coal mine would look like to you inside is to just imagine being up in a helicopter over a city. Remove all buildings, leave all the streets and the blocks. The streets and cross streets are your mine entries, the blocks are a big solid block of coal you leave to support the [roof] top."[3]

Inside the mines, it was easy to become disoriented and lost. One miner from 1910 described his experience as he entered the mine's main entry tunnel by stating, "I stood, half-dazed by the roar of unknown sounds, my eyes blanketed by the absence of light and my whole mind smothered and crushed . . . into a seeming wall of darkness."[4] The darkness continued as he walked through the tunnels, alternately illuminated by the light of the flame in his pit lamp or the headlights of the motors (mine locomotives) hauling men, coal, and other cargo underground. The darkness permeated everything, from the endless walls of coal, to the faces and clothing of the men coated with coal dust, to the emptiness of the tunnel through which he traveled to earn his daily wage. He also recalled a silence, similar to the darkness, but rather a "total absence of sound, rather than stillness." The silence would prove to be unnerving and something he never quite became used to, even after he had worked in the mines for some time.[5]

A great deal of technological advancement took place over the course of the first thirty years of the Stearns mining operations. In the early years men would hand drill holes into the face of the coal and then place explosives into the holes to be fired. Once the coal was blasted, it was torn down and broken into smaller pieces with a pick and then hand shoveled into a coal car. Mules pulled the cars through the mines and then outside, only to return again with an empty car, waiting to be loaded. As early as 1914, and probably prior to this year, Stearns operated his mines with electricity, and some mines replaced mules with electric motors (mine locomotives). As the technology progressed, "machine men" operated electric cutting machines, which looked similar to large chainsaws, that undercut a large section of coal six inches above the room floor and several feet horizontally. Once this had been completed, another crew of "drillers" followed and used air drills to create a series of "shot-holes." A final crew of "shot-firers" filled the holes with powder and "fired" the powder. These blasts were conducted at night, allowing the dust and smoke to dissipate, and the whole process of loading the cars with coal would begin again in the morning. The advancements made in the Stearns mines over the first two decades of the twentieth century demonstrated that "technologically, they were years ahead of other operators in eastern Kentucky."[6]

The air generally felt cool in the mines if one entered in the summer, but warm in the winter as it remained a steady, moderate temperature throughout the year. To preserve safety, it was necessary to maintain a continuous flow of fresh air circulating through the mine tunnels, which could be difficult to accomplish. Prior to the use of electric fans, a chimney had to be drilled through the mine roof above which a furnace ran so the bad air could escape through the chimney as fresh air continued to enter through the mine entrance. In the early years, men took canaries with them underground as a safeguard to detect the presence of dangerous gases. As time went on, electric fans were used to circulate air and the foremen carried a mine safety lamp to detect methane gas to ensure that working conditions remained safe. As the mine tunnels lengthened, crews constructed partitions, called brattices, to maintain the flow of fresh air to each working area. A temporary brattice might be made of canvas, while those that were more permanent were made of wood. Each brattice was designed to improve ventilation by stopping the airflow in a cross-tunnel, while forcing air ahead to new workstations, as teams of miners worked farther into the mountain. Brattice work was a full-time position and several crews might operate in a mine at the same time.[7]

Even by the 1920s and beyond, and most definitely in the first two decades of the Stearns operations, coal was loaded into mine cars by hand. According to operating rules the company established in 1922, either in pairs or alone, men would be given a room in which to work and were required to "work it to completion." The mine foreman had the authority to assign rooms that each miner had to finish or, "work up the place assigned to him." Men could apply for a specific location in which to work, but the foreman was prohibited from promising places in advance. Operating rules stated that room entries were required to be six and one half feet in height, and when working a room, employees were expected to operate in a "workmanlike manner."[8] Armed with a pick and shovel, loaders set to work shoveling coal, which previously had been blasted from the rock face, into a waiting mine car. Even in the cool temperatures, the men often stripped to the waist and set to work lifting each shovelful of coal four feet into the car. At times, they might have to use their picks to break the large coal blocks into smaller pieces. Once the car began to fill, it had to be "trimmed" by placing larger chunks on top of the pile. Their bodies would be covered in sweat, and coal dust clung to their skin. Hands became blistered; muscles ached. Over time calluses developed over the blisters and the difficult work continued.[9]

Individual miners were assigned a number when they began working for the company and each man had several small brass tags upon which his number was stamped. After loading a car, a brass tag was attached to it and then the car was transported by mule (in the early days) or electric-powered motor (mine locomotive) to the mouth of the mine and eventually to the scale house and tipple.

Mining coal was a dirty and dangerous occupation, but it also provided employment and expanded economic opportunities. (Courtesy of McCreary County Museum)

The tipple was a huge building, several stories high, that sorted coal into different commercial grades. Before a mine car was dumped, it had to be weighed and inspected. Often, there were two men who oversaw this process. The weighman was considered a "company man" who maintained the company's records for all the pounds of coal attributed to each miner. This was important because loaders were paid by the weight of coal they mined. To ensure the company did not cheat the men out of their hard days' labor, a check weighman, representing the miners, conferred with the weighman to confirm the men received proper credit. Often the miners elected the check weighman to his position. Each miner's car was inspected for slate or other waste rock. If there was too much, workers faced a fine of $1, a forced layoff of one day, or a discharge for a multiple offense. If miners were found maliciously adding slate or rock to their weight, they faced an immediate discharge, even for a first offense. Once it had been properly weighed and inspected, the coal was put through the tipple. After the raw coal was dumped, the tipple's perforated screens made of sheet steel shook back and forth until the coal dust and smallest particles fell out, with the larger sizes then sorted onto screens with larger perforations. The coal was carefully inspected as it passed over the screens to ensure impurities were removed. Eventually the different sizes of coal were collected and loaded onto rail cars, ready to be transported to customers.[10]

At the end of each shift, the men emerged from the tunnels exhausted from the day's work, covered in coal dust. Stearns miners then could take advantage of something that many other miners did not have: a washhouse. The Stearns Coal and Lumber Company was one of the first organizations in Kentucky to ensure that men could return home clean at the end of the day; the company constructed washhouses at many of its mines. The US Coal Commission report noted there were "very few" washhouses available for miners nationwide in 1923, and a follow-up report from 1946 indicated fewer than half of the mining operations in the United States at that time included washhouses, including only 35 percent of the mines located in the state of Kentucky. Men working for Stearns paid for the privilege of using the company washhouse. Rates were set by a petition signed by at least 75 percent of the men working at each mine. Employees were charged 50 cents per month for the use of the washhouse along with a locker. If no locker was used, they paid 25 cents. It appeared as if most, if not all, Stearns miners took advantage of this opportunity because the washhouses provided easy access to hot and cold water. In the early years company housing did not include running water for a shower or even a bathtub. By keeping a set of work clothes in a locker at the washhouse, at least some of the dust and grime of the mines could be left at the place of work, rather than being brought home.[11]

Miners could earn a decent wage for their work, particularly if the demand for coal was strong and the mines operated at full capacity. Unfortunately, the mines did not always operate at this pace, as demand for coal was sporadic, and other factors influenced how many days each week a miner might work. If the mines operated only part of a week (which was common during the summer when less coal was needed for heating), employees would be forced to rely on income from their farms, or other sources, to make ends meet. A wage scale the company implemented in 1909 revealed the amount of money each miner could earn on a daily basis for much of this early era. Day laborers worked ten-hour days in the early 1900s, but as early as 1922 the eight-hour day was adopted. Miners who chose, or were assigned, to work as day laborers earned $2.25 per day. Men who loaded coal into cars were paid by the tons of coal they loaded. Those working coal where the seam was less than 30 inches earned 67.5 cents per ton, while individuals working in forty-eight inches or over earned at least 50 cents per ton; those working seams between thirty and forty-eight inches were compensated at varying rates.[12]

The highest paid day laborers working for Stearns were blacksmiths and machine runners at $2.50 per day. Blacksmiths sharpened the men's picks and repaired their shovels while working on other projects that required skilled labor. By 1922 miners had $1.00 deducted from their pay each month to ensure the blacksmith properly maintained their equipment. The fact that the position of machine runner was listed in the wage scale for 1909 would indicate that electric cutting machines were being used to undercut coal in at least some of the company's mines by that date. Timbermen were paid $2.00 per day while their helpers received $1.75. The timbermen were responsible for providing support for the tunnels and rooms by placing wooden posts along the roof a few feet from each wall to prevent a roof collapse; slate falls from the roof were one of the most common causes of severe injury the men suffered underground. Trackmen received $2.00 per day to maintain the tracks underground that allowed the cars to travel smoothly with their heavy loads. The lowest paid day laborers were the entry-level positions of mucker ($1.50 per day) and outside laborers ($1.25 per day). Muckers worked above- and belowground and were responsible for shoveling fallen coal out of the way as it accumulated along the tracks. Muckers could be placed at numerous locations in the mines. Outside laborers did not work underground, but might be assigned a variety of jobs strictly aboveground, such as picking slate and other impurities out of the coal, general cleanup, or other tasks.[13]

It can be difficult to predict how much coal each miner could produce in one day because conditions varied greatly from state to state, over time, and even daily, but national averages demonstrated that as mining technology improved, average daily output per man increased. In 1890 the average daily output stood at 2.56 tons, grew to 2.98 tons in 1900, reached 3.46 tons by 1910, and by 1921 averaged 4.19 tons per man. It also remains unclear exactly how Stearns miners compared to the national averages, but data is available for the state of Kentucky. In 1921, the overall average production of coal per man in the state was less than the national average, at 4.1 tons. For coal loaded by hand, it was 3.4 tons, whereas it was 4.2 tons for coal mined by machine. Stearns's employees harvested coal by hand and by machine. It was possible a fast-working miner might be able to load ten tons of coal on a single day; however, this probably could be accomplished only occasionally and might involve more than one miner operating under the same number. For example, a father and son might work together as a team under the same number, shoveling coal into two separate cars, while assigning the father's employee tag to both cars.[14]

Payday for Stearns employees came twice each month, and workers were paid in US currency; however, beginning in October 1914 the company also compensated employees using company scrip when workers requested an advance on their wages prior to a scheduled payday. Scrip initially came in the form of paper coupon books in denominations of 5, 10, 25, and 50 cents as well as $1 and $5. Employees could purchase items from the company store using their scrip, but many other businesses in the area chose to accept Stearns company scrip at a discount or even face value. While the system could be convenient for those in need of money, it also could be problematic. Although metal scrip coins were adopted by the company in later years, in the early days the paper on which the scrip was printed was not very durable, so it did not last as long as regular currency. Also, if a customer paid for items with scrip at the company store, any change they received came in the form of loose coupons, which easily could be lost or destroyed. Probably the largest drawback came from the potential overreliance on scrip by employees. Workers and their families could fall into a pattern of requesting an advance on a paycheck and find themselves caught in a constant cycle of debt. This could happen if an employee became sick, injured, or if their services were not needed for a time because the mines were not running at full capacity. Employees who became too reliant on scrip might discover their paycheck was shrinking over time, which required an additional advance, and only made the cycle more difficult to escape.[15]

There were advantages and disadvantages for Stearns, and other coal operators nationwide, using scrip, but the competitive advantages almost always outweighed the disadvantages. One benefit for the company was that it encouraged employees to shop at the company stores, thereby increasing revenue through retail sales. Similarly, wages paid to workers could simply cycle back to the company when groceries, clothing, or other items were purchased at these stores. In many parts of the country company stores were located in the heart of the mining communities, which tempted employees to take an advance on their pay in scrip to purchase products at the stores. National studies showed that, at times, families felt forced into purchasing goods at the company store. By 1916 the Stearns Coal and Lumber Company operated nine stores in Stearns and other company towns, with combined annual retail sales of about $350,000. Stearns company stores stocked a wider range of items on their shelves than other stores, but at "elevated prices" as compared to prices in nearby counties. Unfortunately for Stearns employees and others living in the area, all stores located in McCreary County appeared to have inflated prices until the county road system was implemented in later years. These came as a result of increased income seen by residents of McCreary County, as opposed to neighboring counties, following the establishment of Stearns's coal operations and the relative prosperity of its workers.[16] Stores operated by coal companies

Stearns offices and stores. By 1916 Stearns Coal and Lumber Company was the third-largest coal producer in Kentucky, and its assets included 450 company houses, nine stores, a hotel, and numerous additional buildings. (Courtesy of Robert E. Gable)

nationwide were accused of establishing "monopolistic prices" with items for sale at prices much higher than independent operators. Many employees also recognized the potential problems associated with the abuse of scrip advances by using the system cautiously. While some workers undoubtedly became indebted to the "company store," this tended to occur only rarely. One disadvantage of using scrip for the companies involved corruption. Because Stearns's coupon books were printed on paper that was readily available, counterfeiting could be a problem. One way the company tried to combat corruption was that Stearns employees who handled scrip, such as bookkeepers, clerks in company stores, or even waiters in the company restaurant, were not allowed to receive it as an advance on their pay. In 1928 Stearns was forced to suspend the issuance of scrip after three employees stole $22,000 worth of coupon books at a company store in Worley and tried to cover their actions by setting fire to the building. The store and its contents were a total loss, but within a short period of time the scheme's ringleader was identified, and the company was able to reissue scrip after three months. By the 1940s, scrip was used in only 17 percent of the mines included in a national study. Unions opposed it and several states either outlawed it or strictly regulated its use as an attempt to protect workers;

however, it was used in the coalfields of southern Appalachia for decades, and the Stearns company did not discontinue issuing scrip until 1964.[17]

Not only would employees see deductions taken from their paychecks if they had taken advances in the form of scrip, but also additional withholdings also lowered their take-home pay. As shown in chapter 5, rent was deducted for those living in company housing and for other items such as health care, blacksmithing, and use of the company washhouse. Employees wishing to heat their homes with coal could carry all they needed from the mines to their houses for a fee of $2.50 per month. It could be delivered for a slightly higher fee. Workers were charged a minimum of $1.50 per month for the use of electricity in company houses. The company also requested employees make a small contribution to a school fund to help defray the costs of school construction. Finally, a committee of employees set an amount to be collected toward a burial fund designed to defray funeral expenses. The expenses outlined above replaced the need for municipal taxes and demonstrated the overarching influence of the Stearns operations in the company towns it established.[18] The deductions also led to resentment on the part of some workers who believed their labor was being exploited unjustly to the benefit of the company. Chapter 7 will address the tension that developed between Stearns miners who sought to form a union and company officials who tried to prevent the union from gaining influence among its workforce.

Mine Workers

The demographics of Stearns's workforce clearly showed that the great majority of the company's employees came from the states of Kentucky and Tennessee. The Stearns company town of Barthell can be used as a representative sample. Census data showed that in 1910, 57 percent of its residents were born in Kentucky, while 36 percent came from Tennessee; 6 percent came from other states, and only 1 percent were born outside the United States. The trend continued with the census of 1920 even more clearly, as 99 percent of Barthell's population was born in either Kentucky (89 percent) or Tennessee (10 percent), leaving only 1 percent from other states. It is possible that if a census had been taken in 1903 or 1904 it would have registered a higher number of foreign-born residents. Company records from those early years reference Italian workers at least twice; however, data demonstrated clearly that locals living in the region of the Big South Fork made up the majority of the employees working for Stearns.[19]

Most living in the Barthell community also lived in nuclear families made up of parents and children. Just over 80 percent of the residents of Barthell were twenty-nine years old or under in 1910, whereas ten years later, the percentage was a little lower, but not much had changed. Each census indicated that at least 60 percent of Barthell's residents were under the age of twenty. These figures reinforce the fact that while mining was exclusively a male occupation, a large percentage of miners occupying company towns lived in family units. While most lived in such families, 40 percent in 1910 either had relatives living with them or housed boarders who were not blood relations. The average household included 6.4 persons in 1910, and dropped to 4.8 by 1920. The large number of boarders and larger household sizes in 1910 probably were due to a lack of housing following the initial establishment of Stearns's mining operations in the area. Over the years, even those living outside the company town of Barthell came to be influenced by Stearns's mining activities. In 1900 only 14 percent of those living in the general area surrounding Barthell were engaged in coal mining as their primary occupation; by 1910 the number had grown to 36 percent, and by 1920 it rose to 78 percent. While it can be predicted that company towns like Barthell would be made up of coal mining families, the fact that 78 percent of those living outside company housing worked as miners, or in a mining-related field, demonstrated the influence held by the Stearns Coal and Lumber Company in the region.[20]

Conditions at Barthell can be compared to those in the United States and the state of Kentucky in this same era. Kentucky had a population of 2,289,905 in 1910. Of these, 88 percent had been born in Kentucky and only about 2 percent were born outside of the United States. Kentucky's lack of a foreign-born population was not unique when compared to other southern states. Many from the South had foreign populations that made up less than 5 percent of their state's population overall. In contrast, many northern and western states had counties in which those born outside the country made up one-third, one-half, or even more of its population. In 1920, about 65 percent of coal miners nationwide were born in the United States; of those, 8.1 percent were African American. About one-third of the country's miners were foreign born. While Kentucky's mining population was not studied in detail in a national report from 1923, in the neighboring state of Indiana, immigrants made up 17.3 percent of its mining workforce, while Alabama's included only 3.6 percent. More than 55 percent of Pennsylvania's mine workers were foreign born. Census data from 1920 also indicated that over 730,000 men worked in coal mines throughout the country, while Kentucky was ranked number five in the nation with over 44,000 miners employed (Pennsylvania had the highest number, with nearly 150,000).[21]

An advertising booklet published by the Stearns Coal and Lumber Company in 1938, five years following the death of Justus Stearns, provided a description of its workforce. The booklet identified its workers as "white American citizens, most of them native to the hills, and many of them have been with the company since they started out to seek their first job. Hundreds are employees of the third generation."[22] The fact that Stearns's labor force had so few immigrants and African Americans made him atypical compared to other mine owners; often, his contemporaries preferred immigrant labor because some believed immigrants worked harder and were more dependable. While it was true most employees were white, company records from the early 1900s reflected the presence of a nearby black community, and small numbers of African Americans worked for Stearns in Kentucky during Justus's lifetime. Ledger books demonstrated the organization's interaction with the black community and some of its charitable contributions with entries such as a gift of $2.00 for the "Danville Colored School" dated May 12, 1903, and 50 cents allocated for a "Negro preacher" on December 31 of the same year.[23] One black employee was Ralph McAdoo. Company records indicated McAdoo was working in Mine 11 in 1925 when he suffered an injury on February 28 in which his "great toe [was] bruised." McAdoo was fifty-eight years old at the time of his injury, and he was unable to work for eighteen days. When his injury occurred, it appeared McAdoo's weekly wages averaged about $25.00. Employees earning a similar wage were entitled to $15.00 per week in compensation if they were injured while on the job. He was able to return to work March 18 and in the end he was awarded a total of $23.56 for his time lost; the same rate granted to white miners. While the top company officials were all white, when it came to workers' compensation benefits, it appeared as if McAdoo, and therefore probably any other black miner, received the same treatment as a white employee.[24]

The Dangers of Mining

Mining coal was a dangerous occupation that could lead to serious injury or even death. According to the US Coal Commission in 1923, coal mining was "more hazardous than the average occupation, but not the most hazardous" occupation in the country. The report continued by declaring the greatest mining hazards came from, "first, falls of roof and coal; second, underground transportation; third, explosions. More men are killed from the first cause than from all other underground causes combined. While mine explosions attract large attention . . . the deaths underground from this cause [explosions] are only twelve percent of the total."[25] Subsequent data demonstrated fatalities nationwide, as well as in

Table 7. Kentucky mine deaths, 1890–1980

Period	Deaths
1890–99	95
1900–1909	274
1910–19	754
1920–29	1,614
1930–39	1,203
1940–49	1,328
1950–59	689
1960–69	451
1970–79	379
1979–80	242

Source: Harrison, *A New History of Kentucky*, 309.

Kentucky, could be significant. A study of American bituminous coal fields revealed the number of fatalities among miners peaked nationwide in the 1920s, which was followed by a steady decline. The study also provided a sample of those killed in specific years; in 1906 there were 1,581 deaths and by 1915 the number of deaths rose to 1,683. The greatest number of fatalities in the sample set took place in 1925 when 1,834 miners were killed. By 1935 (two years after Justus's death) it dropped to 968 and the trend continued in 1945 with 925 deaths; by 1955 the number had fallen to 360.[26] The number of fatalities in the state of Kentucky also peaked in the decade of the 1920s. In that ten-year period, over 1,600 miners were killed, followed by a significant drop in the 1930s as production slowed in the Great Depression. The number rose again in the 1940s as demand for coal increased during the Second World War. See table 7 for specific numbers.

Naturally, accidents took place at the mines operated by the Stearns Coal and Lumber Company, some of which ended in fatalities, but the company's overall safety record was better than most in the state and even the nation. Karen McBride's study of Stearns's Barthell camp argued, "for the most part, the Stearns mines had a reputation as among the safest mines in the country."[27] Documentation from the first decade of operations is sporadic at best, but it appeared that as many as ten men were killed in mine accidents prior to 1906. Five were killed in a single incident on December 29, 1905, when a blast of explosives blew victims from the mine entry to a nearby creek. Prior to this accident, most miners appeared to operate as independent contractors under Louis Bryant. J. E. Butler soon took over as mine superintendent, replacing Bryant. Butler implemented stricter safety standards and mine safety improved dramatically.[28]

Numerous characteristics of the company founded by Justus Stearns can explain why his organization had a better safety record than other coal producers. According to the US Coal Commission, a mine with the best safety record "attempts to produce only a moderate tonnage . . . and operates continuously." It declared furthermore, "mines operated by large companies where supervised from a distance rarely have good accident experiences."[29] The Stearns operations possessed several of the good-safety qualities identified above. From the 1910s to the 1920s, Stearns could be considered a moderate to significant producer of coal. As early as 1916, the company was identified as the third-largest coal mining company in the state of Kentucky, one of the top coal-producing states in the nation. Its mines also operated year-round. During slow periods Stearns's mines might operate only two or three days per week, but they ran continuously throughout the year. The Coal Commission discovered major problems associated with speculative mining operators who came and went with the rise and fall of the industry. These owners were interested strictly in quick profits and uninterested in developing sound management and engineering practices. Some of these operators even earned the nickname "snow birds" because they only "operated when there was snow on the ground and the demand for coal was at its peak." Once Stearns produced its first coal in 1903, it was in the industry for the long haul, not for a quick profit. Finally, the Stearns Coal and Lumber Company was not "supervised from a distance." This was a family owned and operated business. While Justus never resided in Kentucky, his son, Robert L. Stearns, lived in the community for many years and maintained strict attention to detail in regard to the company's day-to-day activities. In later years, Justus's elder grandson, Robert L. Stearns Jr., joined the company shortly after completing his college education and resided in the town of Stearns for the remainder of his lifetime.[30]

Another best practice identified by the Coal Commission declared, "in the better managed mines rule-of-thumb practices have been superseded by sound engineering" and "modern management" practices.[31] Special mine rules adopted in December 1922 demonstrated safety at the Stearns company mines was strictly regulated and enforced by the company's managers. Some of the most detailed rules addressed the use of powder to fire shots. Only specially trained crews were allowed to fire shots, as shown in Rule #3, which declared, "miners must not light their own shots. Shots will be lighted by two regularly appointed shot firers in each mine." Those firing shots were mandated to do so "ten minutes after the regular quitting time where shots are fired at noon," or "fifteen minutes after the regular quitting time."[32] After firing their shots, the men were required to post their activities in a conspicuous place in the mine, and the company maintained records in a permanent record book. Other regulations established the size of proper work rooms, required mine foremen to close down any work area determined to be unsafe, and provided warnings concerning the danger of electric wires, motors, and trolleys. Alcohol was strictly prohibited in the mines and Rule #31 stated, "No person in a state of intoxication shall be allowed in or near the mines."[33] This collective set of rules establishing strict safety standards demonstrated the high level of effort put forth by J. E. Butler in the years following his promotion to the company's general manager.

While mine safety improved in the years following the adoption of the new safety rules, best practices did not eliminate accidents and fatalities. One of the deadliest accidents occurred in 1910 when six miners were killed at Stearns Mine #1, located at Barthell. E. Rye West survived the traumatic accident, and at the age of eighty-seven he recalled the events of the day.

> When Bryant opened up the Barthell mine with the Stearns company I went to that mine and I was working there when the explosion killed six men. I was the only survivor. That was in 1910 or 1912 I believe. There were only seven of us in the mine at the time, about a thousand feet from the drift mouth. We were shooting from the face and had just finished loading the holes. I remained behind to fire the fuses while the other six were on their way out. I don't know what actually happened but two of the men had been drinking. At first I felt a slight shock or jarring sensation and I stepped back into a "manhole" beside the entry, thinking it might be a rockfall. About that time there was a deafening roar and blasting wind, fire and dust filled the mine with flying brattice lumber, tools and everything. It hit the face and the return blast was worse than the first. I was blinded by the dust but I knew I had to get out of there fast or not at all. Holding my coat over my face and mouth I groped my way toward the outside and as I did so I stepped on the dead bodies of each of the other six men. There was nothing I could do and I just barely made it to the outside, more dead than alive. . . . I would have been killed too if I had been in the path of the blast.[34]

One of the men killed in the explosion was Fred Compton, who left behind a wife and five small children. A description of the event appeared in the *Crossville Chronicle,* published in Crossville, Tennessee, shortly after the disaster. It was believed Compton and the other men were ready to quit work about 10:00 p.m. when the explosion occurred, killing the six men instantly. The force of the explosion was terrific and the bodies were burned beyond recognition. Compton had been working long hours prior to his death and previously had been quoted as saying, "I want my children to have an easier life than I have had."[35] The deadly incident reminded members of the community that even when working for an organization with a good safety record such as Stearns, coal mining remained a dangerous occupation.

Not all mining accidents ended in fatalities, and while records covering operations in the early 1900s remain scarce, a great deal of information can be assembled from later records. Court documents from a case decided in 1914 shed light on an accident involving a Stearns employee. Clarence Tuggle had worked for several months operating an underground pump designed to prevent water from collecting in the mine when his pump suddenly exploded on September 14, 1910. A piece of iron struck Tuggle "just over the eye, inflicting a wound to, or about as deep as, the skull bone, and of a size requiring five stitches to close it."[36] The blow left him unconscious, but he recovered his senses, received assistance, and was taken out of the mine. At the time of the incident, Tuggle was eighteen years old. He returned to work after recovering for several weeks, but the accident left him with permanent problems. He never was able to work as he had prior to his injury, one eye was damaged, and his father also swore that "in his opinion, his [son's] mind is affected as a result of the injury."[37] Tuggle sued for damages as a result of his injuries. The company fought his claim, arguing he brought the injury upon himself for operating the pump improperly; a foreman later discovered a discharge valve had been closed, rather than opened, therefore causing the explosion to take place. A jury awarded Mr. Tuggle damages of $1,000. The company appealed the decision, claiming the award was "excessive, and was the result of passion or prejudice on the part of the jury." A Kentucky appellate court denied the appeal and the original judgment of $1,000 was allowed to stand.[38]

The incident involving Tuggle offers insight into an event that involved one employee, but following the passage of a Workmen's Compensation law by the Kentucky legislature in 1916, companies were required to maintain more detailed records and provide a system of compensation for their employees injured while working. A complete list of records is not available for all years, but detailed records from 1924 to 1926 have survived, providing a unique opportunity to study the dangers inherent in the coal mining industry of this era. Between January 1924 and December 1926 over 1,100 workers' compensation reports were recorded on behalf of employees of the Stearns Coal and Lumber Company and its allied interests, including the K&T Railway and sawmill. The types of injuries identified were staggering and included but were not limited to: "mashed foot, finger cut, bad air, eyeball bruised, hernia, dislocated shoulder, thumb nail torn off, finger cut off, toe broken, ball of finger mashed, ankle broken, 3 ribs broken, back strained, face and head burned, scalp wound, hip bruised, killed instantly." Over the course of the three years studied, an average of about one injury per day was reported. Eleven individuals died within this window of time. Between 1924 and 1926, Stearns operated a total of nine mines that employed about two thousand men directly involved with the production of coal. See table 8 for more detailed figures concerning the number of accidents and deaths recorded each month.[39]

A sample of those injured provides insight as to the injuries suffered by employees and the benefits paid by the company. Stephens Paris, age nineteen, was injured November 26, 1924, while working at Mine A. He suffered "bruised fingers." His weekly wage at the time averaged $25.00 and he potentially was entitled to compensation of $15.00 per week; however, he returned to work after two days on November 28 and therefore did not receive any compensation. Employees were compensated only for time lost beyond the first seven days of missed work. Stephens Paris's situation can be contrasted with that of another miner, Pete Sumner, who was working at Mine #4 when he broke his toe. The accident occurred April 20, 1925, and at the time his wages also averaged $25.00 per week. His injuries were so severe he did not return to work until July 15. He missed a total of fifty-five days of work and received $402.12 for his time lost. At the age of thirty-one, George

Table 8. Accidents and deaths: January 1924 to December 1926

Month	1924		1925		1926		Totals for Each Month	
	Accidents	Deaths	Accidents	Deaths	Accidents	Deaths	Accidents	Deaths
January	30	0	34	0	33	0	97	0
February	33	0	21	0	29	0	83	0
March	39	0	17	1	22	0	78	1
April	24	0	24	0	24	0	72	0
May	30	0	11	0	14	1	55	1
June	22	0	28	0	27	0	77	0
July	31	0	36	1	40	0	107	1
August	36	3	34	1	36	0	106	4
September	31	0	49	0	39	0	119	0
October	38	0	50	0	42	0	130	0
November	29	1	46	2	33	1	108	4
December	20	0	32	0	20	0	72	0
Yearly Total	363	4	382	5	359	2	1,104	11

Source: The Records of Accidents of all Employees of Stearns Coal and Lumber Co. and all Allied Interests, Stearns Archive, McCreary County Museum.

Vinson fractured his arm while working at Mine 11 on December 11, 1924. He was employed as a machine runner with an average wage of $30.00 per week. He returned to work the following November, after missing a total of 314 days, and received a total of $1,265.47 in workers' compensation benefits for his time lost. An overall sample of the claims registered by workers showed that about 65 percent of the employees received compensation for their lost time, while about 30 percent did not because they did not miss enough work to qualify, and about 5 percent of the employee claims were denied by the company.[40]

Workers receiving the greatest amount of compensation for injuries were the highest paid employees who missed the greatest number of workdays. If a man was killed, his survivors received a minimum of $4,000. This was noted when George Wilson was "killed instantly" while working at Mine #4 on March 20, 1924, and someone wrote in his record, "Death: $12.00 per week for 335 weeks to wife." Wilson was twenty-three years old at the time of his death.[41] Robert L. Stearns noted the workers compensation statute and the death of two miners in 1916 when he wrote, "Two men killed at Mine #11 this A.M. early account falling slate. In consequence neither Mine 10 or 11 running. We are now under Workman's Compensation and this means Company has to pay $4,000.00 each but has 8 years to do it in."[42] As can be inferred from Robert L. Stearns's diary entry, if a death occurred, the entire mine was closed down for the remainder of the day.

Conclusion

Coal mining was, and remains, a dirty and dangerous job for those who worked underground and even for those who handled coal aboveground. The Stearns Coal and Lumber Company advanced over the years as new techniques and equipment were implemented. The majority of the miners employed by Stearns came from Kentucky and Tennessee and lived in family units. The company placed an emphasis on safety, but accidents did take place. Perhaps the death of Lewis Jones can show how one man's death inaugurated a solemn tradition at the company's mines. According to employee records, Jones had a wife and four children when he completed a set of company paperwork in 1924. At that time, he was twenty-nine years old with thirteen years of mining experience behind him. In November 1927, he was working in Mine #1, had just drilled a hole, cleaned his workspace, and put his powder in the hole when a spark caused the powder to ignite. The blast blew his tamping bar right into his mouth and out the other side of his skull, immediately killing him. Jones had been working Thanksgiving Day that year in preparation of a large run the next morning. According to one veteran miner "this was the last time anybody ever went in on Thanksgiving Day to make coal."[43]

7

Union Conflict and Years of Prosperity

Cancel the insurance on my hotel; am burning it down.

Justus S. Stearns, December 25, 1908, from an interview with Robert E. Gable, the great-grandson of Justus Stearns, on July 31, 2012, and clarified upon subsequent conversations. Several family members handed down the story over the years.

Over the course of the first thirty years of its operations, the company Justus Stearns founded in 1902 transformed the Big South Fork region of Kentucky and Tennessee. It provided employment, access to education, and an improved standard of living to thousands of the region's residents. But the "march of progress" involved a heavy cost, as seen by the difficult working conditions and inherent dangers associated with mining coal. Workers recognized these costs and began to organize labor unions to secure higher wages and job security. Like other industrialists in this era, such as Andrew Carnegie and John D. Rockefeller, as well as others in the coal mining industry, the Stearns interests opposed their efforts. These activities resulted in a confrontation ending in violence and death on Christmas Day in 1908. Less than ten years later, about the time the First World War broke out in Europe, the Stearns Coal and Lumber Company entered into an era of coal production unprecedented in its history. As the nation "roared" during the decade of the 1920s, the tonnage carved from the Stearns mines grew steadily until it reached a peak in 1929. This time period beginning about 1915 and extending to 1929 can be seen as a "golden era" for the company. These two contrasting circumstances demonstrated that Stearns's actions at times could be benevolent; during other times, he was an iron-willed capitalist.

Labor Unions

Labor unions grew in size and power in the late nineteenth and early twentieth centuries, in both Kentucky and the United States. Between 1880 and 1900, 223 strikes occurred in Kentucky, about one-third of which involved the state's coal industry. Miners struck primarily in hopes of gaining wage increases and job security, but they also were concerned with safety. The United Mine Workers (UMW) was formed in 1890 and grew to represent coal miners working in many regions of the nation. Following strikes in 1900, the UMW won a 10 percent pay increase and recognition of the union from coal companies operating in Pennsylvania. Additional victories were seen in 1902 and later years. In 1908 the UMW attempted to organize union representation among miners working for Stearns.[1]

Justus Stearns, like many leading industrialists in his lifetime, was no lover of unions. As a group, coal barons operating in the South were among the strongest opponents of unionization among American business leaders. According to historian Ronald Eller, most coal operators believed that employees who engaged in union organizing were guilty of "mutiny," which provided "grounds for immediate dismissal from the mine."[2] Both Andrew Carnegie and John Rockefeller famously took steps to undermine union organizing at their companies. Just as Rockefeller was described as "unrelenting [in his] opposition to organized labor," Stearns resisted unionization in the coal mines, and other businesses, he operated. Stearns's strong antiunion position could be seen in various articles appearing in the *Stearns Co-Operator*, a monthly journal published by the Stearns organization beginning in 1915. A fictional story included one month described an old-timer named Uncle Bill Mosby. He was a loyal employee who worked for the same company more than twenty-five years. When he was young, he was one of the most efficient workers, but as he aged, he was not as productive as he had been in the past. He also was a strong union man. The company's owner had received pressure from managers to lay off veteran employees, like Uncle Bill, because they could not produce as much as the younger men. Yet the owner recognized Bill's loyalty and years of service, so he refused to let him go. One day, union leaders at the company called for a strike at one of their meetings. While he opposed the strike and spoke out against it at the meeting, Uncle Bill remained loyal to his union and supported the majority vote of its members. The company's owner did not give in to the union demands, so the men went on strike. After three months, a compromise was reached between the workers and company, but not all employees were rehired following the strike. Only the most efficient workers received jobs, which meant that after working over twenty-five years for the same organization, Uncle Bill lost his position. The moral of the story was clear: blind loyalty to, and support for, a union can lead to trouble for workers. This parable, included in the company's monthly journal, demonstrated that top executives working for Stearns did not support the unionization of its workforce. It also seems likely that Stearns saw himself as the paternalistic company owner from the story. He was willing to employ older, even less productive, workers who had a long history with his company; however, he also was willing to let employees go if they engaged in behaviors Justus deemed to be detrimental to the company's interests, such as union organizing.[3]

The Stearns Coal and Lumber Company stubbornly resisted the union's attempts to organize workers even though the company maintained wages at their mines that were either equal to or higher than those provided in union contracts. Members of management perceived many legitimate reasons why the organization should oppose unions, and the diary of Robert L. Stearns can be used to provide valuable insight into the company's thought process. One factor consistent with most business owners in that era was that Stearns wanted absolute control to hire and fire his workers. The company's marketing touted the high quality of its coal and that it was much cleaner than coal produced by others in the industry. To maintain their rigorous standards, careless employees faced fines and sometimes were let go. After having complained about the quality of coal for some time, Robert L. Stearns noted one day that "coal is coming well cleaned but we had to fire 40 or 50 men to get it."[4] Drunkenness and rowdy behavior often characterized life in Kentucky mining and lumber communities. Such behavior was not tolerated by the Stearns company. Justus and Robert L. Stearns were known to lay off or fire employees who abused alcohol or engaged in unruly behavior. The company's operating rules were clear on this subject, and read, "Gambling, shooting, drunkenness or disorderly conduct of any kind whatsoever on the Company's property or in the Company's houses will be penalized by a ten (10) day lay off or a discharge at the option of the Company."[5] The presence of a union with grievance rights would make it more difficult for Justus to fire careless workers or those engaging in behaviors the company found to be disruptive or unsafe.

Another factor that led Stearns officials to fear labor organizing involved the unpredictability of the coal industry, which was characterized by numerous fluctuations in demand throughout the calendar year. Entries in Robert L. Stearns's diary reflected the concerns he felt in regard to low demand for coal. These included comments such as, "Coal business absolutely dead," or "find [coal] market in deplorable condition," and "February just past was the worst month we have ever experienced in the coal business." Other entries addressed rising inventories such as, "57 cars of coal on track tonight with no orders for." The boom/bust nature of the business was characterized by his entry, "It's feast or famine in the coal business."[6] Unionization would have brought pressure to increase the wage scale at the mines when demand for coal was at its height, resulting in potential losses when demand reached its depth. The union presence also would have made it more difficult for company officials to reduce or expand its workforce during market cycles. A national study from 1923 showed that wages made up nearly 70 percent of the costs of production in the coal industry. As far as the company was concerned, workers could not be granted instant raises in the "boom times" because a market downturn could appear just a few months down the road. Furthermore, it could become difficult for company officials to make payroll unless the mines operated efficiently and demand for coal remained steady. Unfortunately, the same study from 1923 determined that mines did not always operate on a regular basis due to lack of demand and other obstacles. If mines had operated five days a week for fifty-two weeks, they would have been open 260 days per year. Between 1916 and 1921 mines located in the state of Kentucky operated only an average of 196 days per year; the national average for the same time period was 214 days.[7] The lack of predictability in the coal industry was something beyond the control of company officials; however, a company could maintain greater control over its labor force by refusing to allow a union to be formed. Therefore, Justus Stearns and other top officials in his organization took strong antiunion positions to avoid risking the capital invested in the company he had founded.

Other coal mining companies in Kentucky were similarly opposed to the unionization of their workers. A major factor that led mine owners in the state to oppose unions was shaped by geography. Kentucky benefited from rich coal reserves, yet its coalfields were long distances from key manufacturing centers. This put them at a competitive disadvantage with coal providers farther north and east because coal mined in Kentucky had to be transported to outside markets, thereby raising costs considerably. Conflict between miners and management in the state would reach its height in the 1930s in "Bloody Harlan" County, located considerably east of Stearns's mining interests; however, even prior to the Great Depression, companies there exhibited control over their labor force. The actions of miners and their families were closely monitored at times and if they violated the company's moral code, which prohibited theft, drunkenness, prostitution, or union organizing, they could find themselves out of a job and evicted from company housing. While conflicts never reached the same level as those in Harlan County, there were confrontations between laborers working for Stearns and management at his company.[8]

When union organizers from the United Mine Workers recruited Stearns miners to join their union and staged a strike in the fall of 1908, executives at the Stearns Coal and Lumber Company sought a temporary restraining order to halt these union activities. Undeterred, a large number of miners joined the union ranks and went on strike, but company officials received the satisfaction that many others remained loyal out of respect for the contributions Justus and Robert L. Stearns made to their community. Some workers simply returned to their farms in the fall that year as tension rose between the company and UMW organizers, while others crossed the picket lines to work for the company as the mines operated on a reduced basis. Federal judge A. M. J. Cochrane granted a restraining order on November 10, 1908, because union members were accused of harassing miners and their actions interfered with business operations. His order identified about thirty former employees who were prohibited from trespassing on company property and interfering with nonunion laborers who continued to work during the strike.[9]

One individual named in Judge Cochrane's order was Berry Simpson. At the time, company officials believed he was the ringleader behind the union activities. Simpson previously had worked for Stearns and even had risen to the position of mine foreman, but had not worked for the company for about one year. When Simpson heard his name was included in the judge's order, he became angry because he maintained he was not involved in the union organizing. After drinking heavily one night, he confronted Superintendent J. E. Butler at Butler's home and demanded his name be removed from the restraining order. While he did not specifically threaten Butler at the time, Simpson was carrying a rifle and had a pistol hanging from his pocket when he arrived at Butler's home. Butler later testified that Simpson started "cursing and swearing very violently" at the front porch of his house with his two young children nearby, who began to cry.[10] Later that same evening, while walking past a Stearns Company store, he used "harsh words and profane language" concerning Superintendent Butler and Mr. Stearns. About one week after this confrontation, Simpson called on Robert L. Stearns at his home and complained bitterly that his name was included in the judge's order. He claimed he was not threatening anyone, but when he spoke with Stearns he again carried a rifle. Robert L. Stearns later testified he was "somewhat intimidated by Mr. Simpson's manner." Due to the increasing tension between Simpson, the union organizers, and Stearns company officials, on December 22 Judge Cochrane issued a warrant for Simpson's arrest. Six additional men were named in the warrant because the judge believed they were members of a gang of armed men led by Simpson. Others named included Elisha and Oliver Slaven, George Stanley, Rube West, and Berry Simpson's two sons, Jesse and Harvey. Court documents later revealed that local officials suspected that Simpson met with these men several times to plot against the company because the conflict

Stearns Hotel and main office. Conflict between the Stearns Company and union members came to a head on Christmas Day in 1908. Here, the Stearns Hotel is shown on fire; the main office of the company is on the right. (Courtesy of McCreary County Museum)

grew more intense. The same day the arrest warrants were issued, company officials requested that Governor August Willson send National Guard forces to Stearns to quell the situation. About thirty troops arrived shortly thereafter.[11]

Events reached a climax the morning of December 25, 1908, in the city of Stearns, when US marshal John Mullins attempted to arrest Elisha Slaven and Rube West. Slaven and West were seen the previous evening drinking heavily at the home of a friend as they celebrated Christmas Eve. Their party continued the next morning as the two men, accompanied by Richard Ross, walked into town carrying a suitcase full of bottled beer and whiskey about nine in the morning. Their suitcase must have been heavy because each man took a turn carrying it, and the trio stopped several times to take a drink. The men eventually made their way to the Stearns Hotel, which was managed by Lula Simpson, Berry Simpson's wife, to pay a debt after which they planned to take the train to Whitely City and the home of Richard Ross. After watching the three men enter the Stearns Hotel, ten or twelve members of the National Guard surrounded the building, followed by a posse that included several local men who had been deputized. A firefight soon followed. Gerald West, the son of one of the men who remained in the hotel, recalled, "The ringleader of that outfit [US marshal John Mullins] came up on the porch and knocked the window out with his pistol, and that's when somebody shot him from inside." Mullins was killed and another officer was wounded.[12]

The shooting took place about nine thirty Christmas morning followed by a siege in which sustained gunfire was exchanged for about thirty minutes between the National Guard forces and the men who remained in the hotel. The men refused to surrender and George Massingale, another deputy US marshal, believed they were waiting for the cover of darkness to make an escape. To prevent this from happening, he requested that F. C. Ebling, the manager of the Stearns Lumber Company, find some dynamite because he wanted to "blow up the hotel." When no usable dynamite could easily be found, Massingale collected some paper, rags, and oil for fuel to start a fire to burn down the hotel. Meanwhile, Lula Simpson, who had been in the hotel when the shooting started, quickly gathered her children and was able to escape down the back steps of the hotel.[13] The building was set on fire following the evacuation of all but Ross, Slaven, and West. The conflict progressed rapidly that morning. At some point Justus Stearns, who was in Ludington at the time, was informed as to the events that were taking place. Stearns must have supported the steps Massingale took, because that day he sent a telegram to his insurance agent that declared, "Cancel the insurance on my hotel; am burning it down."[14]

As the hotel burned, shots continued to be exchanged between the miners trapped inside and the National Guard troops and posse that still surrounded the building. Just as the building was ready to collapse, the men made their run for freedom. Richard Ross was killed immediately as he emerged from the flaming building. Witnesses later testified that members of the posse had been drinking and that Ross initially was shot while holding up his hands in an attempt to surrender. They claimed he was shot again while begging for his life. Other witnesses refuted those arguments and testified Ross was giving the "Odd-fellows distress signal" when he left the building in hopes that a fellow member would come to his aid. Meanwhile, Elisha Slaven wrapped himself in a quilt and dashed outside. He hoped to escape in the confusion surrounding the smoke, flames, and gunshots; however, he was captured and arrested. Only Rube West remained as he pondered which action he should take to best save his own life. While he disliked speaking about the events of that day, years later, through hearsay and a great deal of prodding, his son Gerald was able to piece together what happened next.

> They had to leave, so my father went out the front door, running. This was Christmas Day. He went out the front, where they had a high porch to jump out. But my dad had to jump off of this porch. He has

> been told that there was one man standing out in front of that and he hit him and knocked him down with his feet, as he jumped off the high porch. . . . But he had to run about 400 or 500 feet and a fence to cross. Two or three of these guys were shooting at him at the same time. They split his ear with a high powered rifle bullet, buckshot hit him in the back of the head, and they shot him in the bottom of the foot. Brought the blood in 19 places, but none of them serious.[15]

Luckily for West, none of his wounds were serious enough to stop him, and he continued on toward the nearby railroad, crossing it at one point to gain additional cover and avoid further detection. He walked "three or four miles in the snow with his socks on" and sought help with friends living in the country. He then made his way to Oneida, Tennessee, where several family members lived. For some reason, no attempt ever was made to arrest Rube West, although he apparently never hid from authorities and later established a successful moonshine business, training several other men in the art of distilling whiskey.[16]

Berry Simpson arrived in Stearns about noon the day of the shoot-out, but then he promptly disappeared. Neither he nor George Stanley were involved in the conflict; however, each still faced a warrant for his arrest. Many in town believed Simpson was responsible for the tension between company officials and the miners that resulted in the violence on Christmas Day. It was unclear exactly where Simpson had gone, but authorities believed he had fled to Tennessee. Additional National Guard forces were called in December 26, and when they arrived in Stearns, "a band of 50 armed mountaineers and miners were in ambush to attack the men as they left the train." Fortunately, word of the trap reached the authorities and "the troops detrained from another point," thereby avoiding a confrontation. The National Guard members eventually disembarked from their train and barricaded themselves in the Stearns bank. There was a fear of a general uprising and martial law was declared, but no additional violence occurred and the troops departed after a few days. News reports declared Simpson was hiding along with seventy-five sympathizers, but was willing to turn himself in and even agreed to do so; however, he remained a fugitive after he failed to appear at an assigned location at the proper time. In another bold move, on December 29, he phoned Governor Willson and the two engaged in a long conversation, during which the governor assured Simpson he would receive a fair trial and remain protected while in custody if he turned himself in to authorities. Simpson maintained his innocence and declared he had nothing to do with the death of

Officer Mullins. While Simpson did not agree to turn himself in, he implied that he would very soon. Simpson actually remained at large until he surrendered, unarmed and alone, on Sunday April 4, 1909. While on the run, he allegedly spent time in Kentucky, Tennessee, New Mexico, and Colorado. He gave himself up after learning two of his sons had been arrested for their alleged involvement in the riots that had taken place in Stearns on Christmas Day.[17]

It seemed as if all the cards were stacked against Simpson and the others as the trial drew near. Simpson, Elisha Slaven, and George Stanley were indicted for the murder of US marshal John Mullins. The three men, and several other defendants, also were charged with disobeying the injunction restricting union organizing. The attorney who argued the case for the government was George M. Davison, the assistant US attorney for the eastern district of Kentucky, and a former member of Congress. The presiding judge was Judge Cochrane, the same man who had issued the order that established the initial injunction against the union. Their defense attorney was Edwin P. Morrow, who had just completed a four-year term as the city attorney for the town of Somerset. Morrow's defense of Simpson and the others was surprising as he had close ties with the Stearns Coal and Lumber Company. In 1903, when the company had celebrated its first successful shipment of coal and held a festival to honor its employees, it had been Edwin Morrow who was called upon by company officials to deliver an address to the crowd. He also maintained a close personal relationship with Robert L. Stearns. It was unclear why Morrow chose to defend the group of men accused of murder and violating the order of a federal judge, particularly given his relationship with Stearns company officials. Earlier in his career Morrow had been assigned to defend an African American man accused of murder. In that case from 1902, he had successfully obtained an acquittal for his client. It was possible that Morrow simply sought hard-luck cases and saw one in Berry Simpson, but his motivation continues to remain unclear.[18]

The trial of Simpson and his codefendants began in July 1909. The proceedings generated a great deal of attention, as over one hundred audience members and witnesses were on hand to observe and testify. It was expected the trial would continue over several days. Reporters noted the case was "stubbornly fought" by attorneys on each side because both called numerous witnesses. Robert L. Stearns and J. E. Butler testified as witnesses for the prosecution. Evidence at the trial showed that Slaven was in the Stearns Hotel at the time Mullins was shot and killed. The only other men with him at that time were Richard Ross, who was dead, and Rube West, who was never apprehended. Simpson and Stanley were accused of conspiracy to commit the murder that resulted in the death of Officer

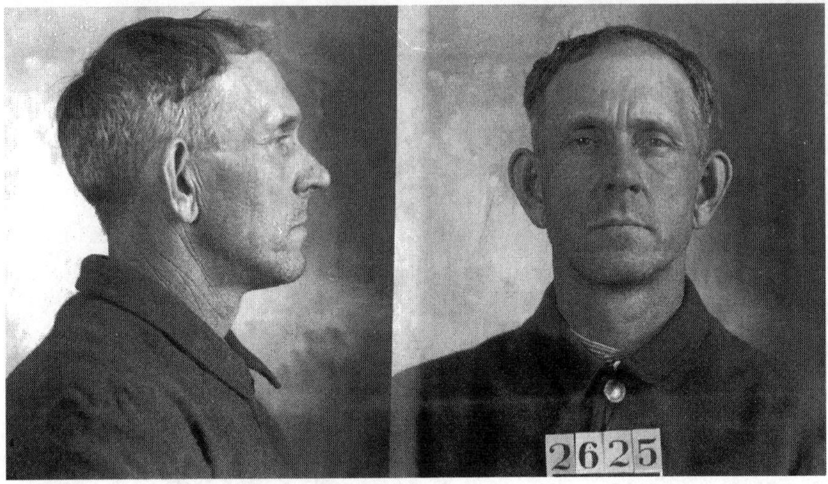

Berry Simpson. Stearns Company officials believed Simpson was the lead agitator whose actions led to the conflict at the Stearns Hotel on Christmas Day in 1908. He was convicted of conspiracy to commit murder, but later was pardoned by President Woodrow Wilson. (Courtesy of the National Archives and Records Administration, Atlanta, Georgia)

Mullins. The prosecution argued that Simpson, in particular, masterminded a scheme to thwart the injunction against the union, even going so far as to declare the strikers should support "killing any officer who attempted to arrest him" or others targeted for arrest. The defense countered that neither Simpson nor Stanley were in Stearns at the time of the murder and that while Simpson may have been guilty of poor judgment when he complained to company officials while carrying his rifle, he never directly threatened the men, nor was he involved in union organizing. After the trial was finished the jury deliberated for only forty-five minutes and handed down a verdict of guilty at midnight July 19, for most of the men involved. Berry Simpson, Elisha Slaven, and George Stanley were found guilty of murder. Simpson and Slaven received life sentences. For a reason the trial judge never articulated, George Stanley received a sentence of only ten years. Berry Simpson, his son Jesse, George Stanley, and Elisha and Oliver Slaven were found guilty of disobeying the judge's injunction concerning union organizing. Oliver Slaven and Jesse Simpson received sentences from three to five years each. Harvey Simpson, another of Berry Simpson's sons, was acquitted of all charges. The wives and children of the convicted men attended the sentencing hearing, which evolved into a "pathetic scene" as family members appealed for sympathy from Judge Cochrane.[19]

While in prison, Simpson took several steps in an effort to receive a presidential pardon. His pardon application was filed in December 1913 and included numerous letters in support of his petition. Remarkably, Simpson's application included two letters from W. A. Kinne, land agent for the Stearns Coal and Lumber Company, indicating company officials had undergone a complete reversal of their position in regard to Simpson. Kinne was one of the longest-serving and most loyal members of the Stearns organization in Kentucky, and it is unlikely he would have written a letter in support of Simpson's pardon without the approval of Justus and Robert L. Stearns. One of Kinne's letters, which was written on Stearns Coal and Lumber Company stationery, indicated the change of heart the company adopted. In addition to showing support for Simpson's pardon, Kinne wrote, "Possibly, he [Simpson] is not near as much to blame as it appeared on the surface." The letter seemed to indicate that in December 1908 he, and other top Stearns officials, believed Simpson was responsible for that year's violence. But with the passage of time and a dispassionate consideration of events, they came to realize their initial conclusions were incorrect. While some have suggested that Justus or Robert L. Stearns personally met with President Woodrow Wilson to request a full pardon for Simpson, there is no record of any such meeting, and therefore it remains unlikely.[20]

Another indication of the change in heart by members of Stearns management was seen with the involvement of Edwin Morrow in Simpson's pardon request. By 1913 Morrow was serving as the US district attorney for eastern Kentucky following his appointment to the position in 1910. Morrow prepared Simpson's pardon paperwork and always had argued in favor of his client's innocence. At least one key member of the Stearns family remained close to Morrow even after he continued to fight on Simpson's behalf. Robert L. Stearns's diary included several references to his interaction with Morrow as the two ate dinner together and their families spent time with each other. In later years, they played poker together, Stearns supported Morrow's bid for the governorship in 1915 and again in 1919 (Morrow won the election in 1919 and served as Kentucky's governor from 1919 to 1923), and they even vacationed together in New Orleans. In a letter to James Finch, the government's attorney in charge of pardons, Morrow argued in favor of a pardon for Simpson and declared his perspective was unique due to his strong "knowledge of both sides of this controversy" and an "intimate acquaintanceship with all the principles of the Stearns Coal company." It was probable that Morrow understood the facts, and individuals, involved in the case more thoroughly than anyone else and used his personal relationship with members of the Stearns family to convince them his client was innocent.[21]

Others who supported a pardon for Simpson included the trial judge, A. M. J. Cochrane, John B. O'Neal, counsel for the prosecution at Simpson's trial, ten members of the original jury (the other two had died by 1913), and several government officials and citizens living in Kentucky. Additionally, three senators and one member of the House of Representatives wrote letters in support of a pardon; however, several local citizens were opposed to any form of clemency for Simpson. They depicted his crime as "one of the worst in the legal annals of the State of Kentucky," and described Simpson as a "vile and vicious man." The editorial staff of Kentucky's *Mount Vernon Signal* wondered why Morrow would seek a pardon for such a "notorious" criminal. Despite the objections of some, on March 22, 1914, President Woodrow Wilson signed the order that commuted Simpson's life sentence and he was released from prison.[22]

Relations between miners and Stearns company officials improved in the months that followed the tragic confrontation as men completed their farm work and slowly returned to their mining positions in the spring and summer of 1909; however, at times tension between labor and management continued. In 1911 Jesse Simpson and Oliver Slaven were released from prison on parole. Robert L. Stearns noted in his diary, "Simpson met me [at] barber shop—looks well." In January 1913 George Stanley was released from prison on parole. Less than one month following his release, he arrived in Stearns with a "heart-rending epistle" asking for a job in the mines. Robert wrote, "George was Berry Simpson's right hand bower during the Simpson riot days and George was sent up with Berry. Through the efforts of some soft-headed prison workers George has been paroled and now desires to return to our camp because (says Dame Rumor) George is extremely interested in the wife of one of his erstwhile friends who lives at Worley." Parole records for George Stanley show that the Stearns Coal and Lumber Company eventually rehired him as early as April 1913. Stanley continued to work for the company for the next two years, until he purchased property and established a farm. Following the pardon of Berry Simpson, Elisha Slaven remained in prison until his sentence was commuted by Woodrow Wilson in 1917, which meant no one ever spent more than eight years in prison for the death of US marshal John Mullins.[23]

Support for a union among the mine workers emerged again in early 1913, and it appeared as if a strike might be imminent. The company hired detectives, and hinted at having spies, to determine the actions the men were considering. Robert wrote, "Our detective leaves today but other sources of information still open. Seems a meeting was held Sunday about 2 miles from Stearns at which about 15 men were present."[24] The men did not decide to strike that February because the injunction was still in effect. The early 1920s saw the United Mine Workers union attempt to organize mine employees. The effort to unionize failed and there was no violence, but according to one study, "every miner who had participated was fired and blacklisted for any future employment by Stearns."[25] One miner fired for his union activities in 1923 was E. Rye West, the sole survivor of the mining disaster from 1910 that had killed six other men. West eventually was forced to leave the area and seek work in the coalfields of eastern Kentucky, along with several other blacklisted men, as the Stearns organization prohibited him from working for the company.[26]

Prosperity and World War I

Although resentment over the company's opposition to unionization continued to exist at times over the next few decades, the era from 1915 to 1930 was characterized by prosperity for the Stearns interests in Kentucky. An article from the *Stearns Co-Operator* offered a valuable overview of the company's assets and position in the mining industry in 1916. Pennsylvania, West Virginia, and Kentucky collectively produced about 64 percent of the coal mined in the United States, or 200 million tons annually. Ever since the first carload of coal was mined in 1903, Stearns's activities had steadily increased so that by 1916 it was the third-largest coal producer in the state, operated four mines with a combined tonnage of 2,800 tons daily, and expected to produce over 650,000 tons that year. The company owned the rights to 78,000 acres of coalfields in five counties in Kentucky and Tennessee. Additionally, Stearns held the Bryant lease, which provided access to coal located on an additional 22,000 acres of property. Taken together, it was estimated the Stearns organization had the rights to over 350 million tons of coal, representing a tremendous opportunity for continued growth in the future, but Stearns's activities were not confined strictly to mining coal. The sawmill, which remained idle from about 1910 to 1926, continued to maintain the capacity to produce 70,000 feet of lumber per day and also included a planing mill and dry kiln. Company assets also included nine stores, along with their inventory of goods, 450 company houses, office buildings, barns, and warehouses.[27]

In 1914 World War I began in Europe, and the United States became involved in 1917. Once the United States became an active participant, demand for coal increased as the nation mobilized in support of the war effort. Even prior to the start of the war, Stearns's coal output increased at a steady pace, but it accelerated after 1915. Prior to that year, the company had produced an annual total of 500,000 tons of coal only twice. After that year, and continuing to the death of Justus Stearns in 1933, the Stearns mines collectively produced a minimum of 500,000 tons each year, with only two exceptions: in 1919, as the nation returned to a peacetime economy following the end of the First World War, and near the depth of the Great Depression in 1932. The peaks and valleys Stearns experienced reflected larger trends in the nation as production levels varied in the years immediately before, during, and after World War I. Table 9 illustrates the tonnage of coal produced by the Stearns Coal and Lumber Company compared to the nation as a whole.

Events that took place during the war years (1917–18) would impact the Stearns family, and residents of McCreary County, in additional ways as well. Ever since Justus Stearns challenged his son in the late 1890s to learn the family business or risk losing his inheritance, the two had worked closely in several business ventures. Robert L. Stearns was most active overseeing the family interests in Kentucky and Tennessee, having served as vice president of the Stearns Coal and Lumber Company for years and acting in the capacity as the organization's managing director. He maintained a rigorous work schedule at the company, but also found time to paint. According to an article published one year prior to his death, his wife Laura encouraged him to resume his artwork. This became Robert's primary form of relaxation, and he found great satisfaction painting with friends such as Lawrence Earle or with his wife Laura. She often painted

Table 9. Bituminous coal produced by Stearns Coal and Lumber Co. and the United States, in tons (original figures rounded to whole tons)

Year	Stearns Coal and Lumber	US
1912	423,291	450,105,000
1913	516,189	478,435,000
1914	500,727	422,704,000
1915	480,161	442,624,000
1916	587,873	502,520,000
1917	553,764	551,791,000
1918	543,856	579,386,000
1919	466,387	465,860,000
1920	610,325	568,666,000
1921	519,988	415,921,000
1922	563,261	422,268,000
1923	751,117	564,564,000

Source: The figures for coal production in the United States are found in Coleman, *Men and Coal*, 311; figures for the Stearns Coal and Lumber Company are found in Stearns Archive, McCreary County Museum.

Robert L. Stearns. Art remained a passion of R. L. Stearns, but he also was a partner in many of his father's business ventures. (Courtesy of Robert E. Gable)

alongside him or read aloud while he painted. It also appeared as if Robert L. Stearns did not take enough time away from work, as he suffered from several health ailments, including "blind spells." He sought the help of medical professionals and even took an extended rest in February 1917, but his health simply did not improve, so he checked into the Battle Creek Sanitarium April 14, 1917, where he spent the next ten days. The "San," as it often was called, had been made famous by Dr. John Harvey Kellogg in the late 1880s. Not only was the "San" famous for providing health care to its clients, it also became known nationwide for its food substitutes for things like coffee and a breakfast cereal that eventually evolved into Kellogg's Corn Flakes. In April 1917, Robert L. Stearns became case #109632 and spent much of his time there "rushing from one examination to another." After several days of tests, it appeared as if he was not suffering from any chronic illnesses, other than a "run down condition and bad cold." On April 24, he checked out after simply resting for much of his stay, and he must have felt much better because he seemed to resume a full schedule of appointments within just a few days.[28]

About two months after his discharge from the "San," Robert L. Stearns received an appointment to the McCreary County draft board and eventually served as its chairman. Additionally, he served on the Liberty Loan campaign committee, which sold Liberty Bonds to raise funds for the war effort. Over the next several months he often worked late on company business, only to be followed by meetings of the county draft board or patriotic rallies. Each county throughout the nation was assigned draft quotas based on the area's population, and residents were asked to contribute to the war effort through the purchase of these bonds. Wounded veterans, including those from England, France, or Belgium, visited the community to describe their experiences in the war. Stearns miners, covered in dirt and coal dust, listened to their stories and purchased thousands of dollars worth of war bonds. Eventually, McCreary County's residents exceeded their quota of war bond purchases by a greater percentage than any other county in the nation. As a reward, the government later christened a ship *McCreary* in honor of the residents' patriotism.[29]

One final event took place near the end of 1917 that further demonstrated the changes taking place in the Stearns household. In November 1917, Robert and his family were in Ludington for Thanksgiving. After breakfast, Justus took Robert into a room for a private meeting; Justus announced he was going to turn over the "greater portion" of his controlling stock in the Stearns Coal and Lumber Company to his son. Robert was shocked and later wrote, "It nearly blew me up as no such bountiful gift had ever entered my mind, and had he said $100,000 of the stock it would have been a most magnificent present. Gee! But I felt rich."[30] The following December, details of the gift were finalized and Robert received over 50 percent of the shares of common stock and just under half of the shares of the company's preferred stock, while his wife Laura purchased additional shares of the preferred stock. Taken together, the value of the stock was about $1 million. At the same time, he owed the company about $50,000, but he also was entitled to company profits of about $150,000. Indeed, it was a large gift.

The gift Justus Stearns granted to his son provides valuable insight in the relationship between the two. Throughout the course of his diary, without exception, Robert refers to Justus as "father." The way in which he used the word "father" implied a level of formality that did not seem to exist when discussing other individuals, particularly members of his immediate family. Justus and Robert worked very closely with each other over the course of several years. When traveling, Robert wrote about meeting his father quite often; the two ate together, spent one or more nights at the same location, and then continued on their separate ways. They spent vacations together and just about every holiday; however, the formal nature of their relationship never seemed to be broken. Even when recalling the day he received the company stock as a gift, Robert wrote, "Father arrived from Ludington and had breakfast with Spencer, Trent, and me."

The day he received the stock he wrote, "Father has had stock of S. C. & L. Co. transferred to me as follows . . ."[31] He never seemed to move beyond a formal relationship with his father.

The relationship between Robert and Justus can be contrasted with the relationship Robert had with his own children. He often commented about the talents of his children, such as when he noted his daughter "Pina [Paulina] shows a decided tendency toward drawing and today made a drawing of a Dutch girl which while not good showed originality." Robert noted that after Paulina drew several figures on the walls of her room at the family's Epworth cottage, "she shows exceptional talent and I hope will continue her work." He even recorded his children's sicknesses, such as when a doctor commented that Bob "has a bad lung and must be careful of colds," and "Freeman has the grippe, but better today."[32] Bob and Freeman Stearns often spent long stretches of time during the summers with their father in Kentucky. The "boys" (including Robert) seemed to have a level of informality, which in some cases was associated with shoes or clothing. When they arrived one June, Robert wrote that Bob and Freeman, "discarded shoes and stockings at once. . . . Did not get home till 8:30 at night and are happy in their freedom. They accosted me with having killed the calf today and I felt as much of a criminal as if it had been a human." That night, he slept in the downstairs bedroom with the boys. On Freeman's birthday in 1914, he was "King" for the day and "commanded we have sausage for lunch and chicken for dinner." Later the "King and his prime minister [brother Bob] go to bed with clothes on but I discovered them and made them undress." One year while staying at Epworth in Ludington, the children staged a production of Shakespeare's "Midsummer Night's Dream." When describing the cast and play, Robert gave credit to Paulina for writing and directing and even took the time to list the entire cast of characters and respective actors. He finally commented, "it was a delightful play and enjoyed by all."[33]

The fact that Robert took the time to compose a playful poem inspired, at least in part, by the names of his children was something that would seem to be completely out of character for Justus Stearns. The text of Robert's poem appeared prior to the start of his diary in January 1913:

Rickety, rickety, rick rack
Zickety zickety zick zack
Rick rack, zick zack
Let's give 'em the horse laugh
Ha—Ha—Ha

Pauleena—Paulina
Ve vobble de shina
Ve vobble das house
Paulina most ouse

Pina bum bina
Ti highly go fina
Tea-legged, tie-legged, bow-legged Pina

Doobly, youbli nobly
Thisbly talkbly

(Spelling Paulina)
Pap A U lal i nan A
(Spelling Freeman)
Faf rarsquare E mam A nan[34]

Robert L. Stearns was in his heart an artist, who happened to become a very successful business leader. While he managed many companies and took over his father's empire in later years, his hobby, and undoubtedly his passion, was art. After traveling and working long hours each week, he longed to work in his studio alone, or with a friend, painting. He also was a skilled writer, as illustrated by his publication of *The Lumberman's Primer* and *The Coalman's Primer* and creation of the fictitious Ossawald Crumb. In 1921 his interest in writing continued with an allegory he titled *The Ass and the Barnacles*, which commented on the problems inherent in excessive government regulation and taxation. Justus Stearns did not take on art as his hobby. He was not a golfer, swimmer, or a tennis player. He only had one hobby—managing companies. It appeared as if father and son respected each other, enjoyed each other's company, shared many of the same successes, and yet the two men differed from each other quite significantly.[35]

Expansion in the 1920s

Following the end of the First World War the Stearns Coal and Lumber Company experienced a slight downturn, but for much of the decade of the 1920s, it prospered. The company's success can be seen in three primary areas. The first involved negotiations to purchase property owned by Louis Bryant, which began in 1923 and eventually became finalized in 1927. The Bryant lease was one of the foundations for Stearns's success in the coal business when it was established in 1902. This granted the organization access to the valuable mineral reserves of approximately 22,000 acres of land. Over the course of the contract, Stearns and Bryant often were at odds with each other. In the company's early years, Bryant served as a consultant and probably coordinated mine operators who worked as independent contractors until 1905, when he was replaced following a series of mine accidents. After this, Bryant operated his own coal mines, independent of the Stearns organization. The two interacted frequently, and Mrs. Bryant received royalties for many years for coal mined on the property leased to Stearns, but Louis Bryant proved to be a difficult person to work with. On more than one occasion he threatened to sue Stearns for violating the terms of the lease. He also tried to pressure Stearns into purchasing the property, yet his asking price was too high. Bryant complained the other members of his family could not agree to an equal division of their father's estate, so he offered to sell all of the acreage for $300,000. Robert L. Stearns estimated its value in 1911 to be around $143,000 as he noted it would be a good purchase at that price, but no agreement was reached until the 1920s. In that decade the company purchased the 22,000 acres of land that previously had been part of the lease for a total of $125,000. This was the last major purchase of property in the region by Justus Stearns, and it served the purpose of uniting his holdings east of the Big South Fork of the Cumberland River with land located west of the river.[36]

The second area of development in the decade involved the resumption of timber and lumber operations in 1926. Ever since 1909 the sawmill had remained largely idle. At the time, he had decided to focus on mining, rather than lumbering, because much of the land where the timber was easily accessible had been logged out. Company officials estimated it would require an investment of $600,000 to construct the necessary improvements and purchase the needed supplies to expand and maintain its logging operations. When the expansion was being considered, Stearns secured the contract to supply coal for the Southern Railway. Therefore, the decision was made to focus on the fulfillment of this contract rather than on an expansion of the lumbering and sawmill operations. There simply was not enough capital available to invest in both ventures simultaneously. At the time, Robert L. Stearns wrote, "Timber is bound to advance and our holdings, if we were financially able to carry them, would be far better to hold than to sell, but with the amount of development we need, it is far better to sell the timber."[37] For several years, they tried to sell the forested land and even the sawmill and yard; however, there were no offers at the price they wanted. Eventually, Stearns decided not to sell, and in the spring of 1926 the company began to cut timber again. Several improvements were made to the sawmill, a rail

Lumberyard, Stearns Coal and Lumber Company. This postcard shows the extensive lumber yard and inventory of the Stearns Coal and Lumber Company in Stearns, Kentucky. (Courtesy of Robert E. Gable)

line was extended into the forest, and the mill began to operate on a regular basis. By 1928, over eighteen million board feet of lumber was produced.[38]

The final growth involving the company, during Justus's lifetime, was demonstrated in its expanded capacity to produce coal. Coal production increased steadily throughout the decade of the 1920s and culminated in the organization's greatest output ever in 1929 at nearly one million tons.

As can be seen when examining the figures in table 10, coal production rose steadily at Stearns's mines throughout the 1920s. To facilitate the sale and distribution of coal, the company established five retail yards located in Chattanooga, Atlanta, Louisville, Fort Wayne, and Frankfort. Production began to slow in 1930 with the onset of the Great Depression. The worst years of the economic downturn did not hit McCreary County until 1931 and 1932, but there was a tremendous expansion prior to those years. A history of the company written at the height of its success in 1929 by W. A. Kinne estimated that the Stearns Coal and Lumber Company employed more than two thousand workers and had a payroll of approximately $1,250,000 that year. Additionally, the company stores had sales of amounting to about $2 million. It was clear that by the end of the 1920s, the organization had come a long way from 1903 and the celebration that accompanied the sale of the first carload of coal from Mine #1.[39]

Table 10. Bituminous coal produced by Stearns Coal and Lumber Co. and the United States, in tons (original figures rounded to whole tons)

Year	Stearns Coal and Lumber	US
1924	775,982	483,686,000
1925	814,712	520,052,000
1926	864,207	573,366,000
1927	903,665	517,763,000
1928	887,095	500,744,000
1929	970,084	534,988,000
1930	783,244	467,526,000
1931	583,743	382,089,000
1932	490,707	309,709,000
1933	504,281	338,630,000

Source: The figures for coal production in the United States are found in Coleman, *Men and Coal*, 311; figures for the Stearns Coal and Lumber Company are found in Stearns Archive, McCreary County Museum.

Conclusion

Justus Stearns deserves enormous credit for the success and accomplishments of his company, but he also took controversial steps to undermine the unionization of his labor force. The company successfully thwarted the efforts of the United Mine Workers to organize unions over the course of its first twenty years: it hired detectives, fired troublesome employees, blacklisted those involved in union activities, and condoned the destruction of its hotel to capture the union men responsible for killing a US marshal. These stern policies proved to be effective until the Wagner Act of the 1930s protected the rights of workers to organize and outlawed tactics such as blacklisting. Stearns was not alone among American industrialists in this era who used similar methods to crush unions. While the confrontation that took place in Stearns, Kentucky, on Christmas Day in 1908 was not soon forgotten, it was not nearly as violent as the events of the 1930s that took place in Harlan County, Kentucky, known as "Bloody Harlan." Stearns's actions in many other areas, moreover, merited recognition. Surely, the fact that Justus Stearns had founded the city of Stearns and contributed so much for the community in the company's formative years played a key role in creating a positive relationship with his workforce and diminishing support for the formation of a union. His company provided access to better jobs with an improved standard of living, constructed its own power plant that brought electricity to residents' homes, established a demonstration farm to help families supplement their diets, encouraged the first medical professionals to settle in the region, and even established schools (including a high school) so future generations could have greater opportunities for advancement. Furthermore, all of these achievements were accomplished without the establishment of municipal taxes. The company was a forerunner in the state, and even the nation, in establishing safety standards, modern mining techniques, and providing access to conveniences such as washhouses for its employees. For several years, his company was the third-largest producer of coal in what was one of the most important coal-producing states in the country. As the nation's appetite for coal grew in the early twentieth century, it was clear that mining coal would remain one of the nation's most harsh and brutal industries; however, Justus Stearns left behind a valuable legacy for his employees and family members when he died in 1933.[40]

8

Entrepreneur and Philanthropist

Mr. Stearns is known in every section of Michigan as Ludington's foremost citizen and benefactor. The constructive work he has accomplished for this city will stand for all time as an enduring monument to the enterprise, loyalty and business acumen of a truly unselfish and public spirited citizen. With Mr. Stearns the welfare of Ludington has ever been the one predominating consideration. For this cause he has for nearly half a century given freely of his time, talent and means. Almost innumerable instances of both private charities and public philanthropies might be cited, but to those who know him this is not necessary.

"Ludington's Foremost Citizen," *Ludington Chronicle*, July 22, 1915, 9

The era beginning about 1900 and ending with the death of Justus Stearns in 1933 saw tremendous expansion of Stearns's business interests. Stearns founded or purchased several new enterprises in his hometown of Ludington, including an electric company, hotel, and firms that manufactured game boards and kitchen utensils. These new businesses helped to diversify the city's economy in the first decade of the twentieth century. The Stearns Salt and Lumber Company continued to serve as the anchor of his Ludington operations for much of this era, but he also expanded his lumbering empire into Michigan's Upper Peninsula and outside the state of Michigan. Beginning in 1909 and continuing into the 1920s, he spent a great deal of his efforts directing the Gile Boat and Engine Company, which was later renamed the Stearns Motor Manufacturing Company. This business specialized in the production of portable generators and high-end motors for boats and tractors. Stearns's actions confirmed he was a successful entrepreneur, while they also demonstrated he was a benevolent philanthropist. Just as other lumbermen who were resident owners, such as Muskegon's Charles Hackley, Stearns's investment in numerous local businesses helped to prepare Ludington for a postlumber economy, while his charitable contributions improved the quality of life for many in the city. His philanthropy was widespread and included contributions to the development of the Epworth Heights community, the establishment of Paulina Stearns Hospital, and numerous additional causes; however, possibly his greatest legacy for the city of Ludington was the beach and park that eventually would bear his name.

Expanding Business Interests

In the early 1900s Stearns expanded his business operations beyond the lumber industry. Many of his investments involved his son Robert L. Stearns and W. T. Culver, Stearns's right-hand man going back to the years at Stearns Siding. Typically, Justus Stearns served as president while Culver served as vice president. The positions of secretary and treasurer often were held by Robert L. Stearns. This triumvirate formed the leadership core for several of Stearns's companies operating inside and outside of Michigan. One example of this successful partnership concerned an electric company.

In 1901 Justus Stearns purchased Ludington's Electric Light Plant. Stearns rebuilt the entire plant using the most modern technology available and relocated the facility near his sawmill operations to increase efficiencies. Sawing lumber created sawdust and other scrap wood, which, rather than being discarded, was recycled and burned to heat water and create steam. This steam was used to generate electricity and to boil brine to make salt. Several lines of steam pipes surrounded the electric plant; some lines carried steam under heavy pressure from boilers, while others carried exhaust used in the salt blocks. According to an article in the *Grand Rapids Press,* "horsepower generated by steam at this plant runs into the thousands," and it probably was the "biggest single power plant north of Grand Rapids." Power at the plant was produced by a large dynamo generator, which had a capacity of 300 kilowatts. Within three years another dynamo was purchased, thereby doubling the capacity to produce power, and by 1908 capacity was doubled once again. Shortly after purchasing the company, Stearns announced a rate decrease of 20 percent to consumers. Additional cost reductions were implemented until rates were less than half of what had been charged in 1901 and were some of the lowest in the state. Prior to these reductions, rates were so high many considered them too costly. By developing efficiencies and investing in the most modern equipment, Stearns was able to produce electricity at a lower cost, and average homeowners could afford to bring electricity to their dwellings. Stearns also began to sell electricity to small businesses and manufacturers in Ludington. Late in 1901 the Stearns Lighting and Power Company announced plans to extend its power lines to Scottville. This had the potential to benefit both large and small farmers living in outlying

Stearns Lighting and Power trucks. Stearns owned and operated a power company in Ludington from 1901 to 1917. (Courtesy of David K. Petersen)

areas, as the electrification of their farms could make rural life easier and their operations more efficient.[1]

The increased efficiencies and rate cuts benefited consumers, but they also benefited Stearns. As rates were lowered, there was a corresponding increase in the number of power customers. Company records indicate that when Stearns purchased the plant in 1901, Stearns Lighting and Power served only residents of Ludington; receipts totaled just under $10,000 with profits of about $3,700. By 1911, the company provided power to four communities: Ludington, Scottville, Pentwater, and Hart. At the end of that year, receipts had increased to nearly $64,000 with profits of more than $27,000. One method the company originally employed to attract customers was to advocate that citizens "show their public spirit by lighting up the streets in front of their homes" with a porch light at the cost of only 25 cents per month.[2] In later years, additional uses of electricity were touted, such as when the company sponsored a week-long exhibit where an "electric cooking apparatus" (an electric cooking stove) was demonstrated. By 1916, the Stearns Lighting and Power Company had 3,383 customers throughout Mason and Oceana Counties, with the largest number (1,896) residing in Ludington. That year receipts totaled over $106,000 with profits of more than $50,000; both were record highs. A year-end report from 1916 indicated that year "was a successful one from the operating standpoint," with "no serious break-down of machinery" or interruption of service. In 1917 Stearns sold the company, probably because he knew its expansion had plateaued and any future growth would require an investment he did not want to make. He most likely drew this conclusion because the same report describing 1916 as a "successful" year also indicated "the prospect of increased business in the future is not good." The only areas into which company officials were prepared to expand were the villages of Fountain and Freesoil. Construction of transmission lines to those communities would require a "high cost" and "large investment." While 1917 saw an end to his ownership, under his direction the Stearns Lighting and Power Company prospered as it adopted the most modern machinery and served an ever-growing number of customers.[3]

Another project involving the trio of Justus, his son Robert, and W. T. Culver was the Stearns Hotel. When the prospect of a new hotel was announced in October 1901, the venture generated considerable excitement in Ludington; the city was becoming recognized as a tourist destination, yet hotel accommodations were considered inadequate. The hotel was to be built of brick at an estimated cost of $25,000. By November that year, the *Ludington Chronicle* announced that Stearns would locate his hotel right on Ludington Avenue, just west of the courthouse, after he paid $2,700 for two corner lots on the city's main thoroughfare. The newspaper was careful to record progress as construction continued into 1903. One article noted the Stearns Hotel would be equipped with "one of the latest innovations in hotel improvements and as yet adopted by only the largest hotels." The "innovation" was the placement of telephones, capable of allowing guests to call long distance, in several of the hotel's rooms. Stearns also applied for a liquor license, as the hotel plans called for the inclusion of a bar, much to the surprise of many in town. The fact that his hotel would serve alcohol also set him apart from some of his contemporary lumber barons and business leaders. Both Charles Hackley and Henry Sage were involved with the temperance movement; Hackley even served as treasurer of Muskegon's temperance society. While Paulina Stearns had once served as an officer in Ludington's Women's Christian Temperance Union, by 1903 she apparently no longer maintained her membership in the organization.[4]

When the hotel officially opened in July 1903, the building stood three stories tall, included ninety rooms, and was made entirely of concrete block. It had a wonderful porch and balcony that ran the length of the building's front entrance. Individual rooms came with electric lights, a phone, and several included a private bath. The hotel's cost had risen substantially: $40,000 for the building, an additional $15,000 for furnishings, and about $5,000 more in other costs, which brought

Stearns Hotel and Bathhouse. The Stearns Hotel opened in 1903; next door is the Stearns Bathhouse. (Courtesy of David K. Petersen)

the total to about $60,000. Prior to the completion of the project, Stearns decided to construct a bathhouse adjacent to the hotel. Plans called for six salt baths and one freshwater bath, six dressing rooms, a steam room, cooling room, and hot room. Salt brine was piped directly into the building from nearby salt wells, and it was hoped its curative powers would help those afflicted with rheumatism, arthritis, or other conditions. The salt baths never proved to be a popular attraction, and within a few years Stearns had the bathhouse remodeled; it served as corporate offices for the Stearns holdings. Despite the failure of the bathhouse, the Stearns Hotel was well received in the community. Justus Stearns actually began living there, at least on a temporary basis, as early as October 1906, about two years following the death of his wife Paulina. In 1923 a forty-two-room addition to the hotel was completed as tourists increasingly turned to Ludington as a vacation destination. As Stearns himself put it, "We are just far enough north to escape the objectionable one-day city excursion crowds, and just far enough south to be reached from Chicago and Milwaukee in a single night's ride." He went on to predict, "I believe Ludington during the next few years will experience a tremendous increase in resort business."[5]

Harry Haskell with the Carrom Company then joined the Stearns, Stearns, and Culver team. Haskell was an inventor from Ludington who created the game of carrom about 1894 as a form of wholesome entertainment for young people. The carrom game grew in popularity and Haskell expanded production, but he was more of an inventor, as opposed to a manager. Beginning in 1905 he leased the manufacturing side of his operations to Stearns, and by 1910 Stearns had

Carrom ad. This advertisement for the Carrom Company demonstrates the strength of their folding tables by having five men stand on one; the men collectively weigh more than 1,000 pounds. (Courtesy of Robert E. Gable)

purchased stock in the company and was named president. Culver became vice president, Robert L. Stearns was secretary, and Haskell served as treasurer, and for many years he remained the company's single largest stockholder. As late as 1912 company records indicate game boards and equipment remained at the core of the organization's mission; sales of those products generated nearly twice as much revenue as any other product line. Literature describing the city of Ludington identified the Carrom-Archarena Company as the "largest game board manufacturer in the world." The company also produced folding tables, billiard tables, and specialty wood parts. An advertisement for the Peerless Folding Table featured a photo of four men weighing a combined 1,002 pounds standing atop the table. During the First World War the company became the largest manufacturer of airplane plywood due to Haskell's development of a special blood albumen glue. The company continued to prosper into the 1920s, and in 1930 Stearns referred to it as a "thriving and profitable industry."[6]

The triumvirate of Justus and Robert L. Stearns and W. T. Culver purchased the assets and property of the Handy Things Manufacturing Company in 1911. The company originally was founded in the 1890s and had been a major Ludington employer for over a decade, but the company fell on hard times and found itself in bankruptcy prior to its purchase by Stearns. Over the years, Handy Things produced numerous kitchen gadgets such as can openers, basting and mixing spoons, cake turners, vegetable and fruit slicers, juicers, and paring knives. Other items such as toothbrush holders, clothes racks, and ironing boards also were manufactured. Company records indicate the best-selling items for 1912 were window cleaners, followed by slicers and squeegees. Handy Things additionally served as the exclusive agent for selling the Rex Brand Stearns Clothespins. Collectively, the manufacturing interests Stearns held made him the largest single employer in the community, representing a diverse number of interests. Investment in the wide range of businesses also represents actions typical of a resident, as opposed to an absentee, owner from this era.[7]

Stearns Salt and Lumber Company

While his business activities were widespread, the anchor of Stearns's operations in Ludington continued to be the Stearns Salt and Lumber Company. Perhaps the headline "Stearns Contribution to City's Prosperity" to an article from the *Ludington Chronicle* dated July 17, 1907, could best illustrate the successes of Stearns's business enterprises. The article reported that Ludington's manufacturing firms paid out approximately $725,000 in wages during 1906, with the Stearns Salt and Lumber Company accounting for $253,000, or about 35 percent of the total. The next highest firm was the Star Watch Company at $100,000. The city's prosperity, the article declared, could be traced back to the purchase of the old Ward Mill and establishment of Stearns Salt and Lumber, as "then Ludington began to recover from the apathy that had overtaken her with the decline of the lumber manufacture." By 1915 Stearns's mill and salt block employed 550, with an additional 300 men working in lumber camps in Kalkaska. The annual payroll was about $500,000. The magnitude of Stearns's business activities also was recognized in an article from the *Michigan Manufacturer and Financial Record* from January 1915. The article predicted that Stearns was "splendidly prepared" to take advantage of a business revival that was sure to arrive soon. Once again the team of Justus Stearns (president), W. T. Culver (vice president), and Robert L. Stearns (secretary and treasurer) provided leadership for the Stearns Salt and Lumber Company, which was capitalized at $500,000 as early as 1905.[8]

The success of the Stearns Salt and Lumber Company came as a result of extensive planning. By the early 1900s it was clear that forested lands near Stearns's Ludington mill were disappearing, and if he were to continue operating, he would have to gain access to additional tracts of timber. In 1903 Stearns negotiated with lumberman R. G. Peters of Manistee to purchase 15,000 acres of hardwood land near Kalkaska. By 1906, Stearns had tapped these tracts, thereby providing him with enough logs to keep his mills running for an estimated fifteen to twenty years. To cut the timber in Kalkaska, which was over one hundred

Stearns camp train in Kalkaska. This lumber camp was designed to accommodate the needs of as many as 150 men. The "camp on wheels" included a dining car, bunkhouse, store, office, and medical car. (Courtesy of Robert E. Gable)

miles north and east of Ludington, Stearns established portable lumber camps. Preparations for the unique camps began with the purchase of eleven railway cars from the Pere Marquette railway. These were cut into two in Ludington and refitted. Once the remodel was completed, the cars were over fifty-six feet long and twelve feet wide, nearly twice the original size. Two cars were reserved as sleeping units with two rows of bunks on either side of the isle. The sleeping cars had cupolas running the entire length of the roof to provide ventilation, and the walls were heavily insulated to protect from the cold. Each sleeper could accommodate seventy-five men, or a total crew of 150. Other rail cars were refitted to create a dining car, which could feed 150 men at one time, a store, blacksmith shop, two lounges, and an office complete with a hospital compartment. This portable camp, which ran on a standard gauge railway, was located near the center of the men's daily operations so that no time would be wasted walking to and from their work area. At the end of the day, men could return to a hot, comfortable dinner and even sleep a bit later the next morning so they could begin that day's efforts refreshed.[9]

Meals at the Stearns Kalkaska camp on wheels were a far cry from the pork and beans, bread, and sugarless coffee that often had been the standard fare in previous lumber camps. Balanced diets, based on a variety of foods, were stressed

to provide "fuel for the human engine." Men could work longer hours and more efficiently if their stomachs were full of food that produced energy and built strong muscles and bones. The Stearns Salt and Lumber Company was recognized for introducing modern methods of food management at their camps with meals that balanced protein, fat, and carbohydrates. One midday Sunday dinner menu began with cream of tomato soup, followed by roast beef and mashed potatoes, buttered bread, pickles, bread pudding, cookies, and tea. While not every meal was as extravagant, it was designed to provide, "energizing carbohydrates and fat, and sufficient protein for the day." Enormous amounts of food were prepared each day by five cooks and fourteen helpers who followed rigorous instructions, designed by an expert, to eliminate food waste. Once adopted, the new system saved the company "thousands of dollars and provided an appetizing and satisfying table for the hands." By the summer of 1908, Stearns's Kalkaska operations were well underway, and in June of that year an average of forty-four cars of logs were being shipped to the mill in Ludington each day.[10]

The salt and sawmill operations in Ludington were organized to monitor costs as much as possible so as to minimize waste. Salt produced by the Stearns Salt and Lumber Company was sold under the Sunshine Salt brand name, and in 1914 nearly 500,000 barrels were shipped to customers all over the country. It operated under the motto of "A Better Salt in a Better Barrel" and exercised care not only in the production of pure and clean salt but also in the construction of each barrel to withstand delivery by wagon and rail. To develop efficiencies,

Dining car. This rail car was refitted as a special dining car for Stearns's operations in Kalkaska. (Courtesy of Mike Hankwitz)

Stearns held an annual education rally and banquet for many of his employees. Training opportunities were made available to personnel in several areas of the company, including those working in sales, clerical work, manufacturing, and at the executive level. One year the head of Chicago's Sheldon School of Business Building was invited to speak on the subject of "The Science of Building Any Business." The company also announced its intention to encourage interested employees to enroll in the Sheldon School's correspondence courses and its willingness to help supplement this instruction by bringing in monthly speakers.[11]

A detailed analysis of two items can demonstrate the efficiency and attention company officials paid to key performance statistics. Company records show all lumber cut at the sawmill was inventoried and identified according to its origin (location of where it was logged) and species (pine, hemlock, maple, elm, cherry, basswood, and such). In 1910 the company cut a total of 27,997,037 feet of timber. From this total, 9,993,753 feet, or 35.7 percent, was made up of pine and hemlock, whereas other species accounted for 64.3 percent of the total. The following year, the company cut 28,662,198 feet; 40.82 percent came from pine and hemlock, while other species accounted for 59.18 percent. The costs involved with the manufacture of salt also were closely scrutinized. In 1910, the company manufactured 350,251 barrels of medium grade salt. Each barrel cost 48.1 cents to produce, while sales brought in revenue of 46.7 cents per barrel. This led to a loss of 1.4 cents for each barrel. The following year the company produced 299,700 barrels of medium grade salt while the cost to manufacture each barrel dropped to 46 cents; however, the price of salt increased and Stearns was able to make sales of 52.4 cents for each barrel sold, thus garnering a profit of 6.4 cents per barrel. Such attention to detail as to the inner workings of his company allowed Stearns to monitor costs and develop efficiencies, enabling him to maximize profits.[12]

Unfortunately for Stearns, his empire grew to be so diverse not all aspects of his operations received the same level of attention. In the fall of 1907 the Stearns Salt and Lumber Company was indicted for "charging secret rebates, amounting to $25,000" in 1905 and 1906 from the Pere Marquette railroad. The rebates came about as a result of contracts negotiated to transport finished lumber from Stearns's mill in Ludington to Toledo, Ohio. Such rebates were made illegal with the passage of the Elkins Act in 1903 and the Hepburn Act in 1906. These pieces of legislation were put into place in the early 1900s in an attempt to regulate the railroad industry. Stearns was charged with twenty counts of violating the laws, which carried penalties of between $1,000 and $20,000 for each count, or a possible total of $400,000 in fines. In March 1908 Stearns entered a plea of guilty

Stearns Salt and Lumber Company loader. Here, two men take a ride on a log as it is placed on a rail car to be transported to the mill. (Courtesy of Mike Hankwitz)

in the US District Court, while maintaining that the company had not purposefully violated the law and the "rebating was not intentional on the part of the company, but was received through the blunders of employees of the company."[13] At the time the plea was made, the presiding judge imposed the minimum fine of $1,000 for each count, for a total of $20,000. Within a few weeks, Stearns still had not paid the fine and the company began a fight to have the judge set aside the guilty plea and the $20,000 judgment. Over the course of the next several months Stearns's attorneys argued in court that they should be allowed to withdraw their guilty plea and instead enter a plea of not guilty. Alternatively, they fought to reduce the fines primarily because company officials had been unaware for some time that rebates had been received in the first place. Eventually, in December 1908 Stearns pled guilty to six offences and paid a fine of $10,000.[14]

Stearns continued to operate his sawmill in Ludington until the fall of 1917. By that time, Mason County's forests had vanished and Stearns's log supply had dwindled in Kalkaska to the point where he sold it to the Antrim Iron Company of Cadillac. While the final whistle brought an end to Ludington's involvement in the lumber era, by that time the city's economy had become more diversified. Stearns himself even commented, "The closing down of the mill is going to bring no hardship on the people of Ludington. . . . All other industries in the city today are handicapped for lack of men and the men laid off at the mill will find employment in the various factories." About the same time the mill was set to close, Stearns announced plans to expand operations at his salt block. A new well was drilled and additional improvements were designed to increase capacity to about 750,000 barrels per year. Stearns continued to manufacture salt in Ludington for a few more years, although production was disrupted for a time in the summer of 1919 when a handful of employees went on strike in hopes of obtaining a nine-hour day and wage increases. Stearns sold his salt block and all twelve acres of property in Ludington's Fourth Ward to Morton Salt in 1923.[15]

The sale of his Fourth Ward properties to Morton Salt took some by surprise in the city of Ludington, but Stearns explained, "We are timber men first; that is our principal business. . . . Manufacturing salt was a side issue carried on to utilize fuel, much of which would otherwise have been wasted." Although Stearns closed his mill in Ludington and developed lumbering operations in Wisconsin and Kentucky, as described earlier, he continued to seek opportunities in other locations. In 1903 Stearns purchased a mill and property in Bagdad, Florida, which operated under the name of Stearns and Culver Lumber Company. By 1908 the Bagdad plant was capitalized at $1,250,000 and Stearns had implemented the use of logging railroads, as opposed to floating logs, to his mill site. In addition to cutting yellow pine, the plant also manufactured turpentine. He eventually sold his holdings in 1919 at a reported price of $3.5 million. Stearns even owned mills and property in Michigan's Upper Peninsula. In 1915 Stearns and Culver took over the Consolidated Lumber Company, located in Manistique, and operated there until the company was sold in the early 1920s. Stearns purchased an additional 36,000 acres of timberland near L'Anse, Michigan, in 1919. This business was organized as the Stearns and Culver Company, which operated in L'Anse until he sold it to Henry Ford in 1922 for $1,850,000. Stearns also expanded into Washington State when he paid $1.5 million for three thousand acres of timberland and the box and veneer plant from the National Lumber and Manufacturing Company near the end of 1919. He operated the business into the 1920s, and by 1923 the mill, located in the city of Hoquiam, Washington, was cutting 75 million feet annually. Stearns served as president of the Marquette Lumber Company too, which manufactured and handled building materials that were sold at the company's retail lumberyards in Grand Rapids.[16]

Stearns Motor Manufacturing Company

Stearns may have described himself as a lumberman, but he devoted the bulk of his energies from about 1914 onward to the direct management of the Stearns

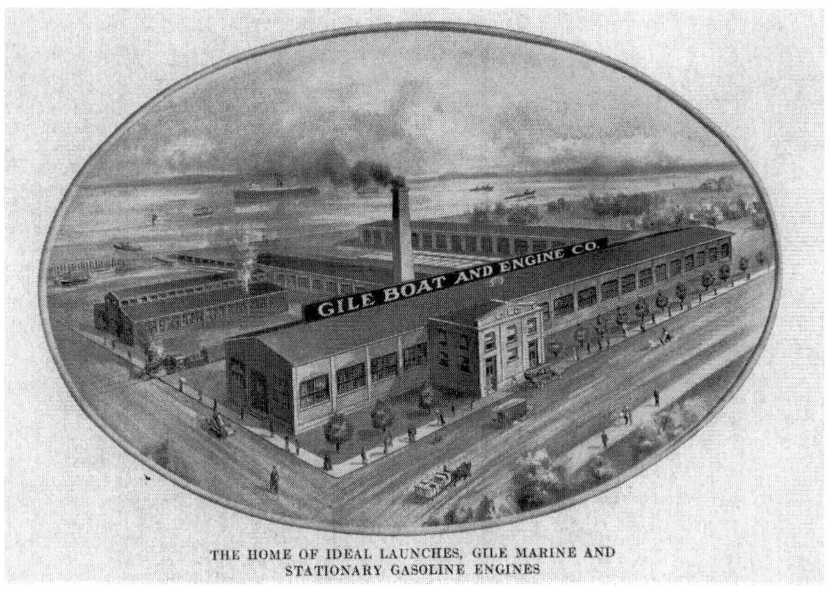

Gile Boat and Engine Company. This image appeared in a company catalog showing the company's factory along Ludington's harbor. (Courtesy of John Holcomb)

Motor Manufacturing Company. It was successful for many years, but nearly bankrupted him in the end. The public became aware of this business in December 1908 when the *Ludington Chronicle* announced that a new gasoline boat factory might come to Ludington. Soon after, the Gile Boat and Engine Company was organized in 1909 with a capitalization of $50,000. Justus Stearns, W. L. Mercereau, and M. B. Danaher served on the board of directors; Stearns was named president. William Gile, who invented and manufactured the engine to be used, was from Muskegon where he was considered a pioneer in the field of gasoline engines. A catalog the company produced from about 1911 highlighted the items available, which included, "Motor Boats, Marine Engines, Marine Hardware, [and] Launch Accessories." The catalog described its "Ideal Launches," which were between sixteen and twenty-six feet in length and could be outfitted with motors ranging from three to ten horsepower each. Company literature emphasized the speed and reliability of its Gile engine. By 1914 Justus Stearns had bought out the other investors, injected an additional $50,000 into the company, and reorganized it as the Stearns Motor Manufacturing Company. The new company continued to produce marine engines, but the product line was expanded to include engines for tractors and lighting plants (portable generators).[17]

In what would become a continuing pattern for the company, it experienced a boom in January 1914 when a very large order for five thousand tractor engines was placed, prompting Stearns to erect another building and expand his operations. This was followed by a bust when production came to a "dead stop" for several weeks as the First World War began and fighting in Europe led to uncertainty and disrupted financial markets. By 1915 the bust had been replaced by a boom, once again, as sales for tractor engines exceeded all previous records; for a time the plant turned out forty engines each day. By March 1915 the *Ludington Chronicle* reported that "Mr. Stearns, notwithstanding his other extensive interests, is devoting almost his entire time and energy personally directing the work and improvements now in progress at the Gile factory."[18]

Throughout the decade of the 1920s, the sale and manufacture of items produced at the Stearns Motor Manufacturing Company expanded, while Stearns continued to invest a great deal of his own money into the company, including an expansion of the foundry. One of the best-selling items produced was the Stearns Lighting Plant. This portable generator was shipped to customers from Australia to England, from Japan to Mexico. Stearns motors also proved to be popular for high-end watercraft, as shown when a new six-cylinder marine engine was the "talk of the show" at a New York motorboat show in January

1926. Stearns motors were used in farm tractors, and their performance at tests conducted at the University of Nebraska proved their power and low fuel consumption. As early as 1924, however, Robert L. Stearns expressed concerns over the management of the company, and he developed a plan to cut costs. By 1927, things had deteriorated to the point where he wrote in his diary, "Father's affairs on my nerves," and conditions at the company were, "all a mess." By December that year, Robert confronted his father to demonstrate "how critical the Motor Company's condition," and "also his [Justus's] own affairs" were at that time; without significant action they would be unable to meet the following week's payroll. The situation became "rather warm," but Justus began to slowly realize the situation. After examining the financial statements, Robert discovered his father's net worth had dwindled to "about $150,000," which could be contrasted to news reports that previously described Justus Stearns as "several times a millionaire." Justus celebrated his eighty-first birthday in 1927, and he no longer was able to oversee his businesses at the same level as he had when he was younger. He decided to turn over management of the plant to his son and others in his family.[19]

The company would operate for three additional years, during which time Freeman Ross Stearns, Justus's grandson, assumed additional responsibilities; however, with the onset of the Great Depression, Stearns's customers stopped placing orders. The business went into voluntary receivership in November 1929 and later was sold at public auction in July 1930. Reflecting back on events, Justus wrote, "I built the Stearns Motor Manufacturing Company, which has always been a losing proposition in a financial way, but which has afforded employment for 200 men ever since that time." These comments were echoed in an article appearing in the *Ludington Daily News* from 1930 that reported that the company had paid over $2.2 million in wages in the previous ten years, making it one of Ludington's most valued industries in that era. As these figures indicate, the wages paid to those employed by Justus Stearns had a substantial impact on the community.[20]

Justus Stearns's Philanthropy

As a group, Michigan's lumber barons donated to numerous causes in the communities where they lived. Henry Sage contributed money to several Bay City churches and as much as $50,000 for the library that continues to bear his name. Sage lived in New York and served on the board of trustees for Cornell University for many years; he gave a great deal of his fortune to the university. The donations of lumberman Ammi Wright led to the establishment of Alma College

Epworth Hotel. Stearns took over management of the Epworth Hotel and restaurant for a period of ten years beginning in 1900. (Courtesy of Epworth Heights Museum)

in Michigan. Charles Hackley was the Michigan timber baron with the greatest reputation for philanthropy; his actions earned him the label "Muskegon's Carnegie." Throughout his lifetime, and in his will, he contributed approximately $6 million to numerous causes, including Muskegon's public schools, Hackley Hospital, numerous parks, and other charities. While Stearns's generosity never reached the level Hackley set, he donated money to a range of causes throughout the course of his lifetime.[21]

Stearns's involvement in the development of Epworth Heights illustrated how his business activities could be closely aligned with his philanthropy. The Epworth League Training Assembly was a Methodist organization incorporated officially in March 1894. It was influenced by the Chautauqua movement, which had become popular throughout the country. Following its incorporation, the Citizens Development Company of Ludington gave the Epworth League $21,000 and 240 acres of property north of town. In return, the Epworth League agreed to develop the property and sponsor two or three weeks of religious and cultural programming in the summers. The arrangement benefited the city of Ludington because it would bring resorters to town, while members of the Epworth League had outgrown its previous encampment at Big Rapids. In subsequent years many famous speakers traveled to Epworth to educate audiences.

Among others, speakers included the famous politician and three-time Democratic nominee for president William Jennings Bryan (1899 and 1918); the Reverend Billy Sunday (1901); Jane Addams, the founder of Hull House (1906); and the Native American activist and writer Charles Eastman (1906). By the late 1890s the momentum associated with Epworth's founding had waned and the organization needed an injection of energy and capital. Stearns became a member of the Epworth League as early as 1900 and later that year assumed management of the hotel, restaurant, and grocery for a period of ten years. He planned to direct numerous projects the following year, including the conversion of the Epworth Hotel into a first-class resort, construction of a large dormitory and several new cottages, and the expansion of educational programming. Remarkably, according to the *Epworth Assembly Quarterly,* "Mr. Stearns has not gone into this enterprise with a view to reaping financial reward." Stearns himself declared, "If I ever get back the money that I am putting into the undertaking, I shall be entirely satisfied without making any profits." Editors of the *Epworth Assembly Quarterly* estimated that by 1901 Stearns had invested no less than $30,000 into the grounds at Epworth. Possibly the greatest transformation came at the Epworth Hotel; it was a losing business financially when Stearns assumed management of the facility, but when he turned it back to Epworth, it was on solid financial footing.[22]

The "Dummy Train" carried passengers from Ludington to Epworth Heights; Stearns obtained control in 1900. It ran until it was discontinued in 1919. (Courtesy of David K. Petersen)

In 1900, Stearns also acquired control of the Epworth League Railroad and reorganized it as the Ludington and Northern. Ever since 1895 the railway had transported Epworth residents from Ludington to Epworth Heights, but once Stearns gained control he extended the line north to Hamlin Lake. Residents referred to it as the "Dummy Train." Ludington historian James L. Cabot offered the best explanation for this name. He explained the train's locomotive had a false exterior because it was designed for use on street railways, to prevent horses from becoming frightened. It was inexpensive to ride the Dummy Train; it cost only 5 cents to travel from Ludington to Epworth, while a trip from Ludington to Lake Hamlin cost 25 cents. Ridership peaked in 1909 when the train carried 200,000 passengers that summer. Stearns operated the Dummy Train until 1919 when it was discontinued. The business had been losing money and ridership ever since 1913 because the automobile became more popular among Epworth residents.[23]

Stearns became an Epworth trustee in 1901, and for many years served as chairman of the committee on grounds. In that capacity he oversaw numerous construction projects. Under his direction, and with his financial support, the dock in front of the hotel was rebuilt in 1902. According to an article in the *Epworth Quarterly,* once it was completed, the dock extended six hundred feet into Lake Michigan. A restaurant was added to the hotel in 1903, and he expanded the store. Stearns also personally supervised repairs following storm damage that took place during the winter of 1905/6. Between 1900 and 1910 numerous renovations were undertaken at the hotel, all of which fell under the responsibility of Stearns. To meet the increasing demand for cottages, the Stearns Improvement Company was formed in 1900. Over the next ten years, it was responsible for the construction of at least eleven cottages; some immediately were purchased, while others were rented out. In July 1901 Stearns's own three-story cottage, with a delightful dining room and wonderful view of Lake Michigan, was built on Epworth's lot described as "Sunset Park." That same year Congressman Roswell P. Bishop built his own cottage, and the two became neighbors. In his annual report to members from 1908, John H. Grant, Epworth's president, highlighted the establishment of the music conservatory building "generously donated" by Stearns. It opened that year and was designed to serve as a location for musical instruction in the summers. Epworth saw remarkable growth in the era from 1900 to 1910, much of which could be attributed to the leadership and financial contributions of Justus Stearns.[24]

Another project in which Stearns's involvement proved to be instrumental was the establishment of Mason County's first hospital. For many years, residents

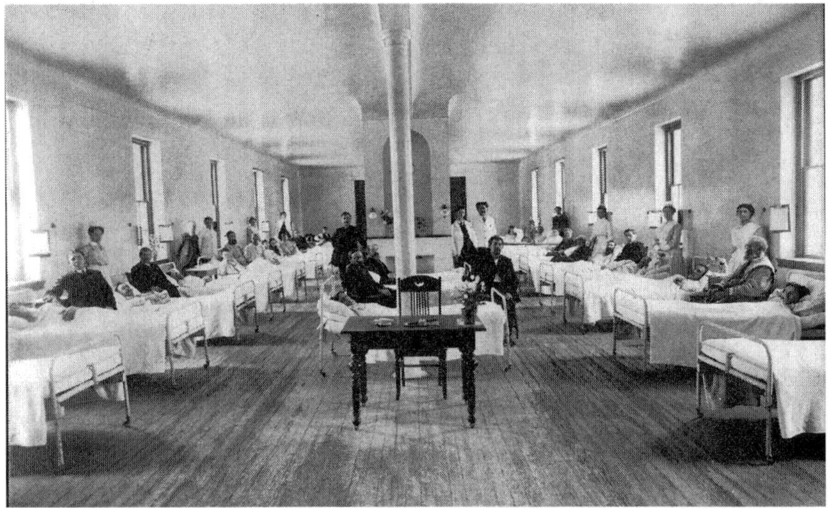

Paulina Stearns Hospital. This photo shows the Men's Wing of the hospital. Originally, the building was the Stearns family home, but it was donated by Justus to serve as the region's first hospital in 1907. (Courtesy of David K. Petersen)

of the county needing hospital services were required to travel to another Michigan city, and in some instances, all the way to Chicago. To rectify this, a group of women met in September 1906 to form the Mason County Hospital Association, which would oversee the establishment of a community hospital in the city of Ludington. They announced their plans to a group of local businessmen at a banquet that month. When their plans for the hospital were revealed, the men declared, "It couldn't be done and was a waste of time." The women were determined to move forward anyway, so they hired a lawyer and developed Articles of Association. Any woman could serve as a member of the Hospital Association upon a majority vote of its members and payment of $5 in annual dues. There continued to be resistance to their efforts by some in the community, while others argued the facility was badly needed. The group received an anonymous donation of $1,000 that December. It later was discovered the anonymous donor was Justus Stearns; it would be the first of many thousands of dollars he would contribute to the hospital.[25]

A train accident the following summer generated additional support for the project, and in September 1907 Justus Stearns announced he would donate the use of his South Washington Avenue home, located in Ludington's Fourth Ward neighborhood, for a period of six months to serve as a temporary hospital. Additionally, he offered to furnish the coal necessary to heat the structure.

Shortly thereafter, members of the Mason County Hospital Association voted unanimously to name the building the Paulina Stearns Hospital, after Justus's wife Paulina who had died in 1904. The first patient was treated prior to the official opening of the hospital that fall. When the hospital officially opened, an article in the *Ludington Chronicle* expressed gratitude for Stearns's contributions, which "made the realization of the long deferred hopes possible." In February 1908 Stearns deeded his home to the Hospital Association. At the time, the residence was worth an estimated $5,000, bringing the total amount of his gifts to more than $6,000. That summer, Robert L. Stearns donated his house, located right next door to the hospital, to be used as a home for nurses. At the same time this was announced, the Paulina Stearns Hospital Nursing School was opened. The school offered two-year nursing degrees and operated until 1922. To accommodate the needs of the new nursing school, Justus Stearns provided several thousand dollars to remodel his son's former home.[26]

With the benefit of Stearns's bequests, along with numerous fund-raisers, the hospital proved to be a major success. Nevertheless, within a few years it was clear the facility was so successful, it suffered from a lack of space. After several months of consideration, a series of major improvements were planned to double the capacity of the institution at a cost of about $15,000. Stearns demonstrated continued generosity when he announced he would pay for the entire expansion, bringing his total contributions to the hospital to more than $30,000. Plans called for the addition of a new wing to be added to the north side of the second floor. Additional improvements allowed for a capacity of at least thirty beds, including ten private rooms, a children's ward, and an operating room. Ludington's first passenger elevator also was installed. It operated with a motor, but riders had to pull a rope if they wanted to be transported from the first floor up to the second floor. In 1921 another major expansion was commenced to remodel the building and purchase new equipment. Construction of the hospital's own boiler plant also was undertaken. Many businesses contributed to help fund these projects, and the hospital sponsored the operetta "Springtime" to raise money, but Stearns contributed an additional $10,000 to make these changes possible.[27]

Stearns left a lasting legacy with his donations to the hospital, but he also contributed his time and money to numerous other causes. For many years he attended Ludington's Congregational Church. In 1903 when the congregation decided to build a new place for worship at a cost of $20,000, Stearns contributed at least $10,000 toward the construction. He continued attending the church for many years, even after it combined with the Presbyterians in 1924 to create the Community Church on Harrison Avenue, just a short walk from the

Stearns Hotel. Stearns also gave many gifts to the Ludington library, including reference works such as the *National Cyclopedia of American Biography* and copies of Ridpath's *History of the World.* When the United States became involved in the First World War, he guaranteed that men who left his employment to serve in the armed forces during the war would be assured of jobs upon their return. Stearns contributed to the war effort by purchasing war bonds, including $50,000 to kick off a Liberty Loan drive in October 1917. In the early 1920s, Stearns also led a petition drive to create a boulevard along Ludington Avenue to Lake Shore Drive to help beautify his hometown and encourage residents and visitors to enjoy the wonderful views of Lake Michigan.[28]

Young people often were the recipients of Mr. Stearns's time and charity, which also spread beyond the city of Ludington. For many years he awarded cash prizes to students receiving the highest grades in their class. In 1917 he offered $10 to each top student in grades nine through twelve and $5 for those ranking second. He also served as chair of the Pere Marquette Council of the Boy Scouts. He described the Boy Scouts as a "worthwhile" organization because it helped to make "good citizens" and encouraged boys to become involved in positive activities in their community. In the final years of his life, Stearns became involved in a statewide project to celebrate Michigan's lumbering heritage. He and his son Robert made "substantial contributions" to a Lumberman's Monument located across the state in East Tawas, Michigan. When the monument was dedicated in 1932, Stearns was eighty-seven years old and the oldest lumberman present.[29]

Perhaps the greatest contribution Stearns made to the residents of Ludington was the beach and park along the Lake Michigan shoreline. He not only donated valuable beach property to the city, but also he did so in such a way as to promote the interests of Ludington's business community at the same time. On July 22, 1909, the *Ludington Record-Appeal* reported there would be a special election to determine if voters would allow the city to issue $50,000 worth of bonds for public improvements. The article continued, "In a nutshell the proposition is to bond the city for $50,000 and purchase the J. S. Stearns property lying along the shore of Lake Michigan north of the avenue, known as the Lakeside addition. The word purchase, in this connection, is really a misnomer because upon the purchase of the property Mr. Stearns will immediately donate to the Board of Trade the sum of $50,000 to be used in securing factories for Ludington, so that the tract of land above mentioned will really be a donation to the city on the part of Mr. Stearns."[30]

The special election for the bond proposal was to be held August 20. The paper described the proposal as a "splendid opportunity for the city" because there was "no better bathing beach in the world than that lying along this land." At the same time Stearns announced his participation in this plan, Antoine E. Cartier, another Ludington lumberman with whom Stearns had carried on somewhat of a friendly rivalry over the years, declared he would donate a large piece of valuable property to the north of the city. Taken together, the two offers, while independent of each other, had the potential to establish an extensive park system in Ludington if the voters approved the proposal the following month.[31]

Articles and advertisements appeared in the *Ludington Chronicle* strongly favoring the bond proposal. More than one article called upon citizens to vote affirmatively because the city needed more industries to employ its citizens and the proposal's passage was sure to bring jobs. An advertisement from August 11, 1909, argued, "If you believe in Ludington, if you believe in its growth and prosperity, if you want to see the value of the city property enhanced and more work provided for the laboring man—you will vote 'YES' on the proposition." As the date for the election drew near, support seemed to grow for the proposal, but a two-thirds majority was required to carry the measure. When the final votes were tallied following the election, the two-thirds majority was exceeded as the proposal passed with 458 residents voting in favor, while 108 were opposed.[32]

In January 1910, about four months after the election, the city of Ludington issued bonds in the amount of $50,000. Later in the month Warren Cartier, the city's mayor, delivered the bonds to Justus Stearns as payment for the lakeside addition, which was purchased by the city to establish a public park. Stearns then turned over the bonds to a committee made up of eight men, which included his partner W. T. Culver, charged with working alongside the Board of Trade, "for the purpose of inducing industrial institutions to locate in" the city of Ludington. At that time the Board of Trade was considered the logical institution to handle the arrangement as it operated similarly to a Chamber of Commerce.[33]

For many years the lakeside addition property Stearns donated was allowed to remain in its natural state, and the city did not take any steps to develop the space into a park. Beginning in 1923, however, Ludington's Public Parks and Grounds Committee took up the issue. The committee was made up of three members of the city council, and it also included members of the community, including Laura Freeman Stearns, the wife of Robert L. Stearns, and Henry Haskell, the partner of Justus Stearns in the Carrom Company. After meeting for several months, the committee recommended that the property along Lake Michigan be named Stearns Park in appreciation for the land that Justus Stearns "generously donated." The committee also recommended an appropriation of $1,000 to landscape the property and to construct a concrete walkway allowing for greater access to the park. Furthermore, the committee supported the adoption of an ordinance regulating the properties abutting the park along Lake Shore Drive "to be strictly a residential district for white families, the buildings to be one-family residences, the cost of which" should be "not less than $5,000."[34] At a subsequent meeting the city council acted on the recommendations and passed Ordinance #405, which created Stearns Park. Ordinance #406 established regulations on buildings fronting the park along Lakeshore Drive. The Jim Crow provision prohibiting nonwhite families from residing in the block was dropped, but one can suspect black families would not have been welcomed in the neighborhood at that time. Other provisions confirmed the requirement that homes be private dwellings each worth a minimum of $5,000.[35]

In subsequent years, Stearns Park gained a reputation for its beaches of pure sand and its family-friendly atmosphere. In 1948 Laura Freeman Stearns purchased a piece of property adjacent to Stearns Park for $4,750. She then donated it to the city, completing the park, with the stipulation the land always be maintained for park purposes, otherwise the title would revert back to Mrs. Stearns or her heirs. With this donation, the land included in the park stretched for more than one-half mile along the shoreline of Lake Michigan. An article in the *Ludington Daily News* from 1956 described Stearns Park as the "Queen" of the Lake Michigan shoreline, attracting thousands of visitors each summer. Farther back from the beach, grass was planted, along with trees memorializing Mason County residents who died fighting in the First World War. Additional memorials have been added over time. A public bathhouse was built for those enjoying the beach, and for many years lifeguards watched over hundreds of swimmers refreshing themselves in the lake's cool waters. Recognition culminated in 2012 when *USA Today* identified Stearns Park Beach as one of the top beaches in the nation that was "family-friendly, with a new skate park, easy access to town and a walkable pier out to North Breakwater Light[house]." It was only through the generosity of Justus Stearns and his heirs that these achievements became possible.[36]

Final Years

Stearns continued to reside in Ludington and remained active in his final years, which also were characterized by numerous events celebrating his lifetime of achievements. As early as the fall of 1907, when he donated his home to serve as the community's hospital, Stearns had lived in the Stearns Hotel in the winters, while spending time at his Epworth cottage in the summer. In 1920 he purchased a house right across from the hotel and began dividing his time between this home and Epworth. He lived alone in this house, with the exception in later years that his maid, Carrie Woodall, lived at the residence as well. In 1923, to celebrate his seventy-eighth birthday, a tribute dinner was held in his honor in Ludington. It was an elaborate affair to which about one hundred citizens were invited. Those attending received a tribute booklet with a biography of Stearns and several pages describing his life and major accomplishments. Following the dinner a silver loving cup was presented to Mr. Stearns, with the inscription, "To Justus S. Stearns . . . an appreciation by the people of Ludington on his 78th birthday anniversary of his worth as a man and a citizen and in recognition of his generosity and conspicuous public service, which for a generation have inspired his townsfolk." When he was presented with the cup, the *Ludington Daily News* reported, "his voice quivered with emotion stirred in his heart by his life-long friends."[37] He soon regained his composure and thanked the crowd of well-wishers. Five years later a similar celebration was held in Stearns, Kentucky, to recognize his eighty-third birthday. Stearns spent the day touring the mill, store, and coal mine operations, but the highlight of his trip was a visit to a school built by the Stearns Coal and Lumber Company. The students wrote personal birthday greetings that were placed in an imitation birthday cake and presented to him. After receiving his gifts, Stearns remarked, "I am proud that I have reached the age of 83 years. . . . I am thankful. Too few persons are accorded the privilege to live as long on this planet. My 83rd birthday anniversary is therefore the happiest of my life."[38]

Stearns received recognition for his accomplishments by other groups and individuals. In 1916 the Michigan Republican Party honored Stearns by choosing him to serve as a presidential elector that year, and in 1928 he was picked to be a delegate to the Republican National Convention. Additionally, in 1925 he was one of only two Michigan residents to represent the state on an advisory committee to commemorate the 150th anniversary of the Declaration of Independence. Michigan's governor, Alex J. Groesbeck, selected him for this position along with William K. Kellogg of Battle Creek. Another Michigan governor, Wilber M. Brucker, later appointed him to serve as a member of a Bicentennial Commission honoring the birth of George Washington. One of the greatest honors he received came in 1930 when Kentucky's governor, Flem D. Samson, appointed Stearns to be an "aide-de-camp on the governor's staff with the rank and grade of colonel." He received this honor "in recognition of his sterling qualities as a business man, and the splendid work he has accomplished in developing a once remote and unproductive section of the state, giving employment to hundreds of men." From that point on, many news articles describing Stearns referred to him as "Colonel" Stearns.[39]

His business interests were at the forefront of his daily activities, even as Stearns grew older. For years he served as president of Ludington's First National Bank. He first was elected to this position in 1909, and subsequently was reelected every year until his death. Articles from the *Ludington Daily News* demonstrated that even when he was well into his eighties, on his birthdays, and most other days, he could be found in his office, working at his desk. On these occasions, he often was seen wearing a finely tailored business suit, while he entertained callers and received letters and telegrams of congratulations from friends and family. In 1928 Justus and Robert purchased a farm in Riverton Township. The plan was to have a small farm with some dairy cows, pigs, and chickens along with some vegetables and fruit. It was not designed to be a large operation, but the intention was to harvest enough to supply the Stearns Hotel. He enjoyed spending time on the farm, and he commented, "It gets me back to the time when I was 16 years old and milked 12 cows on my father's farm."[40]

Stearns's health remained robust for many years, although he did hurt his leg when he was eighty-three. It required a physician's attention, but he recovered quickly. When asked about his vigorous health, he replied, "I have no particular formula; am not a golf player. In fact, I take no set exercises." He also considered vacations unnecessary and believed he received plenty of exercise every day because his daily routine involved considerable walking. The big reason, he continued, "is that I never worry. The philosopher who said worry, not work, kills men spoke an everlasting truth." When others grew concerned during previous financial panics, Stearns declared, "I never lost an hour's sleep over it. . . . We came through all right."[41] Justus may not have worried about things over the years, but his age did eventually catch up with him. Around Thanksgiving in 1932, at the age of eighty-seven, he contracted pneumonia. He was confined to his home for several weeks as he attempted to overcome the illness, but his condition was complicated by his advanced age and arthritis. Prior to his illness, he had been urged to travel south that fall, but he refused, preferring to remain in Ludington. Despite the efforts of his doctors, Justus continued to weaken, and he died at home the morning of February 14, 1933, just two months short of his eighty-eighth birthday.[42]

Funeral services were held at the Community Church later that week, after which his body was laid to rest at Ludington's Lakeview Cemetery. The Ludington Chamber of Commerce asked local businesses to close their operations the day of the funeral out of respect for the contributions of Mr. Stearns to the community. Numerous individuals offered public testimonials in honor of Stearns. One of the most powerful came from Dr. John Loppenthien, a longtime resident of the city. Dr. Loppenthien remembered a story that demonstrated Stearns's generosity as an employer. At a time when the lumber market was in a slump, Mr. Stearns was advised by his business managers to suspend operations and lay off his employees, but he refused. He replied instead, "We'll keep the mill going. The men need work; they've got to live. We'll sell the lumber some day." Loppenthien's father had the contract to handle the finished lumber, which was piled high by the end of the winter. After the market rebounded, Stearns eventually sold the lumber, and at a fair price.[43] An editorial in the *Grand Rapids Herald* the day following Stearns's death described him as "the Pine King of Michigan, but he was more, far more, than that. . . . He was the first citizen of Ludington and one of the first citizens of Western Michigan. His heart was in his home community and his home state. An able, energetic, foresighted, and public-spirited mentor among men, his mark will long endure."[44]

Shortly after the funeral, the *Ludington Daily News* reported that his son and only child, Robert L. Stearns, was the sole beneficiary of his estate. The last will and testament of Justus Stearns was written in 1911, and was modified with a codicil in December 1932. The will confirmed the report from the paper, but it also recognized the faithful services of three individuals who were to receive between $1,000 and $2,000 upon his death. Miss Edna Elizabeth Dickey was one of these individuals. Ironically, Miss Dickey, who never married, served as a secretary for Mr. Stearns and would continue to serve in the same capacity for three additional generations of the Stearns's family. These included Robert L. Stearns Sr., Robert L. Stearns Jr., and Robert E. Gable, the great-grandson of Justus Stearns. When she was interviewed in 1971, she recalled the first letter Justus Stearns dictated to her, which she still had in her possession. The letter was to a clinic on behalf of a disabled Ludington girl. Through Stearns's efforts, and financial assistance, the young girl received the treatment necessary to avoid spending the remainder of her life in a wheelchair. This was just one of the many examples she remembered that characterized the generosity of Mr. Stearns. It also brings to mind Stearns's interaction with Grace Bedell, the little girl who in 1860 had encouraged Abraham Lincoln to grow a beard. Just as Stearns sought to protect the young girl in the wheelchair, he sought out Grace Bedell in 1931, when she was in her eighties, to recognize her interaction with the nation's sixteenth president. These actions, and many others, demonstrated that, indeed, Justus Stearns possessed a very generous heart.[45]

Conclusion

The final years of Stearns's life demonstrated that not only was he a captain of industry, he also was a benevolent philanthropist. Much of Stearns's business success was due to careful negotiation and planning. Stearns was able to intermingle the operations of the Stearns Salt and Lumber Company with his electric company to lower costs and expand his clientele throughout Mason County. These efficiencies, along with those adopted in the lumber camps of Kalkaska and other areas of the Stearns Empire allowed his businesses to profit. He even brought in experts to continually search for efficiencies and improve practices. Stearns did not simply keep these profits for himself; he became a generous benefactor. While Stearns Beach may be the best example of his contribution to the city of Ludington, he donated tens of thousands of dollars to the Paulina Stearns Hospital and improved the lives of many residents with his numerous charitable activities. The communities he touched benefited from his actions, which impacted residents immediately and for many years to come.

9

A Life Considered

"Pine King," utility magnate, financier, hotel man. . . . One of the outstanding characteristics of Mr. Stearns was that he considered it an obligation to furnish steady employment to every person who worked for him.

Associated Press, quoted in "Keen Ability of Pine King Is Traced in Development of City of His Adoption," *Ludington Daily News*, February 14, 1933.

Throughout his career, Justus Stearns demonstrated an exceptional entrepreneurial spirit along with a driving ambition to earn a profit. At times he exhibited the sometimes-harsh attitudes and actions of other well-known captains of industry; he, and his contemporaries, disliked unions while production overrode concern for the environment. Stearns also employed thousands in Michigan, Kentucky, Wisconsin, and other regions of the country, which allowed workers to put food on their tables, a roof over their heads, and improve their standard of living. Several factors influenced his endeavors, thereby allowing him to be a successful business leader. His philanthropy was widespread as it impacted the lives of numerous individuals and groups in his generation and for those to follow. Given his broad range of achievements, Justus Stearns left behind a positive legacy for the communities he served, and his life story helps to show how conditions in the United States were transformed as it entered the twentieth century and the industrial age.

Factors Leading to Stearns's Success

Much of Stearns's success as a business leader can be explained by three factors: his family connections, his willingness to take risks, and his ability to develop efficiencies in the businesses he operated. First, members of his family helped Stearns throughout much of his career. While he did not receive a formal education beyond eighth grade, as a boy growing up on a farm in New York, young Justus was taught a great deal by his father. He rose early every morning to

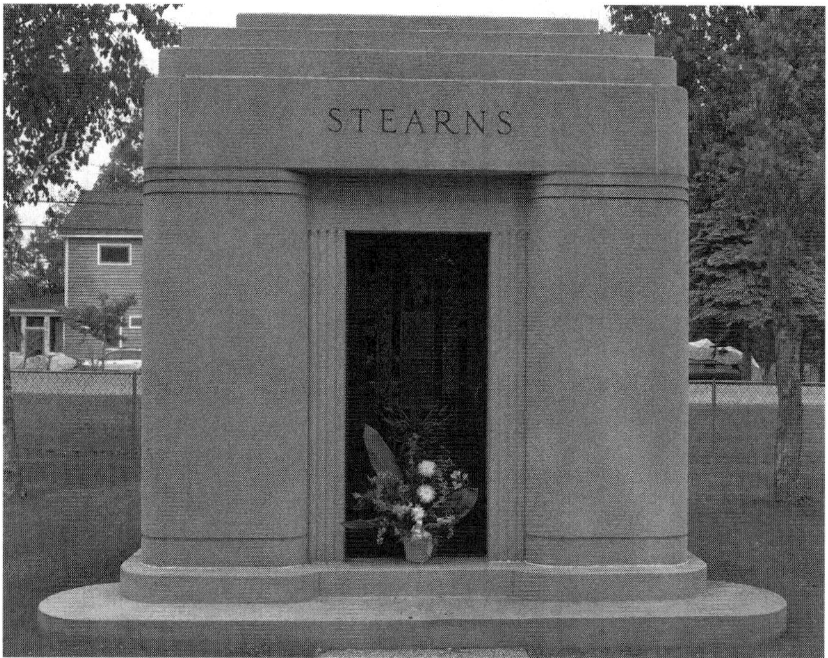

Stearns Mausoleum. The bodies of both Justus and Paulina Stearns, along with several additional family members, have been laid to rest in this mausoleum located at Ludington's Lakeview Cemetery. (Author's collection)

complete his chores, and after returning from school he worked alongside his father at his family's sawmill. The work ethic he developed at a young age would remain with him for life. He also saw his father overcome adversity when he lost everything in Erie, Pennsylvania, only to start over. Following the move to Conneaut, Ohio, the two worked together selling lumber. Conneaut was where Justus met Paulina Lyon, and the two fell in love. Stearns's marriage had a major impact on his subsequent success in business. Paulina's family was more well to do than his own, and following his own financial difficulties, including bankruptcy, Justus and Paulina relocated to Ludington. There, he worked for members of the Lyon family, at the mill previously owned by Eber Ward, until his finances became stable. In later years, Stearns continued to maintain close ties to members of his wife's family. As time went on, his son Robert L. Stearns became a trusted deputy, often serving in a leadership role alongside his father. In 1917 Justus even turned over his share of the controlling stock in the Stearns Coal and Lumber Company to Robert. Additionally, Edward E. Barthell, Robert's brother-in-law, provided the family with legal counsel for many decades. By the late 1920s the tables had turned and Justus had to rely on his son for help. It was Robert who assumed control of the Stearns Motor Manufacturing Company and ensured it would not bankrupt Justus a second time. Family connections can explain some of Stearns's success, but he also was willing to take risks.

On more than one occasion, Stearns ventured out on his own and took risks, most of which paid off for him in the end. One gamble he took was in 1880 when he established Stearns Siding. He left behind a steady job and the family business in Ludington to found an entirely new settlement, the future of which was uncertain. He overcame adversity when a fire in 1882 destroyed his mill, but he quickly rebuilt and maintained this sawmill, and related businesses, for many years. In the early 1890s he took a risk by investing a great deal of money into lumbering operations in Wisconsin. These proved to be successful, but at the time, there was no guarantee. The same was true in 1898 when he purchased the sawmill and property, formerly owned by Eber Ward, in Ludington. In that decade, the city's economy was depressed, but his investment sparked an economic revival. Taking these chances allowed Stearns to become the largest manufacturer of lumber in the state of Michigan by the late 1890s. The greatest risk he took was in 1902 when he purchased and leased thousands of acres of property in the "wilds" of Kentucky and Tennessee. He wasn't from that region; he had been living in Michigan for over twenty-five years prior to the purchase of the land. Yet he founded a coal-mining company that operated for several decades and a town that continues to bear his name. At times, he carried a great deal of debt. He owed about $2.5 million in 1907–8, and his friends expressed their concerns that he was overextended. Nonetheless, he remained steady because he knew the market for his products would improve over time. Not all of his risks paid off. Like his father before him, he had to declare bankruptcy in the 1870s. He also spent a great deal of effort, and money, in an attempt to save the Stearns Motor Manufacturing Company, but the business was forced to close. Even though some investments failed, they did not destroy his ambition to be a successful entrepreneur.[1]

A final factor contributing to Stearns's success involved his ability to organize and manage businesses in ways to create efficiencies. His knack for doing so was demonstrated in his early days in Ludington working at the Ward mill, but they became particularly apparent when he ran his own companies later in his career. The integration of his sawmill and salt block with Stearns Lighting and Power Company in the early 1900s developed efficiencies so great he lowered rates and expanded his customer base while continuing to increase profits each year. The lumber camps Stearns operated in the same era were models of efficiency. Meal preparation took into account the latest knowledge of balanced diets and nutrition while at the same time steps were taken to eliminate waste. Key performance statistics were monitored to keep an eye on costs, and each year education rallies were held for employees. These even featured guest speakers who lectured about best business practices. Furthermore, the founding and establishment of the Stearns Coal and Lumber Company required organization and management skills on the part of Stearns to ensure its success.

Stearns was not alone in his desire to implement efficient business practices based on cutting costs. Andrew Carnegie and John D. Rockefeller, two of the greatest industrialists of this era, were very concerned with costs. Carnegie believed it was more important to know the costs associated with production, as opposed to profits, and partners described him as obsessed with the subject. The sale of goods may go up and down, but his dictum was, "Watch the costs and the profits would take care of themselves." Rockefeller had an eye for detail and once carefully observed a machine filling five-gallon cans with kerosene. An expert explained how the operation worked, and Rockefeller remained silent until he asked about the number of drops of solder used to seal each can. When he learned the number was forty, he asked if thirty-eight drops ever had been tried. When this number was used, the cans leaked, but when thirty-nine drops were attempted, the cans held. One drop of solder may not have seemed like much, but when a company produced several hundred thousand cans of kerosene each year, one less drop of solder could lead to enormous savings.[2] Similarly, Justus Stearns knew exactly how much it cost to produce a single barrel of salt at his Ludington salt block. One could imagine him challenging employees to determine methods to cut costs and save even a fraction of a penny for each barrel of salt produced, or each ton of coal mined, or each carload of lumber manufactured.

Stearns's successful business practices resulted in a prosperous level of activity that peaked during a fifteen-year stretch of time that began in 1895 and extended to 1910. By 1895, Stearns Siding was a thriving lumber town and Stearns had initiated his timber activities on two Wisconsin Indian reservations. Just three years later, in 1898, he moved his base of operations to Ludington and closed down his mill at Stearns Siding. Then he bought an electric company, built the Stearns Hotel, invested in a sawmill and considerable pineland in Florida, assumed control over the Carrom Company, began to cut timber in Kalkaska that then had to be shipped to Ludington, established the Gile Boat and Engine Company, and served as president of the First National Bank of Ludington. Furthermore, he founded the town of Stearns, Kentucky, along with the Stearns Coal and

Lumber Company, and the Kentucky and Tennessee Railway. Between 1895 and 1910 Stearns also was elected Michigan's secretary of state and undertook three campaigns in an attempt to win the Republican nomination for governor. Stearns even took over management of the Epworth Hotel and provided leadership for the organization during a period of exceptional growth. Additionally, many of these endeavors took place after 1904, the year in which Justus buried Paulina, his wife of thirty-six years. Indeed, during this short stretch of time, Stearns's record of activity was remarkable and demonstrated a dazzling level of energy, ambition, and successful entrepreneurship.

Evaluating Justus Stearns and his Legacy

The actions Stearns undertook often were influenced by whether or not he was operating as a resident or absentee business owner. As has been shown, Stearns was a resident owner in the city of Ludington where he ran several diverse businesses, remained active in the community, and contributed to numerous charitable causes. In contrast, when he served as an absentee owner, he often was not invested in the local community and his actions at times merited criticism. For example, Stearns acted as an absentee owner in Wisconsin. After engaging in extensive timber operations on two Indian reservations for nearly thirty years, when the timber ran out, he pulled up stakes and moved on to his next endeavor. He never became involved in the community as he did in Ludington, and there is no record he contributed to any charitable causes in the region. His actions here also were likely influenced by racist attitudes concerning the superiority of whites, attitudes that were commonly held at the time; it appears as if Stearns never challenged these beliefs. By the time he left Wisconsin, life on the reservations was plagued by disease, poverty, and unemployment, leaving a negative legacy for those who remained.

Stearns also was an absentee owner of the Stearns Coal and Lumber Company; however, his actions in this instance were more complex. While Stearns never lived in Kentucky, he visited often. But, most importantly, his son Robert L. Stearns relocated to Kentucky where he lived for several years. Justus Stearns did not simply delegate authority for his company to a paid employee in a faraway region of the country. Instead, his son held this responsibility, and members of the Stearns family maintained strong ties to the area. Robert L. Stearns built a home in the community, lived in it, and for many years raised his family in Stearns. In later years Robert L. Stearns Jr., the grandson of Justus Stearns, would live in the community with his family and run the company. Stearns's great-grandson, Robert E. Gable, also lived in the community and was intimately involved in the company's operations, demonstrating that following the establishment of the company by Justus Stearns, three generations of Stearns men served as resident owners/operators of the Stearns Coal and Lumber Company.

Although members of his family maintained ties to the community of Stearns, Kentucky, this did not prevent Justus Stearns from taking harsh actions to prevent the unionization of his workforce. Like the majority of the leading businessmen of his day, Stearns was no lover of unions. His strong antiunion stance was illustrated best in December 1908 when conflict during a strike involving his mine workers led to the death of a US marshal and a striking worker. Stearns helped to escalate, rather than diffuse, tension during the strike, when he supported the actions of a US marshal who set his hotel on fire so the men trapped inside the building could be apprehended. His actions that Christmas aligned him with Social Darwinists, such as Henry Sage who was willing to use force to protect his investment and prevent the unionization of his workforce. When Sage's employees staged a strike in 1872, he prepared to "arm his mill staff with six-shooters and Spencer rifles, and gave orders to notify the mob [of strikers] that Company officials were armed and would protect the mill property" that he owned.[3]

Finally, neither Stearns nor the majority of his contemporaries did much to halt the impact their extractive industries had on the environment. The fact that Stearns's companies transformed the environment in a permanent manner should not go unnoticed; however, while individuals such as John Muir called for the preservation of the nation's natural resources during Stearns's lifetime, the majority of Americans favored business and economic development at the expense of nature, regardless of its environmental impact. In the 1930s, well after the heyday of Michigan's lumber era, Stearns was asked about the related issue of reforestation of cutover lands. While he did indicate support for replanting land that had been clear-cut because it would be of great value to have "these lands growing pine again," Stearns did not believe the burden for doing so should be left up to individual landowners. Instead, he declared, "I firmly believe it is something that should be taken over by the state or federal government."[4]

Justus Stearns also acted in a benevolent manner throughout his lifetime; this benevolence manifested itself in many ways. The community of Stearns Siding was founded to serve as a fulcrum for his lumber operations in Lake County; as a result of his leadership, a strong sense of community developed. The settlement included homes and a school, which bound the residents together. The same was true for the development of the mining town of Stearns, Kentucky. Beginning with the celebration in honor of the first carload of coal mined in

Justus S. Stearns (older). Stearns was very active throughout his lifetime, even in his old age, yet when he contracted pneumonia at the age of eighty-seven he never recovered. (Courtesy of Robert E. Gable)

1903, the Stearns Coal and Lumber Company sponsored celebrations each July that its employees and their families attended. Stearns's operations were one of the first in Kentucky to offer washhouses at the mines for employees, and the safety procedures implemented in the company's early years helped to reduce the number of accidents among the workforce. Electricity and the prospect of steady employment also were brought to an area known for its poverty. Residents of Ludington labeled him "Ludington's Foremost Citizen" as early as 1915 due to the numerous businesses he owned and operated in the city. These businesses helped to diversify the city's industrial base and prepare it for a postlumber economy. Additionally, his active leadership in state and local politics, particularly his support for the Progressive movement, demonstrated a strong sense of civic duty. He was a vocal advocate of political primaries as a replacement for party conventions. Although he never succeeded in winning the governorship of Michigan, subsequent political leaders eventually implemented many of the causes he initially championed.[5]

The charitable contributions Stearns made demonstrated his greatest impact as a benefactor. Children often were the beneficiaries of his generosity; gifts were given at Christmas, cash was awarded to top students, and time was spent providing leadership to the Boy Scouts. Construction of schools was an important feature of the Stearns Coal and Lumber Company's expansion into Kentucky. This was implemented by J. E. Butler, a former teacher and principal himself. Stearns contributed to numerous additional causes as well. The donation of his home, and subsequent cash contributions to the Paulina Stearns Hospital, improved the well-being of countless residents of Mason County. The leadership he provided Epworth Heights in the early 1900s coincided with the organization's greatest growth in its history. His support for a boulevard along Ludington Avenue and donation of the beach property on Lake Michigan transformed the city's appearance forever.

In many ways, Stearns's actions defy easy categorization due to their complexity. While the same could be true for many of his contemporaries, Stearns's activities were particularly multifaceted. His philanthropic contributions demonstrate he was benevolent, yet his ruthlessness was reflected in the efforts he took to fight unions. More significantly, Stearns's business empire mirrored the nation's transition from a natural resource-based economy to one founded on manufacturing. Initially, he engaged in extractive industries where timber was cut and coal and salt were mined. He also held manufacturing operations that produced finished lumber, motors for boats and tractors, as well as game boards and kitchen utensils. Stearns's ownership of the K&T Railroad, along with the Stearns Lighting and Power Company, exhibited his involvement in the transportation and utility industries. Furthermore, his companies operated in diverse regions of the country: the Great Lakes, the Appalachian South, and even the West Coast. This range of activities represented a unique level of achievement, while the eras during which Stearns operated also set him apart from other industrialists. His career began in the Gilded Age and stretched into the early years of the Great Depression. Most Michigan lumbermen had either retired or died by the late 1800s and early 1900s. Stearns's businesses not only continued well into the twentieth century, but also he expanded his operations into entirely new industries and regions of the country. Because of this, Stearns's career helps to demonstrate the development of the American economy over time as it evolved into a global manufacturing power.

An editorial published shortly after Stearns's death, which appeared in the *Ludington Daily News,* captured the essence of Stearns's driving energy and leadership aimed at forging successful business enterprises, accompanied by a concern for the common good. It read, "Col. Stearns was essentially a builder; he was progressive; he was an unusual organizer. He was one of those men, comparatively rare in the smaller communities, who was literally a captain of industry. He built constructively, and as he built for himself, so did he build for Ludington."[6] Had the editorial been written in other places where Stearns's businesses were located, similar appreciation would surely have been attributed to this exceptional captain of industry.

Appendix A

Partial List of Businesses Founded or Operated by Justus Stearns

Stearns Siding, Bennett, Michigan
Stearns and Mack, Scottville, Michigan
Flambeau Lumber Company, Lac du Flambeau, Wisconsin
J. S. Stearns Lumber Company, Ashland, Wisconsin
Stearns Salt and Lumber Company, Ludington, Michigan
Double Brick Store, Ludington, Michigan
Stearns Lighting and Power Company, Ludington, Michigan
Stearns Improvement Company, Ludington, Michigan
Ludington and Northern Railroad, Ludington, Michigan
Epworth Heights Hotel, Ludington, Michigan
Stearns Coal Company*
Stearns Lumber Company*
Kentucky and Tennessee Railway, Stearns, Kentucky
Stearns Hotel, Ludington, Michigan
Stearns Hotel, Stearns, Kentucky
Stearns and Culver Lumber Company, Bagdad, Florida
Carrom-Archarena Company, Ludington, Michigan
Gile Tractor and Engine Company, Ludington, Michigan (later reorganized as Stearns Motor Manufacturing Company)
Handy Things, Ludington, Michigan
Ludington First National Bank, Ludington, Michigan
Consolidated Lumber Company, Manistique, Michigan
State Bank of Stearns, Stearns, Kentucky
Whiteside-Stearns Coal Company, Chattanooga, Tennessee **
Stearns Coal Company, Atlanta, Georgia **
Stearns Coal Company, Louisville, Kentucky **
Stearns Coal and Lumber Company, Fort Wayne, Indiana **
Stearns-Kelly Coal Company, Frankfort, Kentucky **

Stearns and Culver Company, L'Anse, Michigan
National Lumber and Manufacturing Company, Hoquiam, Washington
Marquette Lumber Company, Grand Rapids, Michigan

* These two later were reorganized as the Stearns Coal and Lumber Company; each was headquartered in Stearns, Kentucky
** These five companies were organized in the 1920s as retail yards for the sale of coal.

Appendix B

Coal Production to 1933

Year	Mine #1	Mine #2	Mine #10	Mine #11	Mine #12	Mine #14
1903	32,595.45					
1904	52,531.26					
1905	35,531.28	6,713.65				
1906	31,174.27	8,571.67				
1907	50,883.22	22,262.92	281.15			
1908	57,887.69	32,330.95	7,753.43			
1909	68,671.36	37,590.10	7,737.97			
1910	67,336.35	49,078.17	37,622.34	60		
1911	65,004.42	41,111.57	81,188.45	10,258.78		
1912	79,178.10	23,211.35	149,035.30	46,156.40		
1913	82,022.35	8,328.20	164,077.00	67,217.75		
1914	95,992.90	2,866.05	150,566.55	85,296.03		
1915	83,930.80	6,212.25	146,939.35	86,249.05		
1916	94,478.80	8,667.60	163,736.60	106,287.15		
1917	73,702.05	2,170.60	103,342.25	110,075.20	11,928.84	
1918	81,922.85	3,575.05	64,624.65	125,831.90	18,650.75	776.1
1919	83,726.55	581.1	39,038.50	119,652.95	1,387.75	233.05
1920	112,164.74		35,611.25	156,027.92		
1921	84,550.35		21,563.45	125,216.05		
1922	78,701.40		21,730.40	121,508.40		
1923	113,980.60		25,692.80	133,058.35		
1924	65,722.55		9,221.35	111,723.57		
1925	39,505.14		12,325.85	102,947.03		
1926	88,478.25		9,530.70	106,441.18		
1927	85,016.70		9,025.85	103,722.10		
1928	84,868.80		8,460.45	121,550.49		
1929	120,979.85		8,261.45	136,775.06		
1930	106,827.70		7,307.65	144,198.25		
1931	39,273.10			102,909.05		
1932	4,845.05			92,044.05		
1933				84,343.20		
Totals	2,161,483.93	253,271.23	1,284,674.74	2,399,549.91	31,967.34	1,009.15

(continued next page)

(continued)

Year	Mine #15	Mine 16	Mine "A"	Co-op	Total
1903					32,595.45
1904					52,531.26
1905					66,557.58
1906					105,724.02
1907					154,712.24
1908					190,182.62
1909					214,087.40
1910					272,837.05
1911					300,030.91
1912					423,291.25
1913					516,188.45
1914					500,726.45
1915					480,161.15
1916			5,618.55		587,872.75
1917			78,311.70		553,764.09
1918			92,702.45		543,855.55
1919			91,142.65		466,386.90
1920			145,287.40		610,325.21
1921			152,446.35		519,987.90
1922			152,797.55	65,367.10	563,261.15
1923	1,840.30		203,272.70	97,585.65	751,117.05
1924	5,575.74	42,477.45	208,166.55	161,227.13	775,982.29
1925	7,940.65	63,476.70	186,351.33	211,853.75	814,711.57
1926	11,462.35	33,680.85	174,070.45	207,235.25	864,207.17
1927	23,337.55	39,527.75	161,378.60	243,656.53	903,664.88
1928	22,437.90	5,799.70	139,901.85	237,821.65	887,095.38
1929	39,014.35		125,601.85	280,102.30	970,083.60
1930	31,799.85		96,073.65	192,256.67	783,243.47
1931	22,480.20		115,485.10	141,525.75	583,743.25
1932	17,422.35		89,849.00	125,112.65	490,706.85
1933	26,290.95		104,292.75	133,908.30	504,280.60
Totals	209,602.19	184,962.45	2,322,750.48	2,097,652.73	15,483,915.49

Notes

Introduction

1. H. W. Brands, *American Colossus: The Triumph of Capitalism, 1865–1900* (New York: Doubleday, 2010), 3–7. The prologue to Brands's book is titled "The Capitalist Revolution," and many of the ideas included in this paragraph come from this section of his book.

2. The traits of paternalistic owners and those influenced by Social Darwinism are discussed in Jeremy Kilar, *Michigan's Lumbertowns: Lumbermen and Laborers in Saginaw, Bay City, and Muskegon, 1870–1905* (Detroit: Wayne State University Press, 1990), 149–52; and Ronald D. Eller, "The Coal Barons of the Appalachian South, 1880–1930," *Appalachian Journal* 4, no. 3/4 (1977): 199–203. An excellent biography of Charles Hackley is Richard Henry Harms, *Life after Lumbering: Charles Henry Hackley and the Emergence of Muskegon, Michigan* (New York: Garland, 1989). For a biography of Henry Sage, see Anita Shafer Goodstein, *Biography of a Businessman: Henry W. Sage, 1814–1897* (Ithaca, NY: Cornell University Press, 1962); the quotation concerning Sage is from 268–69 of this book.

3. Eller, "Coal Barons of the Appalachian South," 202. Another source is Kilar, *Michigan's Lumbertowns,* 149–52.

4. Kilar, *Michigan's Lumbertowns,* 155–62. Another source that describes the positive impact of resident owners is Burton W. Folsom, *Urban Capitalists: Entrepreneurs and City Growth in Pennsylvania's Lackawanna and Lehigh Regions, 1800–1920* (Baltimore: Johns Hopkins University Press, 1981), 64–65.

5. In this paragraph, and throughout much of the text, the "Progressive movement" refers to the reform movement that included both Republicans and Democrats, and was most popular in the United States beginning in the late 1890s and extending to about 1917 and American involvement in World War I. Stearns was very proud of his involvement with the Progressive movement, which, in that era, had goals ranging from the implementation of political reforms to promote democracy, to protection of the environment, and the establishment of Settlement Houses for the immigrants and poor. As will be addressed in chapter 3, Stearns supported the adoption of political primaries to replace party conventions; he also called for the direct election of United States senators. His advocacy for these political reforms demonstrated his support of the Progressive movement, even though he wasn't involved in the movement's other causes.

Chapter 1

1. George A. Dondero, *Why Lincoln Wore a Beard* (Springfield, IL: Journal Printing Company, 1931), 5, reprinted from *Journal of the Illinois State Historical Society,* 24, no. 2 (1931). The archives at the Mason County Historical Society must contain Justus Stearns's personal copy of this

reprint, as it includes an inscription by the author addressed to Stearns. The inscription reads, "To Col. J. S. Stearns, who saw Lincoln kiss Grace Bedell at Westfield N.Y. Feb. 15-1861, from Geo. A. Dondero." Additional sources used include Louis A. Warren, ed., "Lincoln's Beard," *Lincoln Lore* 98 (February 23, 1931): 1, Stearns box, Stearns, J. S. Lincoln Reminiscences Folder, Mason County Historical Society Archive, Ludington, Michigan.

2. Dondero, *Why Lincoln Wore a Beard,* reprint edition, 7, 8. Dondero's article notes that not only did Bedell hold onto her letter from Mr. Lincoln, Lincoln's family preserved her letter as well. Following the death of Robert Todd Lincoln (President Lincoln's son) July 26, 1926, his widow, Mary Harlan Lincoln, returned the original letter to Grace.

3. Ibid., 12.

4. Justus Stearns letter to Dr. McClelland, n.d., taken from *The Mountain Herald,* "How a Friend Remembers Lincoln." While there is no additional information identifying this journal, a photocopy of the letter from it can be found in Stearns box, Stearns, J. S. Lincoln Reminiscences Folder, Mason County Historical Society Archive, Ludington, Michigan.

5. Justus Stearns letter to Mrs. Billings, October 10, 1931, Stearns box, Stearns, J. S., Lincoln Reminiscences Folder, Mason County Historical Society Archive, Ludington, Michigan.

6. Ibid.

7. Heman Stearns was born August 25, 1819. A great story survives concerning Ebenezer Stearns Jr., Justus Stearns's great-grandfather. Ebenezer was born in Plainfield, Connecticut, in 1747 and fought with the Green Mountain Boys of Vermont during the American Revolution. In recognition of his actions at the Battle of Bennington, he was commissioned a lieutenant. His marriage in 1782 to Rachel Jones unfortunately was much too short. The day of their wedding, as was often the custom, the bride was "stolen" and held for ransom. To escape the wedding party, the would-be kidnappers drove her by sleigh to a hotel where she eventually was released, probably after her captors received a small prize or sum of money. Although she had been wrapped in overcoats for her journey, she caught a cold and never recovered from the illness. She died about one year later. The men involved were prosecuted but never punished as public opinion supported the tradition. For this story and other information concerning the Stearns family, see Avis Stearns Van Wagenen, *Genealogy and Memoirs of Charles and Nathaniel Stearns, and Their Descendants,* vol. 2 (Syracuse, NY: Courier Printing, 1901), 342, 343, 350, 379, available at http://books.google.com, accessed August 8, 2011. Joseph Stearns, Justus Stearns's grandfather, was born about 1776 and died October 16, 1855, at the age of seventy-nine. His death notice can be found in the *Fredonia Censor,* October 23, 1855. Justus Stearns's grandmother, Susan (Rogers) Stearns, was born about 1783 and died May 14, 1854, at the age of seventy-one. Her death notice can be found in the *Fredonia Censor,* May 16, 1854.

8. *Fredonia Censor,* September 20, 1837. Other sources include Lois Barris and Donna Johnson, *Selected Information from the 1855 New York State Census for the County of Chautauqua, Vol. II, Harmony thru Westfield* (Fredonia, NY: Chautauqua County Genealogical Society, 2008), 549. The rolls of the Presbyterian Church are available at www.rootsweb.ancestry.com/~nychauta/CHURCH/FredoniaPresby/FPCRosterBookA.html#Top and www.rootsweb.ancestry.com/~nychauta/CHURCH/FredoniaPresby/FPCRosterBookB.html#Top, each roll book was accessed May 21, 2013. The name of "Justis Smith" [*sic*] is listed as being "received" on the rolls of Fredonia's Presbyterian Church on March 2,

1834. This is the same day Perry Smith, the grandfather of Justus Stearns, was "received." Justus Smith was the brother of Mabel Smith and therefore the uncle of Justus Stearns. Dr. Douglas Shepard, who has worked extensively with the sources, noted that "casual spelling is the rule, not the exception." The information that Justus Smith died in a boating accident, and the preceding quotation, comes from Douglas Shepard, e-mail message to author, May 21, 2013. The notice of Smith's death appeared in the *Fredonia Censor* on August 4, 1841. The full article reads, "Found—The body of Justus Smith, son of Captain Perry Smith, of Van Buren Harbor, has been found about twenty miles below Wheeling in the Ohio River. When found, he had about sixty dollars in money in his pocket; no marks of violence could be discovered."

9. S. B. McCracken, *Men of Progress: Embracing Historical Sketches of Representative Michigan Men with an Outline History of the State* (Detroit: Evening News Association, 1900), 133, available at http://name.umdl.umich.edu/BAD6035.0001.001, accessed November 22, 2013. The marriage announcement for Heman Stearns and Mabel Smith is found in the *Fredonia Censor,* April 27, 1842. Additional sources include Van Wagenen, *Genealogy and Memoirs of Charles and Nathaniel Stearns,* 379; William Livingstone, *Livingstone's History of the Republican Party*, vol. 2 (Detroit: Livingstone, 1900), 367, 368; "Stearns, Hon. Justus Smith," *Historical Sketches,* Private Collection of Robert E. Gable, 133; "A Tribute: A Dinner Commemorating the Seventy-Eighth Birthday Anniversary of Justus S. Stearns," Ludington, MI, 1923, Stearns box, Stearns, Justus S. Birthday Dinner Folder, Mason County Historical Society Archive, Ludington, Michigan. An additional copy is available at Special Collections Library, Biography Collection, University of Kentucky, Lexington. Lumberman Charles Hackley had a similar educational background and experience working for his father in the lumber industry. His formal schooling ended at the age of fifteen, but he also attended a business school for several months in Kenosha, Wisconsin, at the age of twenty. He also worked for his father as an unskilled worker in Muskegon. See Harms, *Life after Lumbering: Charles Henry Hackley and the Emergence of Muskegon, Michigan,* 14, 22, 27, 28.

10. Justus Stearns letter to William Stearns, March 27, 1930, Mason County Historical Society Archive, Ludington, Michigan.

11. Alice and Jane Stearns were listed as living in the town of Pomfret, while Annette Stearns was listed as living in Cordova in, Jo Ann Kaufman, compiler, and Lois Barris, transcriber, *Directory of Students Who Attended the Fredonia Academy during the Years 1826–1867* (Fredonia, NY: Chautauqua County Genealogical Society, 1990), 73.

12. Both quotations from this paragraph are from Justus Stearns letter to William Stearns, March 27, 1930, Mason County Historical Society Archive. The author visited the Village of Fredonia in May of 2013. The park remains in the center of town; however, the Presbyterian Church mentioned in the letter was torn down. Records for the Presbyterian Church cited by Stearns are available and indicated that in addition to her deceased brother and parents, Mabel Stearns was "received" as a member April 17, 1840. Neither Justus Stearns nor his father was listed as members. These records are available at www.rootsweb.ancestry.com/~nychauta/CHURCH/FredoniaPresby/FPCRosterBookA.html#Top and www.rootsweb.ancestry.com/~nychauta/CHURCH/FredoniaPresby/FPCRosterBookB.html#Top, each book was accessed May 21, 2013.

13. It is unclear whether Stearns wore a toupee, but photos seem to make this likely. Additionally, the diary of Robert L. Stearns indicates that he wrote "I got hair restorer" after a visit to a hospital where he received an examination from a doctor, so it is possible that thinning hair, and concerns over it, ran in the family. The source for Robert's diary entry is Diary of Robert L. Stearns, June 23, 1911, Stearns Archive, McCreary County Museum, Stearns, Kentucky.

14. Barris and Johnson, *Selected Information from the 1855 New York State Census for the County of Chautauqua,* 549; Lois Barris and Norwood Barris, *Selected Information from the 1860 United States Census for the County of Chautauqua, New York, Vol. II, Towns of Hanover thru Westfield, plus Deaths by Towns* (Fredonia, NY: Chautauqua County Genealogical Society, 2003), 626. The tax rolls for the village of Pomfret were made available in Douglas Shepard, e-mail message to author, May 20, 2013, and can be found in Pomfret Assessment Roll, 1855, Darwin R. Barker Historical Museum, Fredonia, New York. The e-mail message from Douglas Shepard also describes the location of the Stearns' farm as "in what was called Little Canadaway, a small community on Little Canadaway Creek, later called Milford, and today Lamberton. It is at the westernmost part of Pomfret practically in the Town of Portland."

15. Frederick W. Kohlmeyer, "Northern Pine Lumbermen: A Study in Origins and Migrations," *Journal of Economic History* 16, no. 4 (1956): 530–32; Barbara B. Benson, *Logs and Lumber: The Development of Lumbering in Michigan's Lower Peninsula, 1837–1870* (Mount Pleasant, MI: Clarke Historical Library, Central Michigan University, 1989), 212–17. Jeremy Kilar's extensive study of three Michigan lumber towns (Saginaw, Bay City, and Muskegon) shows that in those communities, 55 percent of the leading lumber barons had previous experience in the timber industry and more than half of the lumbermen had a high school education, while one-third attended a private academy or college. See Kilar, *Michigan's Lumbertowns,* 138–41.

16. Justus Stearns letter to William Stearns, March 27, 1930, Mason County Historical Society Archive; it is ironic that Stearns would mention his father's business failure in this letter, yet not mention his own bankruptcy in 1875. This is particularly interesting as Stearns later repaid the creditors to whom he owed money, even though the bankruptcy laws did not require it.

17. Ibid.; "A Tribute: A Dinner Commemorating," Mason County Historical Society Archive. It is possible Justus and his parents moved to Conneaut, Ohio, in 1865, but the date of 1864 appears to be more likely.

18. Sidney Elizabeth Lyon, ed., *Lyon Memorial* (Detroit: Press of William Graham Printing, 1907), 164, 165, available at http://books.google.com, accessed August 9, 2011; Robert Bond Lyon's first wife, Catherine Bacon, was born January 8, 1800, in Bacon's Hill, New York, and she died October 11, 1840, in Conneaut, Ohio. Prior to her death, the couple had five children. William Bacon was born August 15, 1823, in Ogdensburg, New York; Lydia Jane was born September 21, 1826; John Bacon was born April 15, 1829, in Canandaigua, New York; Helen Mary was born August 9, 1832, in Conneaut, Ohio; and Robert Woods was born May 21, 1835, in Conneaut, Ohio. Robert Lyon and Clarissa (Kellogg) Lyon were married in Kelloggsville, Ohio, January 16, 1841. The children of Robert and Clarissa each were born in Conneaut, Ohio. In addition to Paulina,

Catherine was born November 26, 1841; Clarissa was born October 26, 1843; and Thomas Rice was born May 31, 1854.

19. Ibid., 164.

20. *Biographical History of Northeastern Ohio, Embracing the Counties of Ashtabula, Trumbull, and Mahoning* (Chicago: Lewis Publishing, 1893), 481–82.

21. George B. Catlin, *The Story of Detroit* (Detroit: Detroit News, 1923), 493–99; Justus Stearns letter to William Stearns, March 27, 1930, Mason County Historical Society Archive; Lyon, *Lyon Memorial,* 201–2.

22. At least four separate dates have been assigned to the marriage of Justus and Paulina (1868, 1869, 1870, and 1871). The date of March 4, 1868, seems most likely. This date is confirmed in at least four sources: Justus Stearns letter to William Stearns, March 27, 1930, Mason County Historical Society Archive; Lyon, *Lyon Memorial,* 201–2; "Whole City Saddened," *Ludington Chronicle,* May 11, 1904; Doug Coldwell, "Justus Smith Stearns," available at http://en.wikipedia.org, accessed May 22, 2013. The entry on Stearns in Wikipedia is brief, but includes helpful references to several additional sources.

23. Lyon, *Lyon Memorial,* 164; for Paulina's interaction with family members see *Mason County Record,* May 30, 1879; *Mason County Record,* September 2, 1880; *Mason County Record,* October 14, 1880; *Mason County Record,* August 19, 1886; *Mason County Record,* June 16, 1887. Census data concerning Clarissa Lyon, Justus, and Paulina Stearns can be found in United States Census, 1870, Ashtabula County, Ohio, page 261; census data concerning Heman and Mabel Stearns can be found in United States Census, 1870, Ashtabula County, page 28, both are available at www.ancestry.com, accessed March 9, 2012. It appeared as if economic conditions had changed for Heman Stearns, for the worse, following the move from New York.

24. The chaos concerning Ward's estate, and subsequent trial, is chronicled in Justin Wargo, "A Case without Parallel: The Sensational Battle over Eber Brock Ward's Will and Subsequent Legacy of Detroit's First Great Industrialist," *Michigan Historical Review* 39, no. 2 (2013): 77–103. Additional sources include Livingstone, *History of the Republican Party,* 368; "A Tribute: A Dinner Commemorating," Mason County Historical Society Archive; Catlin, *Story of Detroit,* 498, 499. The announcement of Mabel Stearns's death is found in the *Fredonia Censor,* March 3, 1875.

25. The exact location of Pere Marquette's death has been a subject of some dispute. The Michigan Historical Commission has erected *two* separate historical markers that identify the site where Pere Marquette died; one is located in Ludington with another in Frankfort. Most scholars believe he died near the mouth of the Pere Marquette River at Ludington's Buttersville Peninsula. For more information, see Willis F. Dunbar and George S. May, *Michigan: A History of the Wolverine State* (Grand Rapids, MI: Eerdman, 1995), 35; Catherine L. Stebbins, "The Marquette Death Site," *Michigan History* 48 (December 1964): 333–68; Raphael N. Hamilton, "The Marquette Death Site: The Case for Ludington," *Michigan History* 49 (September 1965): 228–48. In 2012, a third historical marker was placed in the city of Manistee. For Manistee's claims, see Robert P. Adams, *The Thirteenth River* (Manistee, MI: Robert P. Adams, 2002).

26. "Reforestation Should Be a Major Function," Stearns box, Stearns, J. S., Stearns Lumber Cos. Folder, Mason County Historical Society Archive, Ludington, Michigan.

27. This outline of Ludington's early lumbering history is taken from several sources. The best surveys of this subject can be found in *History of Mason County Michigan, with Illustrations and Biographical Sketches of Some of Its Prominent Men and Pioneers* (Chicago: H. R. Page, 1882), 49–52; Frances Caswell Hannah, *Sand, Sawdust, and Saw Logs: Lumber Days in Ludington* (Ludington, MI: Frances Caswell Hannah, 1955), 7–15, 26–33; Thomas A. Hawley, ed., *Historic Mason County* (Ludington, MI: Mason County Historical Society, 1980), 9–14; and Paul S. Peterson, *The Story of Ludington* (Ludington, MI: Mason County Historical Society, 2011), 15–29, 38–47; James L. Cabot, *Images of America, Ludington 1830–1930* (Chicago: Arcadia, 2005), 7. The statistic for the manufacture of eighty-three million board feet of lumber in 1873 comes from Peterson, *Story of Ludington,* 43.
28. The "model mill of Michigan" quotation is from Rolland H. Maybee, *Michigan's White Pine Era, 1840–1900* (Lansing: Michigan Historical Commission, 1960), 48; *History of Mason County Michigan,* 50, 51; Hannah, *Sand, Sawdust, and Saw Logs,* 28, 29; Hawley, *Historic Mason County,* 10; Peterson, *Story of Ludington,* 15, 16; Benson, *Logs and Lumber: The Development of Lumbering in Michigan's Lower Peninsula,* 22. Benson's book is an excellent general survey of the lumber history in Michigan's Lower Peninsula in this early era.
29. Justus Stearns letter to William Stearns, March 27, 1930, Mason County Historical Society Archive.
30. "A Tribute: A Dinner Commemorating," Mason County Historical Society Archive; Hawley, *Historic Mason County,* 320.
31. "Reforestation Should Be a Major Function," Mason County Historical Society Archive.
32. *History of Mason County Michigan,* 62; "Reforestation Should Be a Major Function," Mason County Historical Society Archive. The quotation comes from Justus Stearns letter to William Stearns, March 27, 1930. In the letter, Justus writes, "All during this time we were cutting this lumber and she was getting only $7.00 and $7.50 per M ft. delivered, which scarcely paid the expense of manufacturing and getting it to its destination. The best lumbermen in the country looked the tract over and did not or could not buy it because they had not sufficient means, and they said there was more timber in Michigan, Wisconsin and Minnesota than would ever be cut—this same timber that they referred to was practically exhausted ten years ago. However, in 1879—three years after I came here—lumber came up $1.00 per M in Chicago and as Mrs. Ward was cutting 50 million feet a year, she made $50,000.00 that year, and continued cutting from 50 to 60 million feet each year for many years, finally cleaning up in profits over $6,000,000.00 from what she had offered to sell for $250,000.00."
33. H. M. Haff, "One Lumberman Remains True to Ludington, Devoting Time and Finances to Establish Industries That Give Local Employment," *Ludington Daily News,* September 21, 1919; Hawley, *Historic Mason County,* 320; "A Tribute: A Dinner Commemorating," Mason County Historical Society Archive; *History of Mason County Michigan,* 62–64; *Mason County Record,* February 7, 1879; *Mason County Record,* March 21, 1879; *Mason County Record,* January 16, 1880; "Whole City Saddened," *Ludington Chronicle,* May 11, 1904.
34. Hawley, *Historic Mason County,* 12; Peterson, *Story of Ludington,* 43. The quotation is taken from Dell Read letter, no date, L1 box, Lumbering Men Folder, Mason County Historical Society Archive, Ludington, Michigan.

35. The quotations are from *Mason County Record,* April 16, 1880; *Mason County Record,* May 14, 1880.
36. An unpublished pamphlet contains a great deal of information concerning the history of Stearns Siding. See Grace Tillson Smith, "Stearns Siding," Stearns box, Stearns Siding Folder, Mason County Historical Society Archive, Ludington, Michigan. The same pamphlet can be found in the archives of the Lake County Historical Society, but it appears to be a copy of the original from the Mason County Historical Society. Much of this pamphlet also was published in the local newspaper the day Stearns died. See Grace Tillson Smith, "Interesting Experiences of Stearns Siding Days Recalled Graphically," *Ludington Daily News,* February 14, 1933; Justus Stearns letter to William Stearns, March 27, 1930; "A Tribute: A Dinner Commemorating," Mason County Historical Society Archive; *Mason County Record,* May 7, 1880; *Mason County Record,* June 18, 1880; McCracken, *Men of Progress,* 133.
37. Smith, "Stearns Siding," Mason County Historical Society Archive.
38. Ibid.; "A Tribute: A Dinner Commemorating," Mason County Historical Society Archive; Jean Stickney, "Mack, A Scottville Name to Remember," *Ludington Daily News,* July 10, 2003, available at http://news.google.com/newspapers, accessed June 3, 2013; *History of Mason County Michigan,* 64; Hawley, *Historic Mason County,* 261; *Mason County Record,* January 19, 1882; *Mason County Record,* February 2, 1882; *Mason County Record,* April 6, 1882; Lake County Historical Society, *Images of America, Lake County 1871–1960* (Chicago: Arcadia, 2009), 9.
39. Smith, "Stearns Siding," Mason County Historical Society Archive.
40. Ibid. The story of Nels Johnson's life provides another good example of an immigrant from Sweden who lived and worked at Stearns Siding. He was born in 1872 and came to the United States in 1888. He probably began working for Stearns the same year. He cut timber in Fountain, Michigan, and later did the same in Carr Settlement, where he eventually settled on a farm. At times he also worked for Stearns in Wisconsin. See Nels Johnson letter, 1955, L1 box, Lumbering Men Folder, Mason County Historical Society Archive, Ludington, Michigan.
41. Smith, "Stearns Siding," Mason County Historical Society Archive; the quotation is from Stephen Darke letter, no date, L1 box, Lumbering Men Folder, Mason County Historical Society Archive, Ludington, Michigan. In the summer of 2011 the author visited the site of what had been known as Stearns Siding. Bruce Micinski, president of the Lake County Historical Society, was my guide. It was fascinating to see the "basement holes," which were still readily apparent. People from Michigan often refer to them as a "Michigan basement," which often was used to store canned goods, food items that needed to remain cool, or other possessions. Stearns Siding became a ghost town as the village was abandoned after Stearns moved his operations to Ludington and the mill site was destroyed by fire in 1899. In 1900 the abandoned village, along with 8,000 acres of adjacent land, was sold to A. M. Todd of Kalamazoo. Todd was a former member of Congress who planned to establish a large stock-raising business on the property. See *Ludington Record,* May 3, 1900, available at http://news.google.com/newspapers, accessed June 2, 2013.
42. The correspondence between Matt Stevensen and Ingeborg Clomen was made available from the private collection of Bruce and Cindy Bosley, who generously granted

access to much of their correspondence, related the history of the Stevensen family, and provided a photo of the couple with their children. However, all of the letters were written in Norwegian and had to be translated. Gunver Lodge graciously took the time to translate each of them. The Bosleys had several letters, at least seven of which were sent from Matt Stevensen to Ingeborg Clomen. Ingeborg brought them with her when she traveled to the United States. The letters were dated June 25, 1893; April 15, 1894; December 1, 1894; May 20, 1895; September 12, 1895; January 11, 1896; and February 25, 1896. The quotations are from those dated June 25, 1893; April 15, 1894; and February 25, 1896. The photo shows all four children, along with Ingeborg and Matt, who are seated. From left to right, the children are Ida, Herman (sitting on his mother's lap), Ellen, and Martin.

43. *Mason County Record*, June 7, 1883; Smith, "Stearns Siding," Mason County Historical Society Archive.

44. C. C. Peck Jr. letter to Mother, November 1894, Lake County Historical Society, Baldwin, Michigan.

45. Ibid.

46. Stephen Darke letter, Mason County Historical Society Archive.

47. Each quotation from the paragraph comes from Stephen Darke letter, Mason County Historical Society Archive.

48. James P. Miller letter, January 26, 1955, L1 box, Lumbering Men Folder, Mason County Historical Society Archive, Ludington, Michigan.

49. Justus S. Stearns letter to John Danaher, August 10, 1888, Danaher vs. Stearns, 1888, Folder, Lake County Historical Society, Baldwin, Michigan.

50. The court records concerning this case can be found in *John Danaher v. Justus S. Stearns*, Danaher v. Stearns, 1888 Folder, Lake County Historical Society, Baldwin, Michigan. Nick Krieger of the Michigan State Court of Appeals and Bruce Micinski of the Lake County Historical Society provided valuable assistance in the investigation of this case and the court records. There is no record of this appeal ever reaching the Michigan state court of appeals. Any errors concerning the description of events based on fact, interpretation, or omission are the responsibility of the author alone.

51. Ibid. Some of the unique methods in which lumber companies sometimes "acquired" timber from one another, or the United States government, can be found in Lewis C. Reimann, *When Pine Was King* (Ann Arbor: Edwards Brothers, 1953), 27–37; and George M. Blackburn and Sherman L. Richards, "The Timber Industry in Manistee County, Michigan: A Case History in Local Control," *Journal of Forest History* 18 (April 1974): 16, 17. The issue of timber trespass also is addressed in Harms, *Life after Lumbering: Charles Henry Hackley and the Emergence of Muskegon, Michigan*, 129–30.

52. "Want the Stearns Mills," *Mason County Record*, August 6, 1896; "A Good Prospect," *Mason County Record*, August 13, 1896; Smith, "Stearns Siding," Mason County Historical Society Archive.

Chapter 2

1. Hawley, *Historic Mason County*, 29–30; Hannah, *Sand, Sawdust, and Saw Logs*, 45.

2. The first quotation is taken from "Diphtheria," *Ludington Record*, June 2, 1881, 1, available at http://news.google.com/newspapers, accessed May 13, 2014. This article continued by declaring that, "Our cemetery has doubled its occupants in ten months, and three-fourths are" children buried in, "little graves." The second quotation is from the *Ludington Record,* June 16, 1881, 1, available at http://news.google.com/newspapers, accessed May 18, 2012; the diphtheria outbreak also is described in Peterson, *Story of Ludington,* 54–55, 187; and Hannah, *Sand, Sawdust, and Saw Logs,* 50. While the total number of victims is unclear, Hannah's work includes the appraisal of Dr. G. O. Switzer, who estimated that as many as two hundred schoolchildren had died. If this number is accurate, the epidemic was truly devastating to the city, as according to the census of 1880, the total population of Ludington was 4,190 inhabitants.

3. *Ludington Record,* June 16, 1881, 1. The exact number of buildings destroyed by the fire is somewhat unclear. One source determined that "nearly one hundred buildings" were destroyed, "mounting in value to about $200,000." See *History of Mason County Michigan,* 54–57. Another argues, "Sixty-seven buildings were destroyed or heavily damaged." See Peterson, *Story of Ludington,* 52–54.

4. Quoted in Peterson, *Story of Ludington,* 53.

5. Peterson, *Story of Ludington,* 53; *History of Mason County Michigan,* 56–57.

6. Peterson, *Story of Ludington,* 68, 69.

7. Hawley, *Historic Mason County,* 84. The home John S. Woodruff owned was moved later to the corner of Washington Avenue and Foster Street where it became the Alexander-Rye Funeral Home and later the Clock Funeral Home. United States Census, 1880, Mason County Michigan, page 63, and Ashtabula County Ohio, page 22, available at www.heritagequest.com, accessed May 11, 2012; Cabot, *Images of America, Ludington 1830–1930,* 123; "Republican County Convention," *Ludington Record,* May 10, 1888.

8. United States Census, 1880, Mason County Michigan, page 67, available at www.ancestry.com, accessed March 9, 2012; *History of Mason County Michigan,* 59.

9. *History of Mason County Michigan,* 40, 43; a brief history of Royal Arcanum is available at www.royalarcanum.com, accessed May 19, 2012. The author spoke with someone from the organization on May 23, 2012, who described the group as a fraternal benefit society involved in many charitable activities that also provides life insurance.

10. *Mason County Record,* March 21, 1879; January 23, 1880; March 26, 1880; and April 16, 1880; for the editorial, see "An Appeal to Women," *Ludington Record,* January 18, 1883, 9; Dorothy Schneider and Carl J. Schneider, *American Women in the Progressive Era* (New York: Facts on File, 1993), 104, 105.

11. *Ludington Record,* November 25, 1886; March 24, 1892; "A Pleasant Evening," *Ludington Record,* March 10, 1898; *Grand Rapids Press,* January 18, 1902, 7.

12. *Ludington Record,* February 26, 1885, 1, available at http://news.google.com/newspapers, accessed May 21, 2012; Hannah, *Sand, Sawdust, and Saw Logs,* 47.

13. Hannah, *Sand, Sawdust, and Saw Logs,* 47–48; *Ludington Record,* June 19, 1884, 1; the quotation from the Sherman Bros. advertisements is taken from the *Ludington Record,* July 2, 1885, 1, available at http://news.google.com/newspapers, accessed May 18, 2012.

14. *Ludington Record,* July 9, 1885, 1, available at http://news.google.com/newspapers, accessed May 18, 2012.

15. *Ludington Record,* September 2, 1880; October 14, 1880; October 28, 1880; May 19, 1881; January 19, 1882; February 2, 1882; April 6, 1882; December 28, 1882; January 3, 1884;

and February 9, 1888. A sample of the numerous trips within the United States can be seen in the *Ludington Record,* January 3, 1884; July 28, 1884; January 15, 1885; July 19, 1886; June 16, 1887; and September 7, 1899. Robert Stearns's European trip is chronicled in the *Ludington Record,* June 7, 1888; June 14, 1888; June 26, 1888; August 2, 1888; and August 16, 1888.

16. Biographical information covering Robert Stearns is found in "Stearns, Robert Lyon," *National Cyclopedia of American Biography,* vol. 31 (New York: James T. White, 1944), 472–73; Leo Teholiz, "Ludington's Robert Lyon Stearns: The Mark Twain of Art," *Great Lakes Review* 5, no. 1 (1978): 28–41; James S. Pooler, "Ludington Millionaire Found Release in Art," *Detroit Free Press,* April 30, 1950. The quotation is from Bernice Cosulich, "R. L. Stearns Is 'The Mark Twain of Art,'" *Arizona Daily Star,* December 11, 1938, 1. The article by Cosulich is quite extensive and contains helpful information about Robert Stearns's accomplishments as an artist and businessman; much of this article was reprinted in the *Ludington Daily News,* January 7, 1939.

17. *Ludington Record,* November 25, 1897.

18. Cosulich, "R. L. Stearns Is 'The Mark Twain of Art.'"

19. *Ludington Record,* January 20, 1898; February 3, 1898.

20. *Ludington Record,* September 20, 1900; "Stearns, Robert Lyon," *National Cyclopedia of American Biography,* 473; the quotation is from Teholiz, "Ludington's Robert Lyon Stearns," 33. A great overview of Ossawald Crumb can be found in David K. Petersen, "Ossawald Crumb: The Legend of a Pioneer Character Created by Robert Stearns," *Ludington Daily News,* April 27, 2013, 4.

21. Quoted in Teholiz, "Ludington's Robert Lyon Stearns," 33.

22. *Ludington Record,* March 8, 1900; United States Census, 1900, Pere Marquette Township, Mason County Michigan, sheet no. 8, available at www.ancestry.com, accessed March 9, 2012.

23. Hannah, *Sand, Sawdust, and Saw Logs,* 51–52; Peterson, *Story of Ludington,* 70–71. The quotation is taken from the *Ludington Record,* May 3, 1883, 1, available at http://news.google.com/newspapers, accessed May 21, 2012.

24. Hannah, *Sand, Sawdust, and Saw Logs,* 52; Peterson, *Story of Ludington,* 70–71.

25. Hannah, *Sand, Sawdust, and Saw Logs,* 55; Peterson, *Story of Ludington,* 71–72.

26. Efforts by companies in the city of Ludington to drill for salt are chronicled in the *Ludington Record,* February 1, 1883; October 4, 1883, 1; March 26, 1885, 1; and May 21, 1885, 1, available at http://news.google.com/newspapers, accessed May 21, 2012; Hannah, *Sand, Sawdust, and Saw Logs,* 53–54; Peterson, *Story of Ludington,* 64, 65. Additional sources include *History of Manistee County Michigan, with Illustrations and Biographical Sketches of Some of Its Prominent Men and Pioneers* (Chicago: H. R. Page, 1882), 54, 55. Lumbermen in the city of Muskegon attempted to drill for salt, beginning in 1866, but were unsuccessful. According to Harms, "Sufficient brine was never found, even at depths of 5,000 feet." See Harms, *Life after Lumbering: Charles Henry Hackley and the Emergence of Muskegon, Michigan,* 254.

27. Bridger (Billie) Kolberg letter, no date, L1 box, Lumbering Men Folder, Mason County Historical Society Archive, Ludington, Michigan; Hannah, *Sand, Sawdust, and Saw Logs,* 56; Peterson, *Story of Ludington,* 64–66.

28. Frances Lemire letter, January 13, 1952, L1 box, Lumbering Men Folder, Mason County Historical Society Archive, Ludington, Michigan.
29. Nels Johnson letter, 1955, L1 box, Lumbering Men Folder, Mason County Historical Society Archive, Ludington, Michigan.
30. Hannah, *Sand, Sawdust, and Saw Logs,* 58; Peterson, *Story of Ludington,* 73, 74; Hawley, *Historic Mason County,* 11–13.
31. Hannah, *Sand, Sawdust, and Saw Logs,* 58; Peterson, *Story of Ludington,* 66, 73, 74; Hawley, *Historic Mason County,* 511. The attempts to diversify Muskegon's economy in the 1880s and 1890s are described in Harms, *Life after Lumbering: Charles Henry Hackley and the Emergence of Muskegon, Michigan,* 262–72.
32. *Ludington Record,* September 26, 1895, 4, available at http://news.google.com/newspapers, accessed May 16, 2012.
33. The quotation is taken from the *Ludington Record,* July 2, 1896, 5; the election results are found in the *Ludington Record,* July 16, 1896, 1, both are available at http://news.google.com/newspapers, accessed May 16, 2012; Hannah, *Sand, Sawdust, and Saw Logs,* 64.
34. "A Big Deal," *Ludington Record,* February 6, 1896, 1, available at http://news.google.com/newspapers, accessed May 22, 2012; "Development of the Epworth League Railway and Regions About Hamlin," *Ludington Record,* February 13, 1896; "Want the Stearns Mills," *Ludington Record,* August 6, 1896; "Mr. Stearns May Move His Plant from Bennett to This City," *Ludington Record,* August 13, 1896. Each edition of the *Ludington Record* was checked between February 6, 1896, when the deal for Stearns was described as "not quite consummated, but almost certain to be," and August 6, 1896, when the paper's focus began to shift toward Stearns simply moving his base of operations to Ludington. No explanation of why this deal fell apart was registered in the newspaper. In May 1900 the Pere Marquette Lumber Company was sold to the Michigan Salt Association, according to Hawley, *Historic Mason County,* 13.
35. "Mr. Stearns May Move His Plant from Bennett to This City."
36. Ibid.
37. "Where Is the Board of Trade," *Ludington Record,* December 30, 1897; "A New Route Proposed by the F.&P.M. Railway Company," *Ludington Record,* May 12, 1898; "He Will Come If Not Taxed too Heavily," *Ludington Record,* May 19, 1898.
38. "Encouraging Prospects," *Ludington Appeal,* May 5, 1898, 7, available at http://news.google.com/newspapers, accessed May 16, 2012; Hannah, *Sand, Sawdust, and Saw Logs,* 66.
39. "Big Lumber Deal," *Ludington Record,* January 26, 1899; "J. S. Stearns Assumes Management of the Double Brick Store," *Ludington Record,* March 9, 1899; James L. Cabot, "The Double Brick Store," *The Ludington Daily News,* July 31, 2004, 3, available at http://news.google.com/newspapers, accessed May 22, 2012. The advertisements for the Double Brick Store can be found in the *Ludington Record,* April 13, 1899; April 20, 1899; May 4, 1899; July 13, 1899; August 17, 1899; and November 23, 1899.
40. *Ludington Record,* May 26, 1898; March 23, 1899. The quotation is from the *Ludington Record,* September 21, 1899.
41. *Ludington Record,* December 21, 1899, 3, available at http://news.google.com/newspapers, accessed May 22, 2012. The quotation is taken from "Boom for Ludington," *Ludington Record*, September 21, 1899.

42. *Ludington Record,* June 9, 1898; and December 21, 1899.
43. *Ludington Record,* October 5, 1899.
44. Ibid. *Ludington Record,* January 11, 1900; February 25, 1900. "Six Candidates for the Republican Nomination for Governor of Michigan," *Detroit Free Press,* February 25, 1900, and "Big Purchase of Pine," *Detroit Free Press,* November 4, 1899, available at http://proquest.com, accessed May 24, 2011. The claim Stearns was the largest manufacturer of lumber in the world can be found in "Our Next Governor," *Ludington Record,* January 25, 1900. Frederick Weyerhaeuser was arguably the leading lumber baron of his generation. When he died in 1914, the *New York Times* reported he owned over "2,000,000 acres of wooded land, and who, with his associates, silently controlled some 15,000,000 feet of standing pine worth more than $200,000,000." The paper also described him as one of the wealthiest Americans, with a fortune ranging between $20 million and $30 million. See "F. Weyerhaeuser, Lumber King, Dead," *New York Times,* April 5, 1914, available at http://query.nytimes.com, accessed February 1, 2014.
45. *Ludington Record,* October 9, 1901; "Making Improvements," *Ludington Record,* October 12, 1901; "Salt Block at Stearns," *Ludington Record,* December 12, 1901.
46. "A Practical Optimist," *Ludington Record,* April 4, 1901.
47. Ibid. "Big Purchase of Pine," *Detroit Free Press,* November 4, 1899; and the company's reorganization is announced in "Stearns Salt and Lumber Co.," *Detroit Free Press,* January 8, 1902, available at http://proquest.com, accessed May 24, 2011.
48. Mill Reports, 1900, microfilm reel 31, Stearns Salt and Lumber Company Records, 1881–1923, Bentley Historical Library, Ann Arbor, Michigan; "Calendar Year for 1900 (United States)," available at www.timeanddate.com/, accessed May 27, 2012.
49. *Ludington Record,* December 31, 1896.
50. "Half Is Pledged," *Grand Rapids Press,* January 16, 1902; *Catalogue of the Olivet College for 1904–1905* (Olivet, MI: Frank N. Green, 1905), 3, available at http://books.google.com, accessed October 26, 2011; "The History of Olivet College," available at www.olivetcollege.edu/about/history.php, accessed May 22, 2012. The quotation is from "Will Give $1,000," *Ludington Record,* May 2, 1902; also see the *Ludington Record,* May 30, 1901.
51. "Prize Gardens Visited," *Ludington Record,* July 25, 1901; "Contest Inaugurated by J. S. Stearns Shows Beneficial Results," *Ludington Record,* August 31, 1901; "Mr. Stearns Distributes Cash," *Ludington Record,* September 7, 1901; "To Beautify the City," *Ludington Record,* May 13, 1902; "Prizes Are Awarded," *Ludington Record,* September 12, 1902.
52. *Ludington Record,* August 22, 1901; the quotation is taken from "A Big Day Outdoors," *Ludington Record,* September 5, 1901.
53. *Ludington Record,* November 21, 1901; the quotation is from "Justus S. Stearns," *Ludington Record,* December 18, 1901.

Chapter 3

1. The quotation he was "foolish" comes from Justus Stearns letter to William Stearns, March 27, 1930, Mason County Historical Society Archive. He described himself as a "Roosevelt Progressive" in Justus Stearns letter to Woodrow Wilson, October 20, 1913, Woodrow Wilson Papers, Series 2, microfilm reel 51, Library of Congress, Washington, DC. An additional source is Justus Stearns letter to Dr. McClelland, n.d., taken from

the *Mountain Herald,* "How a Friend Remembers Lincoln," Mason County Historical Society Archive.

2. In his profile of lumbermen who operated in the Great Lakes states, Frederick W. Kohlmeyer noted that most were Republicans. Of the fifty-one who identified their political affiliation, forty-five were Republican, four were Democrat, and two supported the Prohibition Party. See Kohlmeyer, "Northern Pine Lumbermen," 537. Jeremy Kilar notes that most lumbermen were Republicans and mentions briefly the party's support of a protective tariff for lumber in Kilar, *Michigan's Lumbertowns,* 141, 158; the Republican Party's support of a high tariff also is addressed in Brands, *American Colossus,* 483, 484. Additional sources include Dunbar and May, *Michigan: A History of the Wolverine State,* 348. The biographer of Charles Hackley describes both Hackley and his partner Thomas Hume as "staunch Republicans" in Harms, *Life after Lumbering: Charles Henry Hackley and the Emergence of Muskegon, Michigan,* 184. A brief profile of Hackley is found in Livingstone, *History of the Republican Party,* 205–8. Henry Sage's political affiliation is found in Goodstein, *Biography of a Businessman,* 45. The company town Sage founded originally was known as Wenona, and then West Bay City.

3. The quotation is from *Mason County Record,* August 7, 1884. Additional sources include *Mason County Record,* September 4, 1884; November 11, 1886; and July 10, 1890; "Republican County Convention," *Mason County Record,* July 31, 1890. Other works that provide a description of his early involvement in politics are Livingstone, *History of the Republican Party,* 369; and Powers, *A History of Northern Michigan and Its People,* 1313.

4. Livingstone, *History of the Republican Party,* 316–19; Dunbar and May, *Michigan: A History of the Wolverine State,* 387–92; Bruce A. Rubenstein and Lawrence E. Ziewacz, *Michigan: A History of the Great Lakes State* (Wheeling, IL: Harlan Davidson, 2002), 129–32.

5. *Ludington Record,* January 17, 1898; February 10, 1898; and November 3, 1898; "Political Pointers," *Detroit Free Press,* July 15, 1898, 5; "Want the O.K. Brand," *Detroit Free Press,* September 21, 1898, 1; "The Republican Ticket," *Detroit Free Press,* September 23, 1898, 4; each article from the *Detroit Free Press* is available at http://proquest.com, accessed May 24, 2011; Jean M. Fox, *Fred M. Warner: Progressive Governor* (Farmington Hills, MI: Farmington Hills Historical Commission, 1988), 55, 56.

6. *Ludington Record,* November 3, 1898; Fox, *Fred M. Warner,* 85; Dunbar and May, *Michigan: A History of the Wolverine State,* 677; Willis F. Dunbar, *Michigan through the Centuries* (New York: Lewis Historical Publishing, 1955), 342, 343. The election results are included in Justus S. Stearns, ed., *Michigan Legislative Manual* (Lansing, MI: Robert Smith Printing, 1899), 611.

7. Stearns, *Michigan Manual,* 673–77; "Thanksgiving Day," *Detroit Free Press,* November 7, 1899, 7, available at http://proquest.com, accessed May 9, 2011; Fox, *Fred Warner,* 58, 59.

8. N. Norton Clark letter to Justus S. Stearns, October 22, 1900, and Eugene D. Goneger to Justus S. Stearns, October 2, 1900, Records Political Parties, Box 20, 21, 22, Michigan State Archives, Lansing, Michigan.

9. *Ludington Record,* February 2, 1899; the quotation is taken from "Stearns for Governor," *Ludington Record,* December 21, 1899.

10. "Stearns a Growing Favorite," *Ludington Record,* January 18, 1900; "Our Next Governor," *Ludington Record,* January 25, 1900; "Stearns Stays In," *Grand Rapids Press,*

December 15, 1899, 1; "Stearns Is Investigating," *Detroit Free Press,* January 2, 1900, 8, available at http://proquest.com, accessed May 9, 2011.

11. "Stearns' Platform," *Ludington Record,* March 1, 1900. The quotation is from Geoffrey G. Drutchas, "Gray Eminence in a Gilded Age: The Forgotten Career of Senator James McMillan of Michigan," *Michigan Historical Review* 28, no. 2 (2002): 104.

12. "Stearns' Platform," *Ludington Record,* March 1, 1900.

13. Ibid.

14. Justus Stearns letter to Woodrow Wilson, October 20, 1913. Additional information is found in Michael W. Nagle, "The Progressive Movement," LecturePoint: U.S. History, Cengage Learning, http://college.cengage.com/history/lecturepoints/index.html, accessed June 21, 2011.

15. Fox, *Fred M. Warner,* 56; Livingstone, *History of the Republican Party,* 62–65.

16. Livingstone, *History of the Republican Party,* 168–72; "Six Candidates for the Republican Nomination for Governor of Michigan," *Detroit Free Press,* February 25, 1900, 3, http://proquest.com, accessed May 9, 2011.

17. Livingstone, *History of the Republican Party,* 301, 302; "Six Candidates for the Republican Nomination for Governor of Michigan," *Detroit Free Press,* February 25, 1900, 3, available at http://proquest.com, accessed May 9, 2011.

18. *Ludington Record,* May 10, 1900; and June 14, 1900.

19. "Fifteen Hundred Men Parade for Stearns," *Grand Rapids Press,* June 23, 1900, 2; "Stearns Big Parade," *Ludington Record,* June 28, 1900.

20. "Col. Bliss for Governor," *Ludington Record,* June 28, 1900; "All Here," *Grand Rapids Press,* June 26, 1900, 1; Livingstone, *History of the Republican Party,* 369; "A Tribute: A Dinner Commemorating," Mason County Historical Society Archive. The *Grand Rapids Press* reported that Stearns was introduced by Judge Palmer, but this probably was a mistake as there was no Judge Palmer from Ludington. The program created in celebration of Stearns's seventy-eighth birthday (cited above) identifies Judge McMahon as the individual who spoke on behalf of Stearns. The *Grand Rapids Press* also reported that Bliss "claimed" 298 votes while Ferry "claimed" 270 on the first ballot. While supporters made these claims, it appears as if a great deal of posturing was going on. The claims made were different from the official results, as operatives for both Bliss and Ferry believed it was a good tactic to keep some of their votes in reserve to then be announced at a later time when it was best strategically. The official results of the first ballot, as described, were reported in the *Ludington Record.*

21. "Stearns and Sinbad," *Detroit Free Press,* June 19, 1900, 4, available at http://proquest.com, accessed May 10, 2011.

22. "Season of 1900," *Epworth Assembly Quarterly* 6, no. 3 (1900): 9.

23. "For Pure Politics," *Ludington Chronicle,* January 17, 1902.

24. Ibid. The quotation is from Justus Stearns letter to William Stearns, March 27, 1930, Mason County Historical Society Archive. While the source for Stearns's complaint that Bliss "bought the nomination through money furnished by the railroads" comes from a letter written nearly thirty years later; sequent actions demonstrate he held this belief at the time he ran for the nomination in 1902 and again in 1904.

25. "Mr. Stearns on Lobbying," *Grand Rapids Press,* January 15, 1902, 2.

26. "Has It Hurt Him," *Grand Rapids Press,* January 16, 1902, 1; "Heard in the Hotel Corridors," *Detroit Free Press,* January 2, 1902, 8; "Heard in the Hotel Corridors," *Detroit Free Press,* January 16, 1902, 3; each *Detroit Free Press* article is available at http://proquest.com, accessed May 11, 2011; "Not His Funeral," *Grand Rapids Press,* February 4, 1902, 2; Drutchas, "The Forgotten Career of Senator James McMillan of Michigan," 102.

27. "Stearns Will Make the Run," *Ludington Chronicle,* April 15, 1902; "Stearns out for the Fight," *Detroit Free Press,* April 13, 1902, 3, available at http://proquest.com, accessed May 11, 2011.

28. "Another Open Letter Issued by Stearns," *Grand Rapids Press,* May 5, 1902, 1; "Stearns Issues Another," *Detroit Free Press,* May 5, 1902, 1; "Stearns to Bliss: Offers to Pay Half the Cost of a Special Session," *Detroit Free Press,* April 22, 1902, 3; each *Detroit Free Press* article is available at http://proquest.com, accessed May 11, 2011; "It's up to Mr. Bliss," *Ludington Chronicle,* April 22, 1902.

29. "Kent County Republican Party Statement," Stearns Collection, Box 3, Politics, ca. 1900 and later Folder, Bentley Historical Library, Ann Arbor, Michigan.

30. Livingstone, *History of the Republican Party,* 90, 91. The quotations are from Open Letter from Edward Cahill, June 5, 1902, Stearns Collection, Box 3, Politics, ca. 1900 and later Folder, Bentley Historical Library, Ann Arbor, Michigan.

31. "For Second Term," *Ludington Chronicle,* June 27, 1902; "They May Bolt It," *Grand Rapids Press,* June 27, 1902, 3; "No Sore Spots on Stearns," *Detroit Free Press,* June 27, 1902, 2; "What the Michigan Editors Are Saying," *Detroit Free Press,* July 7, 1902, 4; each *Detroit Free Press* article is available at http://proquest.com, accessed May 12, 2011; "Thomas, Henry Franklin," *Biographical Directory of the United States Congress,* available at http://bioguide.congress.gov/, accessed September 30, 2012.

32. "There's No Doubt about What He Means," *Ludington Chronicle,* February 17, 1904; "Enters the Race," *Grand Rapids Press,* February 15, 1904, 6; "No Doubt about It: Stearns Says He Will Run for Governor," *Detroit Free Press,* February 14, 1904, 1; "Stearns Makes His Bid," *Detroit Free Press,* February 15, 1904, 1; each *Detroit Free Press* article is available at http://proquest.com, accessed May 13, 2011; Drutchas, "The Forgotten Career of Senator James McMillan," 108; Dunbar and May, *Michigan: A History of the Wolverine State,* 391.

33. "For Governor, Justus S. Stearns of Ludington," *Grand Rapids Press,* April 27, 1904, 3; "Primary Reform Ballot," *Detroit Free Press,* April 29, 1904, 3, available at http://proquest.com, accessed May 14, 2011.

34. "Mrs. J. S. Stearns Very Low," *Ludington Chronicle,* May 4, 1904.

35. "Resolutions of Sympathy," *Ludington Chronicle,* May 11, 1904. The quotation is from "President's Report," *Epworth Assembly Quarterly* 10, no. 4 (1904): 3.

36. "Whole City Saddened," *Ludington Chronicle,* May 11, 1904; "Her Life Ended," *Grand Rapids Press,* May 6, 1904, 5.

37. Dunbar and May, *Michigan: A History of the Wolverine State,* 444, 445; Fox, *Fred M. Warner,* 70–75; "Palaver of the Politicians," *Detroit Free Press,* June 23, 1904, 4, available at http://proquest.com, accessed May 14, 2011.

38. "Conceded to Warner," *Detroit Free Press,* June 30, 1904, 1, available at http://proquest.com, accessed May 14, 2011; "Fight for Primary Reform," *Grand Rapids Press,* June 30,

1904, 1; "Warner in Saddle," *Grand Rapids Press,* July 1, 1904, 5; "The Detroit Convention," *Ludington Chronicle,* July 6, 1904; "Mr. Stearns's Reclamation," *Detroit Free Press,* July 5, 1904, 4, available at http://proquest.com, accessed May 15, 2011.

39. "Favor Mr. Stearns," *Grand Rapids Press,* July 20, 1904, 5; "Respectfully Referred," *Grand Rapids Press,* July 22, 1904, 4; "Just Stands Pat," *Grand Rapids Press,* July 26, 1. The wonderful political cartoon of Stearns as the Sphinx can be found in the *Grand Rapids Press,* July 27, 1904, 9.

40. "Willing," *Grand Rapids Press,* July 30, 1904, 1. Charles Hackley was another Republican lumberman who was tempted to run as a Democrat. He ran for mayor of Muskegon in 1873 and 1877 on the Republican ticket, although in 1878 the Democrats asked him to run for mayor again as a Democrat; he declined the offer from the Democrats. See Harms, *Life after Lumbering: Charles Henry Hackley and the Emergence of Muskegon, Michigan,* 114.

41. "Democrats Not All for Stearns," *Detroit Free Press,* July 31, 1904, 9, available at http://proquest.com, accessed May 16, 2011.

42. "Ferris Was Named," *Grand Rapids Press,* August 4, 1904, 2.

43. "Lost Their Opportunity," *Grand Rapids Press,* August 4, 1904, 4; "Mr. Stearns Is Down and Out," *Detroit Free Press,* August 5, 1904, 4, available at http://proquest.com, accessed May 16, 2011.

44. "Stearns Hits Out," *Grand Rapids Press,* November 3, 1904, 1; Fox, *Fred M. Warner,* 102; Dunbar and May, *Michigan: A History of the Wolverine State,* 445.

45. "Not a Candidate," *Grand Rapids Press,* September 22, 1906, 3; "To Run Mr. Stearns," *Grand Rapids Press,* February 23, 1907, 2; "Stearns Makes Denial," *Detroit Free Press,* September 23, 1906, 7; "Political Gossip," *Detroit Free Press,* February 17, 1914, 6; the quotation is from "J. S. Stearns Glad to Be out of Politics," *Detroit Free Press,* May 26, 1912, 6; each *Detroit Free Press* article is available at http://proquest.com, accessed May 17, 2011.

46. "Ludington's Foremost Citizen Is Honored," *Ludington Chronicle,* May 14, 1916; United States Assistant Secretary of State (name unintelligible) letter to Justus S. Stearns, October 20, 1925, Private Collection of Robert E. Gable, Lexington, Kentucky; Funeral Booklet, "Justus Smith Stearns," Private Collection of Robert E. Gable; Wescott H. Read letter to Robert L. Stearns, February 22, 1933, Private Collection of Robert E. Gable.

47. Justus Stearns letter to William Stearns, March 27, 1930, Mason County Historical Society Archive.

48. "Mr. Stearns's Reclamation," *Detroit Free Press,* July 5, 1904, 4, available at http://proquest.com, accessed May 15, 2011.

Chapter 4

1. Justus Stearns letter to William Stearns, March 27, 1930, Mason County Historical Society Archive.

2. The transitory nature of the lumber industry as the pinelands disappeared is described in Kohlmeyer, "Northern Pine Lumbermen," 534–36. The movement of Michigan timber operations to the South, Minnesota, and the West Coast is mentioned in Maybee, *Michigan's White Pine Era,* 51, 52. Charles Hackley's investments outside of Michigan are chronicled in chapters 8 and 9 of Harms, *Life after Lumbering: Charles Henry Hackley and* *the Emergence of Muskegon, Michigan,* 187–227; Henry Sage's activities can be found in Goodstein, *Biography of a Businessman,* 138, 151, 162.

3. Thomas R. Cox, "Frontier Enterprise versus the Modern Age," *Pacific Northwest Quarterly* 84, no. 1 (1993): 21.

4. In addition to the excellent article by J. M. Pond noted in the epigraph, and the article by Thomas R. Cox, the best sources for background information concerning Fred Herrick, include Wilbur W. Hindley, "His $20 Log Started $12,000,000 Fortune," Spokane *Spokesman Review,* May 26, 1929. The articles by Pond and Hindley are both easily accessible at www.senecakids.org/SenecaProject/Herrick/FredHerrickHome.html. Additional sources include Arthur Earl Victor, "Fred Herrick and Bill Grotte: Idaho's Paul Bunyan and His Bull of the Woods," *Pacificnorthwesterner* 16, no. 3 (1972): 33–48.

5. Pond, "Fred Herrick," 18, 42.

6. The proper spelling is Cushway, although in some sources it is spelled Cushaway. "Joseph Cushway Wielded Power among Indians," *Ludington Daily News,* February 13, 1916, available at http://news.google.com/newspapers, accessed December 6, 2011; "Mason County Indian Pottawatomie Leader," *The Ludington Daily News,* June 15, 1954. An article from the *Ludington Record-Appeal* credits Cushway with successfully negotiating a sum of $384,000 for the Potawatomie Indians as a result of land claims in the Chicago area based upon a treaty from 1837. The article, "Mason County's Most Famous Indian Chief," *Ludington Record-Appeal,* September 10, 1903, 1, is available at http://news.google.com/newspapers, accessed May 26, 2013.

7. Roswell P. Bishop served in Congress from 1895 to 1907. The total cost of Ludington's new harbor was estimated to be over $1.5 million. In July 1914 the city of Ludington celebrated its completion in grand style. As many as forty thousand people participated in the festivities, which took place over two days. Unfortunately, Congressman Bishop was unable to attend the celebration, as he was living in California by 1914. Sources for Ludington's only congressman are surprisingly scarce, but information can be found in Livingstone, *History of the Republican Party,* 53–55; *History of Mason County Michigan,* 62; Rose D. Hawley, "Recalls When Bishop Family Resided on Harrison Street," *Ludington Daily News,* August 6, 1953, available at Biography Files, A–K Drawer, Bishop, Roswell P. Folder, Mason County Historical Society Archive, Ludington, Michigan; "R. P. Bishop Was in Every Sense Representative," *Mason County Enterprise,* March 9, 1920, available at Obituary Files, B Section, Mason County Historical Society Archive, Ludington, Michigan; Peterson, *Story of Ludington,* 123.

8. *Grand Rapids Press,* September 17, 1906, 2; Rufus H. Thayer letter to Thomas J. Morgan, August 6, 1892, RG 75, Entry 102, Special Cases, Special Case 32, Timber Contracts, LaPointe, Authority 39351-1894, National Archives and Records Administration, Washington, DC.

9. Edmund Jefferson Danziger Jr., *The Chippewas of Lake Superior* (Norman: University of Oklahoma Press, 1978), 7; Anthony Godfrey, *A Forestry History of Ten Wisconsin Indian Reservations under the Great Lakes Agency, Precontact to the Present* (Salt Lake City: U.S. West Research, 1996), 5; Michelle M. Steen-Adams, Nancy E. Langston, and David J. Mladenoff, "Logging the Great Lakes Indian Reservations: The Case of the Bad River Band of Ojibwe," *American Indian Culture and Research Journal* 34, no. 1 (2010): 43.

10. Danziger, *Chippewas of Lake Superior,* 7.

11. A good, brief survey of policies the United States adopted in the nineteenth century can be found in Philip Weeks, *Farewell, My Nation: The American Indian and the United States, 1820–1890* (Arlington Heights, IL: Harlan Davidson, 1990); Michael W. Nagle, "Transforming the West," LecturePoint: U.S. History, Cengage Learning, http://college.cengage.com/history/lecturepoints/index.html, accessed January 2, 2012.

12. Danziger, *Chippewas of Lake Superior,* 3–5; Godfrey, *A Forestry History,* 5–10.

13. The statistics addressing acreage and population can be found in House of Representatives, *Annual Reports of the Department of the Interior for the Fiscal Year Ended June 30, 1897, Report of the Commissioner of Indian Affairs* (Washington, DC: Government Printing Office, 1897), 308, available at http://googlebooks.com/, accessed September 28, 2011; Carolissa Levi, *Chippewa Indians of Yesterday and Today* (New York: Pageant Press, 1956), 65.

14. Once again, the statistics addressing acreage and population can be found in House of Representatives, *Annual Reports of the Department of the Interior, Report of the Commissioner of Indian Affairs,* 308; Levi, *Chippewa Indians of Yesterday and Today,* 85; Godfrey, *A Forestry History,* 10.

15. J. P. Kinney, *Indian Forest and Range, A History of the Administration and Conservation of the Redman's Heritage* (Washington, DC: Forestry Enterprises, 1950), 79; additional sources include Levi, *Chippewa Indians of Yesterday and Today,* 239–40; Godfrey, *A Forestry History,* 33–34, 58; Steen-Adams, Langston, and Mladenoff, "Logging the Great Lakes Indian Reservations," 47.

16. Godfrey, *A Forestry History,* 58, 59; the quotation is taken from Department of Interior, *Report on Indians Taxed and Indians Not Taxed in the United States (Except Alaska) at the Eleventh Census: 1890* (Washington, DC: Government Printing Office, 1894), 625, available at http://googlebooks.com/, accessed August 26, 2011.

17. Department of Interior, *Report on Indians Taxed and Indians Not Taxed,* 625.

18. Wa-se-gwan-ne-bi letter to Thomas J. Morgan, July 2, 1892, RG 75, Entry 102, Special Cases, Special Case 32, Timber Contracts, LaPointe, Authority 39351-1894, National Archives and Records Administration, Washington, DC. This letter is taken from a large compilation of correspondence, all revolving around the issue of logging on the Lac du Flambeau Reservation land.

19. Wa-se-gwan-ne-bi letter to Thomas J. Morgan, August 31, 1892, RG 75 Records of the Bureau of Indian Affairs, Entry 102, Special Cases, Special Case 32, Timber Contracts, LaPointe, Authority 39351–1894, National Archives and Records Administration, Washington, DC.

20. The correspondence is also discussed extensively in Kinney, *Indian Forest and Range,* 29–31; Godfrey, *A Forestry History,* 74.

21. Godfrey, *A Forestry History,* 74.

22. Kinney, *Indian Forest and Range,* 33.

23. Patty Loew, *Indian Nations of Wisconsin: Histories of Endurance and Renewal* (Madison: Wisconsin Historical Society Press, 2001), 70; Godfrey, *A Forestry History,* 85.

24. Godfrey, *A Forestry History,* 74, 75.

25. According to Forest Service employee E. R. Hudson, burned timber was not as valuable as mature, green timber, but it still was marketable and had a wide range of uses.

Depending upon its level of fire damage, it was used regularly in mines and for railroad ties. Such timber also was in demand as wood for boxes and crates, as well as for telephone and telegraph poles. The phrases "dead timber" or "dead and down timber" commonly were used to describe timber killed by fire, insects, or storms that were found in varying forms of decay and quality. Because the good and bad were classified together, in some regions of the country a prejudice existed in regard to its use. Hudson argued that "sound dead timber, and particularly sound fire-killed timber, has decided value and that it keeps this value for a considerable length of time. Decay does not readily affect it and its strength is not impaired by standing in the dead condition." For the full text of Hudson's arguments, see E. R. Hudson, "Dead Timber in the National Forests," *Forestry and Irrigation* 13, no. 7 (1907): 363–66, 383, available at http://googlebooks.com/, accessed May 15, 2014.

26. D. M. Browning letter to John W. Noble, October 26, 1893, RG 75, Records of the Bureau of Indian Affairs, Office of Indian Affairs, Correspondence Land Division, vol. 134, Oct. 14, 1893 to Nov. 21, 1893, Letter Book 267, National Archives and Records Administration, Washington, DC.

27. D. M. Browning letter to John W. Noble, November 18, 1893, RG 75, Records of the Bureau of Indian Affairs, Office of Indian Affairs, Correspondence Land Division, vol. 134, Oct. 14, 1893 to Nov. 21, 1893, Letter Book 268, National Archives and Records Administration, Washington, DC.

28. Ibid.

29. An extensive profile of L. K. Baker can be found in *American Lumbermen: The Personal History and Public and Business Achievements of One Hundred Eminent Lumbermen of the United States, Second Series* (Chicago: American Lumberman, 1906), 173, 174, available at http://googlebooks.com/, accessed January 20, 2012. It is likely Baker was a distant relative of Paulina (Lyon) Stearns. Each had ancestors who hailed from Kelloggsville, Ohio, and each could trace the "Kellogg" family name through their mother's family line; Baker's middle name was Kellogg. Additional sources include the *Ludington Record,* October 25, 1895; July 14, 1898.

30. Godfrey, *A Forestry History,* 64, 65; Kinney, *Indian Forest and Range,* 34; Steen-Adams, Langston, and Mladenoff, "Logging the Great Lakes Indian Reservations," 50–53.

31. Godfrey, *A Forest History*, 66.

32. House of Representatives, *Annual Reports of the Department of the Interior, Report of the Commissioner of Indian Affairs,* 313.

33. An excellent summary of the entire case, including appeal, can be found at "Seymour et al. v. Cushway et al.," *Northwestern Reporter, Containing All the Decisions of the Supreme Courts of Minnesota, Wisconsin, Iowa, Michigan, Nebraska, North Dakota, South Dakota,* vol. 76 (St. Paul: West Publishing, 1898), 769–74, available at http://googlebooks.com/, accessed August 14, 2011. An additional source is "Suit for a Big Sum," *Milwaukee Journal,* February 24, 1897, 1, available at http://news.google.com/newspapers, accessed December 6, 2011.

34. "Seymour et al. v. Cushway, et al.," *Northwestern Reporter,* 771; Perry F. Powers, *A History of Northern Michigan and Its People* (Chicago: Lewis Publishing, 1912), 969–70 and 1187–90; for the rivalry between Stearns and Cartier, see James Jensen, "Ludington's Angels: Antoine Cartier and Justus Stearns" (unpublished manuscript, 2010).

35. "Seymour et al. v. Cushway, et al.," *Northwestern Reporter,* 771.
36. Ibid.
37. Ibid.
38. Ibid., 771, 772; the quotation is from Pond, "Fred Herrick," 42.
39. "Seymour et al. v. Cushway, et al.," *Northwestern Reporter,* 772.
40. Ibid., 774.
41. *Ludington Record,* February 24, 1898.
42. Godfrey, *A Forestry History,* 68, 77; Kinney, *Indian Forest and Range,* 52–54.
43. Godfrey, *A Forestry History,* 68; additional information is found in Kinney, *Indian Forest and Range,* 52–54. Kinney indicated there were four bids, but Godfrey reported there were five.
44. "Stearns Big Lumber Deal," *Ludington Chronicle,* May 27, 1903, 1. Other sources used include Kinney, *Indian Forest and Range,* 53–54; "Under a New Deal," *Grand Rapids Press,* May 19, 1903, 1.
45. Godfrey, *A Forestry History,* 68; "Stearns Long Job," *Grand Rapids Press,* May 22, 1903, 1.
46. Kinney, *Indian Forest and Range,* 55–61.
47. Godfrey, *A Forestry History,* 68, 119–22; Danziger, *Chippewas of Lake Superior,* 117–18.
48. Godfrey, *A Forestry History,* 69. Other sources include Godfrey, *A Forestry History,* 108–9; "Will Log Burned Tracts," *Detroit Free Press,* November 29, 1908, C6, available at http://proquest.com, accessed May 29, 2011; Kinney, *Indian Forest and Range,* 100.
49. Kinney, *Indian Forest and Range,* 102. Other sources include Danziger, *Chippewas of Lake Superior,* 112; Will H. Chapple, "Practical Help for Reservation Indians," *National Magazine* 17, no. 6 (1903): 721, 722; *Ludington Record,* March 21, 1895. Godfrey provides the statistics about the numbers of Indians working for Stearns in 1915 and 1920. For some reason there were far fewer Indians working for Stearns in 1920, but he does not offer an explanation. See Godfrey, *A Forestry History,* 66, 111–13. Other sources include "Ashland County's Largest Town—Sanborn; Its Resources and Advantages," *The Wisconsin Municipality* 14, no. 4 (1914): 875, available at http://googlebooks.com/, accessed December 14, 2011.
50. Godfrey, *A Forestry History,* 121. Other sources include Levi, *Chippewa Indians of Yesterday and Today,* 241; Godfrey, *A Forestry History,* 67–68 and 121. Godfrey argues on pages 67–68 the Indians did not receive fair market value for their timber beginning in 1900 due to the lack of an escalator clause in the initial contracts.
51. Kinney, *Indian Forest and Range,* 60. Steen-Adams, Langston, and Mladenoff, "Logging the Great Lakes Indian Reservations," 56, chronicles the accusations tribal members made against Stearns that his crews improperly logged green, instead of fire-damaged, timber. The accusation also is mentioned in Statement Made by Charles D. Armstrong to Louis R. Glavis, no date, RG 46, Records of the United States Senate, Committee on Interior and Insular Affairs, Wisconsin-Menominee, Sen 83A-F9 (70th–82nd), Box 150, Folder: La Pointe Reservation (also Bad River and Odanah), National Archives and Records Administration, Washington, DC. Other sources include Levi, *Chippewa Indians of Yesterday and Today,* 73.
52. *Survey of Conditions of the Indians in the United States, Hearings before a Subcommittee of the Committee on Indian Affairs, United States Senate* (Washington, DC: Government

Printing Office, 1930), 1964, available at http://content.wisconsinhistory.org/cdm/ref/collection/tp/id/26289, accessed November 24, 2013.

53. Ibid., 1891, 1892, 1894.

54. Ibid, 1911.

55. The "exorbitant prices" quote is from Loew, "Natives, Newspapers, and 'Fighting Bob': Wisconsin Chippewa in the 'unprogressive' Era," *Journalism History,* 23, no. 4 (1998): 4. The author accessed this article from the questia.com website, so the page numbers are slightly different in this note, as opposed to the article's original page numbers. For a full citation of the article and the page numbers as they originally appeared, see the bibliography. Additional sources include *The Twentieth Annual Report of the Executive Committee of the Indian Rights Association, for the Year Ending December 10, 1902* (Philadelphia: Office of the Indian Rights Association, 1903), 57, available at http://googlebooks.com/, accessed November 24, 2012; "Ashland County's Retail Establishments," *Wisconsin Municipality* 14, no. 4 (1914): 856, available at http://googlebooks.com/, accessed December 14, 2011. The quotation about the octopus is quoted in Steen-Adams, Langston, and Mladenoff, "Logging the Great Lakes Indian Reservations," 57.

56. Both quotations are quoted in, Reimann, *When Pine Was King,* 28, 31.

57. Patty Loew is a professor in the Life Sciences Communication Department at the University of Wisconsin–Madison and is affiliated with the American Indian Studies program at the school. In addition to her works cited above, she also is the author of a popular text commonly used in Wisconsin's elementary schools titled *Native People of Wisconsin.* Furthermore, she is an enrolled member of the Bad River Band of Lake Superior Ojibwe. The quotations are from Loew, "Natives, Newspapers, and 'Fighting Bob': Wisconsin Chippewa in the 'Unprogressive' Era," 7, 1; an additional source is "Patty Loew," University of Wisconsin–Madison, available at http://lsc.wisc.edu/faculty/patty-loew/, accessed May 27, 2014. As will be shown in chapter 7, Stearns only used scrip in Kentucky to pay employees (most of whom were white) who wanted an advance on their paycheck prior to payday. In Wisconsin, white employees were paid in cash, while Indians were compensated in scrip. Stearns left behind no direct evidence of his attitudes toward American Indians, but his views were likely similar to those expressed in Loew's quotation.

58. *Survey of Conditions of the Indians in the United States, Hearings before a Subcommittee of the Committee on Indian Affairs, United States Senate,* 2049; the statement from Father Chrysostom is quoted from Levi, *Chippewa Indians of Yesterday and Today,* 75. Father Chrysostom worked for decades as a parish priest and missionary in the Bayfield-Ashland area of Wisconsin beginning in 1882 and extending to his retirement in 1912. A brief biography of Father Chrysostom can be found at "Verwyst, Chrysostom Adrian," Dictionary of Wisconsin History, available at www.wisconsinhistory.org/dictionary, accessed November 27, 2013; Patty Loew, "Natives, Newspapers, and 'Fighting Bob': Wisconsin Chippewa in the 'Unprogressive' Era," 5. Information concerning Sage's activities on the Isabella Reservation, including the quotation concerning Sage's actions, can be found in Goodstein, *Biography of a Businessman,* 143, 144. Another example of a timber trespass not addressed in the text, which took place on the Winnebago reservation, is mentioned briefly in Godfrey, *A Forestry History,* 80. In this case, the perpetrators were successfully prosecuted.

59. Steen-Adams, Langston, and Mladenoff, "Logging the Great Lakes Indian Reservations," 51–54; Loew, *Indian Nations of Wisconsin,* 75; "Sued by Indians," *Grand Rapids Press,* December 28, 1904. Forester J. P. Kinney defends the actions of Campbell in this case and argues, "that great injustice was done him in the dismissal." For Kinney's explanation of the events surrounding S. W. Campbell and his dismissal, see Kinney, *Indian Forest and Range,* 94–96.
60. *Grand Rapids Press,* September 17, 1906, 2. Levi argues the Stearns Lumber Company received its initial contracts, "probably because of political influence." See Levi, *Chippewa Indians of Yesterday and Today,* 241.
61. Godfrey, *A Forestry History,* 66, 67.
62. Steen-Adams, Langston, and Mladenoff, "Logging the Great Lakes Indian Reservations," 51–54; Loew, *Indian Nations of Wisconsin,* 51; the quotations are from *The Twentieth Annual Report of the Executive Committee of the Indian Rights Association, for the Year Ending December 10, 1902,* 57, 58.
63. Loew, "Natives, Newspapers, and 'Fighting Bob': Wisconsin Chippewa in the 'Unprogressive' Era," 6; Loew, *Indian Nations of Wisconsin,* 75.
64. *Twenty-Seventh Annual Report of the Board of Indian Commissioners, 1895* (Washington, DC: Government Printing Office, 1896), 14, available at http://googlebooks.com/, accessed August 26, 2011.
65. Chapple, "Practical Help for Reservation Indians," 32.
66. Godfrey, *A Forestry History,* 112, 113; Steen-Adams, Langston, and Mladenoff, "Logging the Great Lakes Indian Reservations," 57, 58; Danziger, *Chippewas of Lake Superior,* 119–23; O. J. Little, "Report to the League of Women Voters," (no date), RG 46, Records of the United States Senate, Committee on Interior and Insular Affairs, Wisconsin-Menominee, Sen 83A-F9 (70th–82nd), Box 150, Folder: La Pointe Reservation (also Bad River and Odanah), National Archives and Records Administration, Washington, DC. A letter written by Oliver Olson and sent to Special Investigator Louis Glavis represented the frustration that many Indians must have felt in the late 1920s, as he complained the Indians had "virtually NOTHING" after many years of logging on Indian land. See Oliver Olson letter to Louis R. Glavis, December 10, 1928, RG 46, Records of the United States Senate, Committee on Interior and Insular Affairs, Wisconsin-Menominee, Sen 83A-F9 (70th–82nd), Box 150, Folder: La Pointe Reservation (also Bad River and Odanah), National Archives and Records Administration, Washington, DC.
67. Danziger, *Chippewas of Lake Superior,* 112; Godfrey, *A Forestry History,* 113, 114; Levi, *Chippewa Indians of Yesterday and Today,* 72–74.
68. Michelle Steen-Adams, e-mail message to author, January 9, 2012. In her e-mail, Steen-Adams argues that based upon her research, "no material suggests philanthropic activity by Stearns [in Wisconsin], but rather strongly suggests to the contrary." For the attitudes and actions of absentee lumber barons, see Kilar, *Michigan's Lumbertowns,* 150, 155–58; and Goodstein, *Biography of a Businessman,* 112, 134.

Chapter 5

1. The bologna sandwich story was included in an interview of Dr. Frank Thomas, the former president of Stearns Coal and Lumber. The full interview transcript can be found in Kim A. McBride, "A Background Archival and Oral Historical Study of the Barthell Coal

Camp, McCreary County, Kentucky": Report 280, 1993, 276, Special Collections, University of Kentucky Libraries, Lexington, Kentucky. An additional copy is on reserve at the McCreary County Public Library. Thomas goes on to say the story was even confirmed by the late Howard Baker, the former US senator from Tennessee, who was related to John Toomey. Portions of the story are confirmed in Edward E. Barthell, "Mountain Stories," 1933, available at http://freepages.folklore.rootsweb.ancestry.com/~smokymtnman/stories/mountainstories.html, accessed June 29, 2012. The statistics concerning the company's activities in 1929 can be found in Benita J. Howell, *Folklife along the Big South Fork of the Cumberland River* (Knoxville: University of Tennessee Press, 2003), 27. The fact that Michigan lumbermen began investing their capital in properties outside the state as the forested lands began to disappear in the 1880s and 1890s is described in Harms, *Life after Lumbering: Charles Henry Hackley and the Emergence of Muskegon, Michigan*, 187; Charles Hackley's purchases of land outside of Michigan, including some in the South, are addressed in the same book, pages 222–38.

2. Howell, *Folklife along the Big South Fork of the Cumberland River*, 1, 14, 15; McBride, *Barthell Coal Camp*, 12, University of Kentucky Libraries; Robert F. Collins, *A History of the Daniel Boone National Forest, 1770–1970* (1975; Forest History Society, 2010), chap. 34, available at www.foresthistory.org/ASPNET/Publications/region/8/daniel_boone/contents.htm, accessed July 10, 2013.

3. Michael E. Birdwell, "The Stearns Company, A History, 1902–1975," prepared by the Big South Fork Scenic Recreation Area by the Upper Cumberland Institute, Tennessee Technological University, 1988, 4, 24, 25, Stearns Archive, McCreary County Museum, Stearns, Kentucky; Ralph Coghlan, "City of Stearns Became a Coal & Timber Center," *Louisville Post*, December 6, 1922, described Stearns as an "industrial monarch" who exercised his powers "benevolently." Birdwell labels Stearns a "benevolent dictator." Ronald Eller demonstrates that not all of the changes brought about by the industrialization of the region were positive. See Ronald D. Eller, *Miners, Millhands, and Mountaineers: Industrialization of the Appalachian South, 1880–1930* (Knoxville: University of Tennessee Press, 1982), xv–xxvi.

4. Eller, "The Coal Barons of the Appalachian South, 1880–1930," 197–98.

5. Ibid., for both quotations. The first quote is from page 198 and the second is from page 196.

6. Ibid., 196–98. Much of the information included in the profile of the various coal barons of the Appalachian South, included in notes 4, 5, and 6, also can be found in Eller, *Miners, Millhands, and Mountaineers*, 201–19.

7. Sources used for the profile of Louis E. Bryant include L. E. Perry, *McCreary Conquest, a Narrative History* (Whitley City, KY: L. E. Perry, 1979), 8–10; Birdwell, *Stearns Company*, 7, 23, Stearns Archive, McCreary County Museum; McBride, *Barthell Coal Camp*, 11, University of Kentucky Libraries; J. Patrick Thomas, *Lore and Legend* (Stearns, KY: J. P. Thomas, 1989), 16–17; and Frank Thomas, "Louie Bryant—A Visionary Scott Countian," *First National Bank Chronicle* 3, no. 2 (1992): 1, 2, available at www.tngenweb.org/scott/fnb_v3n2_louie_bryant.htm., accessed June 27, 2012.

8. Perry, *McCreary Conquest*, 8–10; Birdwell, *Stearns Company*, 7, 23, Stearns Archive, McCreary County Museum; McBride, *Barthell Coal Camp*, 11, University of Kentucky Libraries; Thomas, *Lore and Legend*, 16–17.

9. Samuel Perry, *South Fork Country* (Detroit: Harlo Press, 1983), 203–6. The quotation is from page 205. The pattern that often evolved for purchasing land by the agents working for coal companies, some of which led to conflict, is addressed in Eller, *Miners, Millhands and Mountaineers*, 54–58.
10. W. A. Kinne, *The Gum Tree Story* (Stearns, KY: 1929), 21–22.
11. Kinne, *Gum Tree Story*, 24–26.
12. Ibid.; the entire story involving the Troxells is quoted from Kinne's original in Perry, *South Fork Country*, 206–9; additional information is found in Birdwell, *Stearns Company*, 10; Perry, *McCreary Conquest*, 13; Amy Combs, e-mail message to author, July 4, 2012.
13. "Articles of Association, The Stearns Coal Company, Limited, 1909," Land Acquisitions Folder, Stearns Archive, McCreary County Museum, Stearns, Kentucky; McBride, *Barthell Coal Camp*, 277, University of Kentucky Libraries; Kinne, *Gum Tree Story*, 6, 7; Birdwell, *Stearns Company*, 7, Stearns Archive, McCreary County Museum; information concerning Barthell's relationship to the Stearns family is found in http://michigan.maripo.com/justus_1.htm, accessed 7/1/2012. Both Edward E. Barthell and his wife Florence were buried in Ludington's Lakeview Cemetery, not far from the resting place of Justus and Paulina Stearns. The Barthell family also owned a cottage in Ludington's Epworth Heights community.
14. Birdwell, *Stearns Company*, 25, Stearns Archive, McCreary County Museum. An additional source is Kinne, *Gum Tree Story*, 10–11.
15. McBride, *Barthell Coal Camp*, 11, University of Kentucky Libraries; coal production figures are found in Stearns Archive, McCreary County Museum, Stearns, Kentucky. More detail concerning coal production from 1903 to 1933 can be found in the appendix.
16. Perry, *McCreary Conquest*, 108. Additional information comes from Birdwell, *Stearns Company*, 89, Stearns Archive, McCreary County Museum. Eller argues the Stearns Coal and Lumber Company was the "best known example" of a company engaged in both logging and mining activities. See Eller, *Miners, Millhands, and Mountaineers*, 95.
17. Perry, *McCreary Conquest*, 108; McBride, *Barthell Coal Camp*, 276, University of Kentucky Libraries; Birdwell, *Stearns Company*, 88, 89, Stearns Archive, McCreary County Museum; Howell, *Folklife along the Big South Fork of the Cumberland River*, 72, 73.
18. Kinne, *Gum Tree Story*, 6, 7; J. R. Thompson letter, December 23, 1902, Operations, Construction K & T folder, Stearns Archive, McCreary County Museum, Stearns, Kentucky; "Kentucky & Tennessee Railway," General Information, K & T Folder, Stearns Archive, McCreary County Museum, Stearns, Kentucky; the quotation is from Coghlan, "City of Stearns Became a Coal & Timber Center," *Louisville Post*, December 6, 1922.
19. "Kentucky & Tennessee Railway," Stearns Archive, McCreary County Museum; Coghlan, "City of Stearns Became a Coal & Timber Center," *Louisville Post*, December 6, 1922; "Kentucky and Tennessee Railway, Tentative Valuation No. 860," Kentucky & Tennessee Railway Binder, Stearns Archive, McCreary County Museum, Stearns, Kentucky.
20. Elmer G. Sulzer, *Ghost Railroads of Kentucky* (Bloomington: Indiana University Press, 1998), 212; Doyle B. Inman, "In the Hills of Kentucky," *Trains* 9, no. 9 (1949): 12–13; Birdwell, *Stearns Company*, 10, 90, Stearns Archive, McCreary County Museum; Kinne, *Gum Tree Story*, 12.
21. Birdwell *Stearns Company*, 27–28, 90, Stearns Archive, McCreary County Museum; "Statement of Monies Expended by Kentucky and Tennessee Railway for Construction

from September 1, 1910 to January 1, 1913," Operations, Construction K & T Folder, Stearns Archives, McCreary County Museum, Stearns, Kentucky; Sulzer, *Ghost Railroads of Kentucky,* 213.

22. Perry, *South Fork Country,* 209–10; Kinne, *Gum Tree Story,* 5, 7, 14; Perry, *McCreary Conquest,* 15; "History of the Hotels in Stearns," General History–Stearns Folder, Stearns Archive, McCreary County Museum, Stearns, Kentucky; "Biographical Burnishings," *Stearns Co-Operator* 2, no. 5 (1916): 13.

23. Mabel Brown Ellis, "Children of the Kentucky Coal Fields," *American Child* 1, no. 4 (1920): 359, available at http://books.google.com, accessed April 29, 2013. Additional sources include Thomas, *Lore and Legend,* 6, 13; *Forty Years of Industry* (Stearns, KY: Stearns Coal and Lumber Company, 1938), this is available at multiple locations, including Special Collections, University of Kentucky Libraries, Lexington, Kentucky; the Stearns Archive, McCreary County Museum, Stearns, Kentucky; and Mason County Historical Society Archive, Ludington, Michigan; "McCreary County, Kentucky (Formed 1912)," available at http://ukcc.uky.edu/census/21147.txt, accessed July 6, 2012; Harry M. Caudill, *Night Comes to the Cumberlands* (Ashland, KY: Jesse Stuart Foundation, 2001), 131; United States Coal Commission, *Report of the United States Coal Commission,* September 22, 1923, Records of the United States Coal Commission, Reports of the Coal Commission, Jan–Sep 1923, Entry 36, Box 53, Reports of the Coal Commission E-36 L Folder, National Archives and Records Administration, College Park, Maryland. In notes and text, this will be referred to as U.S. Coal Commission Report, National Archives and Records Administration, College Park, Maryland along with a description of the specific folder location.

24. Harry M. Caudill, *Theirs Be the Power: The Moguls of Eastern Kentucky* (Chicago: University of Illinois Press, 1983), 113.

25. Lowell H. Harrison and James C. Klotter, *A New History of Kentucky* (Lexington: University Press of Kentucky, 1997), 222; William "Doc" Coffey, personal interview with author, March 27, 2012, in Stearns, Kentucky.

26. Birdwell, *Stearns Company,* 89, 90, Stearns Archive, McCreary County Museum. Birdwell identifies the water tank as being located in Stearns, but it appears as if this was situated at Barthell. Additional sources include Perry, *McCreary County Conquest,* 113; U.S. Coal Commission Report, E-36 L Folder, National Archives and Records Administration, College Park, Maryland.

27. Howell, *Folklife along the Big South Fork of the Cumberland River,* 87; McBride, *Barthell Coal Camp,* 14, 17, University of Kentucky Libraries. A 1920 study of coal-company housing located in Kentucky's Harlan County (to the east of McCreary County) provided a breakdown of the monthly rental scale in that community and demonstrated that rents established by Stearns Coal and Lumber were typical. The rental scale identified in this study showed, "The monthly rent is usually about $2 a room. Typical of the rent scale in one of the better type towns is the following: a plastered house of four rooms with electric light and garden plot rents for $8.25 per month; the same house, sealed instead of plastered, rents for $7; a box house of three rooms, rents for $6 with the lights installed; for $3 without lights; a two room house rents for $4.75." The quotation is from Ellis, "Children of the Kentucky Coal Fields," 329.

28. Perry, *McCreary Conquest,* 116; Kinne, *Gum Tree Story,* 34, 35; "History of the Hotels in Stearns," General History—Stearns Folder, Stearns Archive, McCreary County Museum, Stearns, Kentucky; *Forty Years of Industry;* Birdwell, *Stearns Company,* 92, Stearns Archive, McCreary County Museum; Articles of Incorporation, State Bank of Stearns, Private Collection of Robert E. Gable, Lexington, Kentucky; William Faricy Condee, *Coal and Culture: Opera Houses in Appalachia* (Athens: Ohio University Press, 2005), 69.
29. Eller, "The Coal Barons of the Appalachian South, 1880–1930," 202–3; additional information is found in Eller, *Miners, Millhands, and Mountaineers,* 166–68.
30. Perry, *McCreary Conquest,* 15, 114; Thomas, *Lore and Legend,* 7; "R. L. Stearns Led A Creative Life," *Pick and Powder* 1, no. 3 (1939): 3; Diary of Robert L. Stearns, May 6, 1911; August 29, 1912; May 13–21, 1914; June 26, 1917, Stearns Archive, McCreary County Museum. Robert's extensive journeys via train and ferry are reflected in a nine-day stretch from May 13 to May 21 in 1914 when he combined business travel that ended in a family vacation in Florida. He started out in Stearns on Wednesday, May 13, and then traveled to Cincinnati the next day. By Friday, May 15, he was on to Grand Rapids and then to Ludington, where he caught a ferry to Chicago, which first stopped in Milwaukee. After spending Sunday and Monday in Chicago for a series of meetings, he met his family in Cincinnati on Tuesday, spending one night, after which they all traveled to Chattanooga on Wednesday. Then it was on to Mobile for one night. On Thursday, May 21, they arrived in Pascagoula, Florida, where he spent several days with his family on a vacation. Another diary entry from April 11, 1917, reflects frustration with his extended travel requirements. "As I had no alarm clock last night, and desired to catch 2 a.m. train to Cincinnati this a.m., I sat up and read, then at 2 went to chute but train did not arrive till nearly 4."
31. Diary of Robert L. Stearns, April 11, 1912, Stearns Archive, McCreary County Museum.
32. Herman R. Lantz, *People of Coal Town* (Carbondale: Southern Illinois University Press, 1971), 90–91; additional information taken from the same book is found on pages 122–23. Apathy, which was common among miners who had no control (or believed they had no control) over their work and living conditions, is described in Ellis, "Children of the Kentucky Coal Fields," 317.
33. Perry, *McCreary Conquest,* 17; Kinne, *Gum Tree Story,* 32. After the creation of McCreary County, the company had recorded property deeds for its Kentucky property in four different courthouses. This was sometimes inconvenient if a title search had to be conducted requiring travel not only to the McCreary County Courthouse for deeds made after 1912 but also to one of the other three counties for earlier decades.
34. Birdwell, *Stearns Company,* 3, 4, Stearns Archive, McCreary County Museum; McBride, *Barthell Coal Camp,* 60–62, University of Kentucky Libraries; Howell, *Folklife along the Big South Fork of the Cumberland River,* 87. Some families living in the coalfields of Kentucky's Harlan County could supplement their diets with produce from family farms, whereas many others were unable to do so. See Ellis, "Children of the Kentucky Coal Fields," 385.
35. Robert L. Stearns Diary, May 7, 1911; April 1, 1913; the bonus system is discussed in Robert L. Stearns Diary, March 6, 1917, Stearns Archive, McCreary County Museum; Eller describes the tendency of mine workers to take off at certain times of the year in order to work on their farms, go hunting and fishing, or for other reasons. See Eller, *Miners, Millhands, and Mountaineers,* 167.

36. George Riley Tubbs, "A Doctor Goes to Work," Practitioners Folder, Stearns Archive, McCreary County Museum, Stearns, Kentucky.
37. Ibid.; Operating Rules, Stearns Coal and Lumber Company, September 1, 1922, Labor—Stearns Coal and Lumber Co. Folder, Stearns Archive, McCreary County Museum, Stearns, Kentucky; *Forty Years of Industry,* University of Kentucky Libraries; Caudill, *Night Comes to the Cumberlands,* 115; Stearns Coal Co. Ledger 1902–1904 Book B, Stearns Archive, McCreary County Museum, Stearns, Kentucky. The figure of $1.00 to $1.50 was a typical for 1920. A study of Harlan County miners from that year showed single men paid between 75 cents and $1.00 per month if they were single and $1.50 if they were married to have access to the company doctor. It appeared as if by 1938 the figure of $2.00 was more common in Kentucky. See Ellis, "Children of the Kentucky Coal Fields," 341, 342.
38. Tubbs, "A Doctor Goes to Work"; other information is found in Frank Thomas, "Medical and Dental Practice in McCreary County," General History—Stearns, Dr. Frank Thomas Folder, Stearns Archive, McCreary County Museum, Stearns, Kentucky; Stearns Coal Co. Ledger 1902–1904 Book A, Stearns Archive, McCreary County Museum; "Names of Doctors," Stearns Archive, McCreary County Museum, Stearns, Kentucky.
39. U.S. Coal Commission Report, E-36 L Folder, National Archives and Records Administration, College Park, Maryland.
40. "Dr. Mitchell Thomas," General History—Stearns, Dr. Frank Thomas Folder, Stearns Archive, McCreary County Museum. The direct quote is from Robert E. Gable, personal interview with author, July 9, 2013.
41. Thomas, *Lore and Legend,* 8; Howell, *Folklife along the Big South Fork of the Cumberland River,* 26.

Chapter 6

1. McBride, *Barthell Coal Camp,* 7, University of Kentucky Libraries; Birdwell, *Stearns Company,* 90, Stearns Archive, McCreary County Museum.
2. The description of the mine's layout comes from two primary sources. The first is from Robert E. Gable letter to author, March 4, 2013; and William "Doc" Coffey, personal interview with author. Gable, the great grandson of Justus Stearns, worked in the coal mining industry beginning in the late 1950s, and Coffey worked for Stearns Coal and Lumber for over thirty years and was heavily involved with the mapping of the company's mines. While Coffey was most familiar with the layout of the mines in the later years (1960s onward), he was very knowledgeable of the older mines and often was called upon in later years to identify the entry points of some of the older, and newer mines. Additional sources include Birdwell, *Stearns Company,* 27, Stearns Archive, McCreary County Museum; Howell, *Folklife along the Big South Fork of the Cumberland River,* 80; "Coal in Kentucky," *Stearns Co-Operator* 2, no. 5 (1916): 9; Eller, *Miners, Millhands, and Mountaineers,* 176.
3. William "Doc" Coffey, personal interview with author; additional sources include Birdwell, *Stearns Company,* 22, Stearns Archive, McCreary County Museum; Robert E. Gable, letter to author, March 4, 2013.
4. Joseph Husband, *A Year in a Coal-Mine* (New York: Arno Press, 1977), 9.

5. Ibid., 14.
6. Ibid., 18–19; the quotation is from Birdwell, *Stearns Company,* 27, Stearns Archive, McCreary County Museum; Howell, *Folklife along the Big South Fork of the Cumberland River,* 80–81.
7. Husband, *A Year in a Coal-Mine,* 39; Howell, *Folklife along the Big South Fork of the Cumberland River,* 80–81; William "Doc" Coffey, personal interview with author.
8. *Operating Rules,* Stearns Coal and Lumber Company, 1922, Stearns Archive, McCreary County Museum.
9. Husband, *A Year in a Coal-Mine,* 20–22.
10. Ibid., 24–25; William "Doc" Coffey, personal interview with author; Operating Rules, Stearns Coal and Lumber Company, 1922, Stearns Archive, McCreary County Museum. A good, concise description of a tipple and its operation is found in Howell, *Folklife along the Big South Fork of the Cumberland River,* 82; "Coal in Kentucky," 9.
11. *Forty Years of Industry,* University of Kentucky Libraries; Operating Rules, Stearns Coal and Lumber Company, 1922, Stearns Archive, McCreary County Museum; Perry, *McCreary Conquest,* 113; U.S. Coal Commission Report, E-36 L Folder, National Archives and Records Administration, College Park, Maryland; U.S. Department of the Interior, directed by Rear Admiral Joel Boone, *A Medical Survey of the Bituminous-Coal Industry,* Report of the Coal Mines Administration (Washington, DC: Government Printing Office, 1947), 52–58. In notes, this will be referred to as Boone Report.
12. Information concerning wages can be found in Wage Scale Adopted at Stearns Mines Feby. 19/1908, and In Force May 18, 1909, Labor—Stearns Coal and Lumber, Stearns Archive, McCreary County Museum; *Operating Rules,* Stearns Coal and Lumber Company, 1922, Stearns Archive, McCreary County Museum; William "Doc" Coffey, personal interview with author. The wage scale put into place in 1909 for those working in Mines 1 and 2 called for miners working seams between 30 to 33 inches received 62.5 cents per ton; between 33 to 36 inches received 60 cents per ton; between 36 to 42 inches received 55 cents per ton; between 42 and 48 inches received 52.5 cents per ton. Eller argues that while wages varied greatly for coal miners working in Southern Appalachia, in general, miners working in this region of the country "lagged behind those of the rest of the nation." See Eller, *Miners, Millhands, and Mountaineers,* 176.
13. Wage Scale Adopted at Stearns Mines Feby. 19/1908, and In Force May 18, 1909, Labor—Stearns Coal and Lumber, Stearns Archive, McCreary County Museum; *Operating Rules,* Stearns Coal and Lumber Company, 1922, Stearns Archive, McCreary County Museum; William "Doc" Coffey, personal interview with author. Company records indicate that by the mid-1920s average weekly wages for miners working in many different positions was $25, although machine runners often earned $30, while a locomotive engineer earned $50. See Records of Accidents of all Employees of Stearns Coal and Lumber Co. and all Allied Interests, Commencing January 1, 1924 to March 7, 1928, Stearns Archive, McCreary County Museum.
14. U.S. Coal Commission Report, E-36 M Folder, National Archives and Records Administration, College Park, Maryland.
15. Fran Maierhauser, "They Printed Their Own Money . . . and Got Away with It!" *Rural Kentuckian Magazine,* November 1975, 14, available at Stearns Archive, McCreary County

Museum; a diary entry from Robert L. Stearns indicates the company began to issue coupon books in October 1914. The entry specifically reads, "Coupon books substituted for brass checks today at all mines." Robert L. Stearns Diary, October 1, 1914, Stearns Archive, McCreary County Museum.

16. The "elevated prices" quote is from Perry, *McCreary Conquest,* 124, 125. Perry argues that the Stearns Company established elevated prices, which were copied by outside wholesalers who used the opportunity to "make huge profits by ripping off other consumers" in the region. Additional sources include "Biographical Burnishings," 13; U.S. Coal Commission Report, E-36 L Folder, National Archives and Records Administration, College Park, Maryland; Howell, *Folklife along the Big South Fork of the Cumberland River,* 87; Boone Report, 215–17. The higher prices at company stores were typical throughout the industry. See Eller, *Miners, Millhands, and Mountaineers,* 188.

17. Crandall A. Shifflett, *Coal Towns: Life, Work, and Culture in Company Towns of Southern Appalachia, 1880–1960* (Knoxville: University of Tennessee Press, 1991), 179–83. Concerning the issuance of scrip, Shifflett argued on pages 182–83 that, "If the operators intended to entrap miners in a web of debt through the scrip system, miners seem to have thwarted them by using it judiciously. Admittedly, it would have been easy to have become overextended, and some did, because the coal companies encouraged easy credit. . . . Scrip was like today's credit card; it did not seem to be like money." At least in the towns he studied, "miners recognized the inherent dangers." He continued by declaring, "In spite of the miners of legend who 'owed their souls,' evidence suggests that 'debt peonage,' was rare at the company stores. An analysis of the records of the Stonega Company, for example, found that outstanding debts at the company stores averaged less than 2 percent of sales between 1910 and 1947." Additional sources include Maierhauser, "They Printed Their Own Money . . . and Got Away with It!," 14; the story of the stolen coupon books and arson is chronicled in Robert L. Stearns Diary, September 23, 25, 27; October 23; and December 10, 1928, Stearns Archive, McCreary County Museum; Boone Report, 217–18.

18. *Operating Rules,* Stearns Coal and Lumber Company, 1922, Stearns Archive, McCreary County Museum; *Forty Years of Industry,* University of Kentucky Libraries.

19. McBride, *Barthell Coal Camp,* 41, 42, 295, 297, University of Kentucky Libraries.

20. Ibid., 41–43, 296–98. It appears that women are underrepresented in these statistics. The percentages discussed include several occupations, such as "Miner," "Laborer," "Blacksmith," and such. While the typically female occupations of "Cook," "Maid," and "Laundress" are included, "Homemaker" is not identified as an occupation. Therefore, women who stayed home to take care of their house and raise children were not included in these statistics.

21. Caudill, *Night Comes to the Cumberlands,* 103–6; Harrison, *A New History of Kentucky,* 344; Paul Boyer, *The Enduring Vision* (Boston: Wadsworth, Cengage Learning, 2013), 450; U.S. Coal Commission Report, E-36 L Folder, National Archives and Records Administration, College Park, Maryland.

22. *Forty Years of Industry,* University of Kentucky Libraries.

23. Eller, *Miners, Millhands, and Mountaineers,* 172. The entry for the $2 charitable donation can be found in Stearns Coal Co. Ledger 1902–1904 Book A, and the entry for 50 cents is found in Stearns Coal Co. Ledger Book B, both are located in Stearns Archive, McCreary County Museum.

24. In the "Remark" section of the workman's compensation record for Ralph McAdoo was the word, "Nigger." This can be found in Records of Accidents of all Employees of Stearns Coal and Lumber Co. and all Allied Interests, Commencing January 1, 1924 to March 7, 1928, Stearns Archive, McCreary County Museum. Another entry involving John Simpson demonstrated McAdoo's treatment was not isolated. Simpson received a bruised finger while working as a driver (probably a mule driver) in Mine #1 January 19, 1925. In the "Remark" column for his entry, the word "Negro" was written. His weekly wages averaged $16.54 and he received $10.75 in compensation for each week lost for a total of $17.14. Other employees earning the same weekly wages were compensated at the same rate.
25. U.S. Coal Commission Report, E-36 Folder, National Archives and Records Administration, College Park, Maryland.
26. Boone Report, 110.
27. McBride, *Barthell Coal Camp*, 49, University of Kentucky Libraries. Other sources recognizing the Stearns Company's safety record include Perry, *McCreary Conquest*, 117; Birdwell, *Stearns Company*, 9, 26, Stearns Archive, McCreary County Museum; and Howell, *Folklife along the Big South Fork of the Cumberland River*, argues on page 83, "coal mines in the Big South Fork area have had relatively good safety records."
28. Birdwell, *Stearns Company*, 9, 26, Stearns Archive, McCreary County Museum; Thomas, *Lore and Legend*, 7.
29. U.S. Coal Commission Report, E-36 Folder, National Archives and Records Administration, College Park, Maryland.
30. The "snowbird" quotation is from Eller, *Miners, Millhands, and Mountaineers*, 154; "Coal in Kentucky," 7; U.S. Coal Commission Report, E-36 M Folder, National Archives and Records Administration, College Park, Maryland.
31. U.S. Coal Commission Report, E-36 M Folder, National Archives and Records Administration, College Park, Maryland.
32. Special Mine Rules, Stearns Coal and Lumber Company, Stearns Co-Operative Coal Company, 2-28-22, Labor—Stearns Coal and Lumber Co. Folder, Stearns Archive, McCreary County Museum.
33. Ibid.
34. Perry, *McCreary Conquest*, 116, 117.
35. "Disaster," available at http://kyknfolk.com/mccreary/coalmining/coalmining.htm, accessed June 11, 2012. The incident was also covered in Michigan, as seen with "Explosion Kills Six," *Grand Rapids Press*, 1, February 9, 1910.
36. "Stearns Coal & Lumber Co. v. Tuggle," *The Southwestern Reporter, Containing All the Current Decisions of the Supreme and Appellate Courts of Arkansas, Kentucky, Missouri, Tennessee, and Texas*, vol. 164 (St. Paul: West Publishing, 1914), 75, available at http://googlebooks.com/, accessed May 23, 2011.
37. Ibid.
38. Ibid.
39. The workmen's compensation law is mentioned in Lowell H. Harrison, *Kentucky's Governors* (Lexington: University Press of Kentucky, 2004), 107, 109. The list of injuries is taken from The Records of Accidents of all Employees of Stearns Coal and Lumber Co.

and all Allied Interests, Stearns Archive, McCreary County Museum; Coghlan, "City of Stearns Became a Coal and Timber Center," *Louisville Post*, December 6, 1922.

40. The Records of Accidents of all Employees of Stearns Coal and Lumber Co. and all Allied Interests, Stearns Archive, McCreary County Museum.

41. Ibid.

42. Robert L. Stearns Diary, September 21, 1916, Stearns Archive, McCreary County Museum.

43. "Lewis M. Jones," Stearns Coal and Lumber Company Employee Records, Stearns Archive, McCreary County Museum; McBride, *Barthell Coal Camp*, 242, 243, University of Kentucky Libraries.

Chapter 7

1. The history of the United Mine Workers of America is chronicled in McAlister Coleman, *Men and Coal* (New York: Arno and the New York Times, 1969), 54–74. Additional information is taken from Harrison, *A New History of Kentucky*, 365–66.

2. Eller, "The Coal Barons of the Appalachian South, 1880–1930," 201.

3. The quotation describing Rockefeller's views concerning unions is found in Ron Chernow, *Titan: The Life of John D. Rockefeller, Sr.* (New York: Random House, 1998), 574. Other sources include "On and Off the Payroll," *Stearns Co-Operator* 2, no. 2 (1916): 3–4, 12–13. Another antiunion story is included in "Getting His Goat," *Stearns Co-Operator* 2, no. 3 (1916): 3–4. This describes an employee of the Federation of Labor with a "cushy" job who becomes a tool for the unions, and he is only concerned about his paycheck.

4. Robert L. Stearns Diary, September 21, 1916, Stearns Archive, McCreary County Museum.

5. Howell, *Folklife along the Big South Fork of the Cumberland River*, 76; *Operating Rules*, Stearns Coal and Lumber Company, 1922, Stearns Archive, McCreary County Museum. Stearns's desire to have total control over his workforce is reminiscent of the attitude of the lumberman Henry Sage who was strongly opposed to the unionization of the workforce at his mills. For many years he also served as a member of the board of trustees at Cornell University. When conflict developed between the faculty and trustees at the university, Sage wrote a colleague that all the faculty should be fired. The trustees then would rehire "only those we know we can work with." See Goodstein, *Biography of a Businessman*, 23, 235.

6. Robert L. Stearns Diary, January 8, 1915; February 13, 1915; March 1, 1915; June 13, 1912; May 7, 1911, Stearns Archive, McCreary County Museum.

7. U.S. Coal Commission Report E-36 M Folder; U.S. Coal Commission Report E-36 Q Folder, National Archives and Records Administration, College Park, Maryland.

8. John W. Hevener, *Which Side Are You On? The Harlan County Coal Miners, 1931–39* (Chicago: University of Illinois Press, 2002), 10, 20; Harrison and Klotter, *A New History of Kentucky*, 366.

9. Edwin P. Morrow Letter to James A. Finch, December 26, 1913, File 28-189, Berry Simpson, Pardon Case Files, 1853–1946, Box 652, Records of the Office of the Pardon Attorney, Record Group 204–230/39/45/02, National Archives and Records Administration, Washington, DC (this set of files will hereinafter be referred to as Berry Simpson, Pardon Case Files); Kinney, *Gum Tree Story*, 27–30.

10. *Bill of Evidence and Exception, Volume I, Plaintiff's Witnesses,* 64, 65, Law and Equity Cases 1910–1911, Case No. 115 (part), Box 20, Record Group 21, U.S. Circuit Court, Eastern District of Kentucky, Richmond Term, National Archives and Records Administration, Atlanta, Georgia (this set of files will hereinafter be referred to as *Bill of Evidence and Exception, Volume I, Plaintiff's Witnesses*). W. A. Kinne later testified that on another occasion, when Berry Simpson was angry, he heard Simpson declare, "Bob Stearns; the God damn son-of-a-bitch is to blame for the whole thing . . . J. E. Butler! The biggest liar that ever came to this country," and, "I will kill the damn son of a bitch," and, "God damn cock-sucking sons-of-bitches! I will drive every one of them out." The testimony from Kinne can be found in, *Bill of Evidence and Exception, Volume I, Plaintiff's Witnesses,* 109.
11. *Bill of Evidence and Exception, Volume I, Plaintiff's Witnesses,* 43–55, 64–66. Additional information is found in James A. Finch Letter to James C. McReynolds, March 4, 1914, Jurors' Petition to President Woodrow Wilson, January, 1913 and Edwin P. Morrow Letter to James A Finch, December 26, 1913, each is from Berry Simpson Pardon Case Files, National Archives and Records Administration, Washington, DC. The quotations are taken from the Jurors' Petition, which includes a detailed history of events.
12. McBride, *Barthell Coal Camp,* 230, University of Kentucky Libraries. The description of the men drinking and walking into town is found in Jurors' Petition to President Woodrow Wilson, January, 1913, Berry Simpson Pardon Case Files, National Archives and Records Administration, Washington, DC. Contemporary news accounts used include "Soldiers Arrive to Arrest Miners," *New York Times,* December 27, 1908, available at http://select.nytimes.com, accessed October 26, 2010. "Stearns Is a City of 1500 Inhabitants," *Winchester News,* January 2, 1909, 2; "State Troops Go to Stearns Camp," "Excitement Is Intense," *San Francisco Call,* December 27, 1908, 46, each is available online at http://chroniclingamerica.loc.gov, accessed July 3, 2012. Secondary sources describing the events of 1908 include Perry, *McCreary Conquest,* 109; Birdwell, *Stearns Company,* 12, Stearns Archive, McCreary County Museum; Howell, *Folklife along the Big South Fork of the Cumberland River,* 88; Kinne, *Gum Tree Story,* 27–28. Most, but not all, of the newspaper articles identify Officer Mullins's first name as William. All of the government documents associated with the case identify his name as John, including petitions signed by what appeared to be members of the Mullins family; therefore, Officer Mullins's first name is identified in the text as John.
13. *Bill of Evidence and Exception, Volume I, Plaintiff's Witnesses,* 196. Both Kinne and Ebling testified that Massingale wanted to use dynamite to blow up the hotel. Kinne testified that Massingale declared, "We are going to burn the hotel. . . . This is a government affair and you haven't got anything to do with it; a man has been killed and I am a Government officer, and I am in charge here." He then asked for paper and rags to start a fire. Their testimony can be found in *Bill of Evidence and Exception, Volume I, Plaintiff's Witnesses,* 196–98, 105. Lula Simpson's description of her escape from the hotel can be found in *Bill of Evidence and Exception, Volume II, Defendants' Witnesses,* 734, 749–52, Law and Equity Cases 1910–1911, Case No. 115 (part), Box 20, Record Group 21, U.S. Circuit Court, Eastern District of Kentucky, Richmond Term, National Archives and Records Administration, Atlanta, Georgia (this set of files will hereinafter be referred to as *Bill of Evidence and Exception, Volume II, Defendants' Witnesses*).

14. Interview with Robert E. Gable, July 31, 2012. A similar quote is found in Birdwell, *Stearns Company,* 12, Stearns Archive, McCreary County Museum. The story also appears in Caudill, *Theirs Be the Power,* 113, but the author confuses Robert and Justus Stearns. Caudill contends that Stearns "ordered his building torched so they [miners holed up in the Stearns Hotel] could be shot as they fled the flames." Thomas, *Lore and Legend,* 8, argues that J. E. Butler received a wire from Ludington (presumably from Justus) with instructions to torch the hotel. An additional source comes from testimony offered by W. A. Kinne and is found in *Bill of Evidence and Exception, Volume I, Plaintiff's Witnesses,* 93–103.

15. By piecing together secondary sources, government documents, and contemporary newspaper accounts, it appeared as if the oral account Gerald West offered included some minor mistakes covering details involving men other than his father. He reported George Stanley had been killed, rather than Rich Ross, and believed Elisha Slaven escaped wrapped in a carpet. George Stanley was not present in the hotel at that time but later was arrested and convicted for his involvement in the conspiracy. It appeared as if Slaven tried to escape by wrapping himself in a carpet, but was apprehended that day. The quotation, including West's account, can be found in McBride, *Barthell Coal Camp,* 230, University of Kentucky Libraries. Additional sources include "Ross Also Buried," *Winchester News,* December 28, 1908, 1; June 23, 2012, each is available at http://chroniclingamerica.loc.gov, accessed June 23, 2012; Perry, *McCreary Conquest,* 110; Jurors Petition to President Woodrow Wilson, January, 1913, Berry Simpson, Pardon Case Files, National Archives and Records Administration, Washington, DC.

16. McBride, *Barthell Coal Camp,* 230, University of Kentucky Libraries; Howell, *Folklife along the Big South Fork of the Cumberland River,* 89.

17. "Mountaineers Defy Soldiers Sent to Fight," *San Francisco Call,* December 28, 1908, 1; "Quiet Prevails in Stearns, Some Soldiers Ordered Home," *Winchester News,* December 28, 1908, 1; "Martial Law at Stearns," *Paducah Evening Sun,* December 28, 1908, 1; "Desperado Sends Word to Officers," *Winchester News,* December 29, 1908, 1; "Hello Gov., This Is Berry Simpson," *Bourbon News,* January 1, 1909, 5; "Surrenders to Officers," *Winchester News,* April 5, 1909, 6; "Berry Simpson Surrenders," *Bourbon News,* April 9, 1909, 2; "Gives Up," *Mount Vernon Signal,* April 16, 1909, 4, each is available at http://chroniclingamerica.loc.gov, accessed June 23, 2012.

18. "Berry Simpson on Trial," *Richmond Climax,* July 14, 1909, 5; "President Pardons Berry Simpson," *Interior Journal,* April 3, 1914, 1, each is available at http://chroniclingamerica.loc.gov, accessed June 23, 2012; "Davison, George Mosby," Biographical Directory of the United States Congress, available at http://bioguide.congress.gov, accessed August 26, 2012; Melba Porter Hay, "Edwin Porch Morrow," in *Kentucky's Governors,* ed. H. Harrison Lowell (Lexington: University Press of Kentucky, 2004), 152–53.

19. The quotation, "killing any officer who attempted to arrest him," is from James A. Finch Letter to James C. McReynolds, March 4, 1914, Berry Simpson Pardon Case Files, National Archives and Records Administration, Washington, DC; "Hundred Witnesses on Hand," *The Bee,* July 15, 1909, 2; "Stearns Murderers," *Daily Public Ledger,* July 19, 1909, 1; "Ten Years Is the Period Added to Life Imprisonment for Three Men," *Marion Daily Mirror,* July 20, 1909, 1; the quotation "stubbornly fought" is from "Berry Simpson

Convicted," *Richmond Climax,* July 21, 1909, 5; "Kentucky Kernels," *Hazel Green Herald,* July 22, 1909, 3; the phrase "pathetic scene" is found in "Taken to Atlanta Jail," *Mt. Sterling Advocate,* July 28, 1909, 1, each is available at http://chroniclingamerica.loc.gov, accessed June 25, 2012.

20. W. A. Kinne Letter to Edwin P. Morrow, November 20, 1913, Berry Simpson Pardon Case Files, National Archives and Records Administration, Washington, DC. Other sources used include W. A. Kinne Letter to President Woodrow Wilson, November 21, 1913, Berry Simpson Pardon Case Files, National Archives and Records Administration, Washington, DC. There is no record that either Justus or Robert Stearns actually visited President Wilson at the White House. But the following sources indicate at least one of the men made the trip in secret. These sources are Howell, *Folklife along the Big South Fork of the Cumberland River,* 88; Perry, *McCreary Conquest,* 110, 111.

21. Edwin P. Morrow Letter to James A. Finch, December 26, 1913, Berry Simpson Pardon Case Files, National Archives and Records Administration, Washington, DC. Other sources used include Robert L. Stearns Diary, September 3, 1912; September 14, 1912; April 13, 1914; December 31, 1914; February 28, 1915; July 3, 1915; June 25, 1927; March 2, 1929, Stearns Archive, McCreary County Museum; Hay, "Edwin Porch Morrow" in Harrison, *Kentucky's Governors,* 153.

22. Numerous letters of support and opposition are seen in the Berry Simpson Pardon Case Files. Senators John K. Shields (TN), John H. Bankhead (AL), and W. O. Bradley (KY) wrote letters in support of a pardon as well as Congressman A. O. Stanley from Kentucky. It is unclear why Bankhead became involved, but Berry Simpson had been born in Alabama. In addition to being a member of the US Senate in 1913, Bradley was a former governor of Kentucky and Edwin Morrow's uncle. Stanley later would serve one term as Kentucky's governor. The quotations are taken from T. R. Mullins Letter to President Woodrow Wilson, April 9, 1913, Berry Simpson Pardon Case Files, National Archives and Records Administration, Washington, DC. Other sources used include "Here and There," *Mount Vernon Signal,* December 19, 1913, 2; "President Pardons Berry Simpson," *Interior Journal,* April 3, 1914, 1, each is available at http://chroniclingamerica.loc.gov, accessed June 25, 2012.

23. The quotations are from Robert L. Stearns Diary, August 12, 1911; February 1, 1913, Stearns Archive, McCreary County Museum. Additional sources include George Stanley Letter to Frank Rogers, April 22, 1913, Monthly Parole Report of Paroled Prisoner to the Warden, May 1, 1913, and July 1, 1915, all of which can be found in George Stanley, Inmate No. 2627 Folder #2, Record Group 129, U.S. Bureau of Prison, Atlanta Federal Penitentiary Inmate Case Files 1899–1921 ACC No. 129–62–0269, Box #122, National Archives and Records Administration, Atlanta, Georgia (this set of files will hereinafter be referred to as George Stanley Inmate Files). The National Archives in Atlanta contains information about the inmates who served at the prison. Zina Rhone, an archival technician at the NARA facility, located information on several of the men involved in the events of 1908 who were convicted. Zina Rhone, e-mail message to author, September 4, 2012; Amy Combs, e-mail message to author, September 18, 2012. Another example of the good will that later developed between Stearns Company officials and those initially involved in the union organizing involved Oliver Slaven, who originally had been sentenced to five years in prison. After he was paroled in August 1911, Slaven later worked for the Stearns Coal and Lumber Company. In a letter from Ida Cayas, an employee of the Stearns Company, Slaven was described as a "good citizen" following his return to Stearns after his release from prison. He also later served as a local deputy sheriff until he was killed in the line of duty in the spring of 1920. Ms. Cayas, using Stearns Company letterhead, made a request on behalf of Slaven's family for a photo of Mr. Slaven. See Ida Cayas Letter to Warden, Federal Prison, Atlanta, Ga., August 20, 1920, Oliver Stanley, Inmate No. 2624 Folder, Record Group 129, U.S. Bureau of Prison, Atlanta Federal Penitentiary Inmate Case Files 1899–1921 ACC No. 129–62–0269, Box #121, National Archives and Records Administration, Atlanta, Georgia.

24. Robert L. Stearns Diary, February 19, 1913, Stearns Archive, McCreary County Museum.

25. Howell, *Folklife along the Big South Fork of the Cumberland River,* 89.

26. Perry, *McCreary Conquest,* 117.

27. "Coal in Kentucky," 7, 9. The article states the company had four mines in operation in 1916, but other production records at the Stearns Archive indicated there were six. This difference in reporting is likely due to the relatively small amount of coal produced from Mine #2 and Mine A that year. See Appendix B for specific detail concerning the amount of coal produced at each mine. While company officials estimated they would produce 650,000 tons, only about 587,873 tons actually were produced in 1916.

28. "Biographical Burnishings," 11; Cosulich, "R. L. Stearns Is 'The Mark Twain of Art,'" 1; Pooler, "Ludington Millionaire Found Release in Art." A sample of some entries concerning Robert Stearns's painting can be found in Robert L. Stearns Diary, April 22, 1912; January 24, 1914; April 5, 1917. Stearns's health problems can be found in Robert L. Stearns Diary, February 9, 1914; February 17–March 6, 1917 (this is one entry). Information about the Battle Creek Sanitarium is found in Dunbar and May, *Michigan: A History of the Wolverine State,* 397–98; and the quotations from his stay at the "San" are found in entries from Robert L. Stearns Diary, April 14, 1917–April 24, 1917, Stearns Archive, McCreary County Museum.

29. Robert L. Stearns Diary, June 30, 1917; August 8, 1917, Stearns Archive, McCreary County Museum; an entry on September 1, 1917, demonstrates how complicated his working days had become; Caudill, *Theirs Be the Power,* 113; "Stearns, Robert Lyon," *National Cyclopedia of American Biography,* 473; Kinne, *Gum Tree Story,* 33.

30. Robert L. Stearns Diary, November 27, 1917; December 5, 1917, Stearns Archive, McCreary County Museum.

31. Ibid.

32. Ibid., March 21, 1911; July 2, 1914; February 25, 1912.

33. The quotation concerning his time with the boys is taken from Robert L. Stearns Diary, June 11, 1912; Freeman's birthday is January 2, 1914; the description of the play is found August 29, 1913, Stearns Archive, McCreary County Museum.

34. Robert L. Stearns Diary, prior to the entry for January 1, 1913, Stearns Archive, McCreary County Museum.

35. Robert L. Stearns, *The Ass and the Barnacles* (Stearns, KY: Stearns Coal and Lumber Company, 1921). Stearns mentioned his lack of a hobby, or interest in golf or vacations, when

interviewed by the *Ludington Daily News* in 1926. The full article can be found in "Pays Tribute to J. S. Stearns, Foremost Citizen Of City," *Ludington Daily News,* August 9, 1926.
36. McBride, *Barthell Coal Camp,* 11, University of Kentucky Libraries; Robert L. Stearns Diary, April 11, 1911; April 12, 1911; September 20, 1911, September 22, 1911, Stearns Archive, McCreary County Museum; Kinne, *Gum Tree Story,* 34.
37. Kinne, *Gum Tree Story,* 34; Robert L. Stearns Diary, March 5, 1911; April 2, 1911, Stearns Archive, McCreary County Museum; McBride, *Barthell Coal Camp,* 7, 11, University of Kentucky Libraries.
38. Kinne, *Gum Tree Story,* 34.
39. Ibid., 35. The retail coal yards were Whiteside-Stearns Coal Company, Chattanooga, Tennessee (1922); Stearns Coal Company, Atlanta, Georgia (1924); Stearns Coal Company, Louisville, Kentucky (1925); Stearns Coal and Lumber Company, Fort Wayne, Indiana (1927); and Stearns-Kelly Coal Company, Frankfort, Kentucky (1928). Information concerning the retail coal yards is found in *Minutes of the Board of Directors Meetings of the Stearns Coal and Lumber Company, Vol. I, January 18, 1928 through December 2, 1935,* 2, 3, 4, 6, 20, Private Collection of Robert E. Gable, Lexington, Kentucky.
40. Harrison, *A New History of Kentucky,* 366; Howell, *Folklife along the Big South Fork of the Cumberland River,* 89.

Chapter 8

1. The announcement that Stearns had purchased the electric plant is found in "Electric Light Plant, Property Was Sold Yesterday by Frank Filer to Hon. J. S. Stearns," *Ludington Record,* February 7, 1901. The quotation is from "Waste Not Known," *Grand Rapids Press,* August 14, 1911, 11. Additional information is found in "Stearns Industries," Scrapbook 201, Mason County Historical Society Archive, Ludington, Michigan; *Ludington, Gateway of the Northwest* (Ludington, MI: Record-Appeal, ca. 1908), Business Advertisement Folder, Mason County District Library, Ludington Branch, Local History Special Collection; "Electric Light Plant, Negotiations in Progress to Sell the Property to Hon. J. S. Stearns," *Ludington Record,* January 10, 1901; "One of the Best," *Ludington Chronicle,* September 7, 1901; "Electric Lights for Scottville," *Ludington Record-Appeal,* November 28, 1901; "Electricity on the Farm," *Ludington Record-Appeal,* December 5, 1901; "Will Double Their Capacity," *Ludington Chronicle,* July 6, 1904; Place Big Order, *Ludington Chronicle,* May 6, 1908.
2. The statistics concerning the company's receipts and profits are found in Report of the Stearns Lighting and Power Company Year-Ending-December 31, 1916, Stearns Salt and Lumber Company Records, 1881–1923, Box 3, Stearns Lighting and Power Company, Ludington Folder, Bentley Historical Library, Ann Arbor, Michigan; "Bubble Burst," *Ludington Chronicle,* May 17, 1911. The quotation is from the *Ludington Chronicle,* October 16, 1901.
3. The quotations and company statistics are from Report of the Stearns Lighting and Power Company Year-Ending-December 31, 1916, Stearns Salt and Lumber Company Records, 1881–1923, Box 3, Stearns Lighting and Power Company, Ludington Folder, Bentley Historical Library, Ann Arbor, Michigan. Additional information is from "Are

in Earnest about It," *Ludington Chronicle,* March 15, 1905; "Electric Cooking Exhibit," *Ludington Chronicle,* April 5, 1905.

4. "In Fifty Rooms," *Ludington Chronicle,* December 24, 1902. Other sources include "Stearns' New $25,000 Hotel," *Ludington Record-Appeal,* October 24, 1901; "Is a Sure Thing," *Ludington Chronicle,* October 26, 1901; "Things Are Coming Our Way," *Ludington Chronicle,* October 26, 1901; "Location Decided," *Ludington Chronicle,* November 9, 1901; "At the New Hotel," *Ludington Record-Appeal,* March 4, 1903; *Ludington Chronicle,* July 8, 1903. Information concerning the temperance movement outside of Ludington can be found in Harms, *Life after Lumbering: Charles Henry Hackley and the Emergence of Muskegon, Michigan,* 285; and Kilar, *Michigan's Lumbertowns,* 152, 153.

5. The first guests stayed overnight at the hotel the week of July 15, 1903, according to the *Ludington Chronicle,* July 15, 1903. Other sources include Peterson, *Story of Ludington,* 107; "Opening of The Stearns," *Ludington Chronicle,* August 12, 1903; "Bath House Plans Accepted," *Ludington Chronicle,* June 17, 1903. The Stearns bath house was torn down about 1953 and is described in "Stearns Office Building, Erected 50 Years Ago as Bath House, Wrecked," *Ludington Daily News,* February 27, 1953; *Ludington Chronicle,* October 10, 1906, related that Stearns would spend that year's winter at the hotel. Other sources include "Addition Complete at Stearns Hotel," *Ludington Daily News,* May 27, 1923; and the quotation is from "New Addition to Stearns Hotel," *Ludington Daily News,* March 19, 1922.

6. Haskell originally founded the Ludington Novelty Works in 1889 and eventually absorbed the Archarena Company of Peoria, Illinois, after which it became known as the Carrom Archarena Company. The first quotation is from "Ludington, Michigan as a Place to Live and a Place to do Business," ca. 1904, Ludington, City of Box, Ludington, City of Citizens Ass. Brochure T. M. Sawyer, Sec. Tourism Folder, Mason County Historical Society Archive, Ludington, Michigan. Other sources include "The Carrom Company," *Stearns Co-Operator* 1, no. 8 (1915): 12; Lenore P. Williams, "Industry on Parade: Carrom Industries, from Lumber to Game Boards," *Ludington Daily News,* December 22, 1952; "Carrom History Described in Speech by Lee Smith," *Ludington Daily News,* April 19, 1958; "Annual Reports," *Ludington Chronicle,* May 11, 1910; Carrom-Archarena Company Sales 1912, Stearns Salt and Lumber Company Records, 1881–1923, Box 1, Carrom-Archarena Folder, Bentley Historical Library, Ann Arbor, Michigan; Peterson, *Story of Ludington,* 77; James L. Cabot, "Henry Haskell—Local Inventor," *Ludington Daily News,* January 7, 1989. The "thriving and profitable industry" quotation is from Justus Stearns letter to William Stearns, March 27, 1930, Mason County Historical Society Archive.

7. "The Handy Things Mfg. Co.," *Stearns Co-Operator* 1, no. 8 (1915): 12; Peterson, *Story of Ludington,* 77; "Fate Decided," *Ludington Chronicle,* November 1, 1911; "Products of Handy Things Co. Find Their Way 'Round World, in Business for 26 Years," *Ludington Daily News,* January 13, 1937; "Ludington, Michigan as a Place to Live and a Place to do Business," ca. 1904, Ludington, City of Box, Ludington, City of Citizens Ass. Brochure T. M. Sawyer, Sec. Tourism Folder, Mason County Historical Society Archive, Ludington, Michigan; Handy Things Manufacturing Company Year-End Report, 1912, Stearns Salt and Lumber Company Records, 1881–1923, Box 1, Handy-Things Manufacturing

Company Folder, Bentley Historical Library, Ann Arbor, Michigan; Kilar, *Michigan's Lumbertowns,* 155–58.

8. "Stearns Contribution to City's Prosperity," *Ludington Chronicle,* July 17, 1907. Other sources include "Stearns Salt and Lumber Company," *Stearns Co-Operator* 1, no. 8 (1915): 7. Several annual reports describing the organization and capital stock included in the company were published in the *Ludington Chronicle.* The article for 1905 can be found in "Annual Reports," *Ludington Chronicle,* April 19, 1905. The "splendidly prepared" quotation is from "Stearns Plants Do Big Business," *Michigan Manufacturer and Financial Record* 15, no. 1 (1915): 15, available at http://googlebooks.com/, accessed November 7, 2011.

9. "Outlook Is Very Bright," *Ludington Record-Appeal,* December 10, 1903, available at http://news.google.com/newspapers, accessed December 4, 2012; "Lumber Cut 1907," *Ludington Chronicle,* March 18, 1907; "Stearns Unique Logging Camp," *Ludington Chronicle,* November 7, 1906.

10. "Feeding Men in Lumber Camps," *Ludington Chronicle,* January 21, 1915, available at http://news.google.com/newspapers, accessed December 4, 2012. The average of forty-four carloads of logs each day is mentioned in the *Ludington Chronicle,* June 17, 1908.

11. "Stearns Salt and Lumber Company," *Stearns Co-Operator* 1, no. 8 (1915): 7; "Hear Lectures," *Ludington Chronicle,* December 31, 1913.

12. The Stearns Salt and Lumber Company Statements for the Year 1910 and 1911, Stearns Salt and Lumber Company Records, 1881–1923, Box 3, Stearns Company Miscellaneous Folder, Bentley Historical Library, Ann Arbor, Michigan.

13. "Gave Rebates to Stearns Co.," *Detroit Free Press,* December 20, 1907, 6, available at http://proquest.com, accessed May 17, 2011; *Ludington Chronicle,* December 25, 1907, available at http://news.google.com/newspapers, accessed February 21, 2013; "Reformer Stearns Took Rebates," *Detroit Free Press,* March 26, 1908, 4, available at http://proquest.com, accessed May 17, 2011. The second quotation is from "Stearns Company Is Fined $20,000," *Grand Rapids Press,* April 9, 1908, 1.

14. "Stearns Company Fined $20,000 for Rebating," *Detroit Free Press,* April 9, 1908, 10, 6, available at http://proquest.com, accessed May 17, 2011; "To Fight $20,000 Fine," *Detroit Free Press,* April 29, 1908, 7, available at http://proquest.com, accessed May 17, 2011. Paperwork associated with the federal indictment, including the indictment itself, and correspondence between Stearns Salt and Lumber Company employees and their attorneys can be found in Stearns Salt and Lumber Company Records, 1881–1923, Box 3, Stearns–Pere Marquette Federal Indictment Folder, Bentley Historical Library, Ann Arbor, Michigan. Key sources and correspondence in this folder include Receipt for $10,000 from the District Court of the United States for the Western District of Michigan, Southern Division dated January 11, 1909; Victor Gore letter to W. T. Culver, September 26, 1906; Victor Gore letter to Stearns Salt and Lumber Co., November 14, 1908; C. M. Letter to Victor Gore, November 17, 1908; Kleinhans and Klappen letter to Stearns Salt and Lumber Co., November 21, 1908; Victor M. Gore letter to Stearns Salt and Lumber Co., November 20, 1908; Justus S. Stearns letter to Victor M. Gore, November 21, 1908.

15. "With Passing of Stearns' Mill the Book of Mighty Pines and of Hardwood Closes Forever," *Ludington Daily News,* August 26, 1917; "Larger Salt Block to Be Built Here at Stearns Plant," *Ludington Daily New,* August 5, 1917; "Stearns Co. Drives New Salt Well on Fourth Ward Site," *Ludington Daily News,* March 11, 1918; "Stearns Men Hold Fast to Principles," *Ludington Daily News,* July 2, 1919; "Morton Buys Stearns Salt Holdings," *Ludington Daily News,* January 21, 1923. Unfortunately, there isn't much information concerning the strike by Stearns's employees at the salt plant (such as its length), which began in late June of 1919. Several editions of the *Ludington Daily News* are unavailable from that summer, and this author could not uncover an article identifying the date on which the strike ended. According to Wilmer Culver, the company's vice president, the strike was mostly confined to five leaders. The men complained the company paid "starvation wages." Interestingly, the men targeted their anger at Culver, as opposed to Stearns. See "Hostility to Culver Evidenced in Vote of Commissioners on Monday Night," *Ludington Daily News,* July 8, 1919, available at http://news.google.com/newspapers, accessed January 7, 2013; the "starvation wages" quotation is from "Stearns Men Hold Fast to Principles," *Ludington Daily News,* July 2, 1919.

16. "Morton Buys Stearns Salt Holdings," *Ludington Daily News,* January 21, 1923; "Business in Brief," *Detroit Free Press,* April 5, 1903, available at http://proquest.com, accessed May 24, 2011; Augustus H. Gansser, *History of Bay County, Michigan, and Representative Citizens* (Chicago: Richmond and Arnold, 1905), 580, available at http://googlebooks.com/, accessed August 1, 2011; "A Change in Management," *Pensacola Journal,* June 30, 1908, available at http://chroniclingamerica.loc.gov, accessed May 18, 2011; "Lumber Holdings of $3,500,000 in Florida Sold by J. S. Stearns," *Ludington Daily News,* October 26, 1919; M. Luther King, *History of Santa Rosa County, a King's Country* (Milton, FL: Micanopy, 1973), available at www.friendsofpacelibrary.org/History/King%20History/Bagdad.htm, accessed December 27, 2012; Larry Peterson, e-mail message to author, January 8, 2013. Robert L. Stearns describes some of the assets and business practices of the Consolidated Lumber Company in Diary of Robert L. Stearns, May 3, 1915, Stearns Archive, McCreary County Museum. Additional sources include "Stearns-Culver Co. Make Big Purchase," *Ludington Daily News,* November 21, 1919; Memorandum of Agreement, November 25, 1922, Stearns Salt and Lumber Company Records, 1881–1923, Box 2, L'Anse Property Sale to Ford Motor Company Folder #3, Bentley Historical Library, Ann Arbor, Michigan. The sale of property to Henry Ford is also mentioned in Theodore J. Karamanski, *Deep Woods Frontier: A History of Logging in Northern Michigan* (Detroit: Wayne State University Press, 1989), 162. Additional sources include "Immense Lumber Deal Closed in the Northwest," *Lumber Manufacturer and Dealer* 64, no. 26 (1919): 31, available at http://googlebooks.com/, accessed August 1, 2011; Charles Moore, *History of Michigan,* vol. 2 (Chicago: Lewis Publishing, 1915), 1073–74; Marquette Lumber Company Report for Year Ended December 31, 1923, Box 3, Marquette Lumber Company Folder #2, Bentley Historical Library, Ann Arbor, Michigan; "Death Takes City's Foremost Citizen Today," *Ludington Daily News,* February 14, 1933.

17. *Gile Boat and Engine Co. Catalog* (Grand Rapids, MI: Etheridge Press, ca. 1911), 1, from the private collection of John Holcomb, Ludington, Michigan. Other sources include "New Industry," *Ludington Chronicle,* December 30, 1908; "Want Factory," *Ludington Chronicle,* January 6, 1909; "Local Men Will Give Ludington Big New Motor Boat Factory," *Ludington Chronicle,* January 13, 1909; "Start May First," *Ludington Chronicle,* April 21, 1909; "Annual Reports," *Ludington Chronicle,* May 11, 1910; "Stearns Motor

Manufacturing Company—A Brief History," from the private collection of David K. Petersen; Hawley, *Historic Mason County,* 515; *Gile Boat and Engine Co. Catalog,* 6–20; "Annual Reports," *Ludington Chronicle,* October 1, 1914.

18. The "dead stop" quotation is from "Ludington Concern Revives," *Michigan Manufacturer and Financial Record* 15, no. 18 (1915): 39, available at http://googlebooks.com/, accessed November 7, 2011. Other sources used include "Large Contract," *Ludington Chronicle,* January 28, 1914; "Motors for War," *Ludington Chronicle,* November 12, 1914. The second quotation is from "100 Are at Work," *Ludington Chronicle,* March 25, 1915. Additional sources include "Stearns Motor Co. Enlarges Foundry," *Ludington Daily News,* September 14, 1919.

19. The "talk of the show" quotation is from "Ludington Motor Was Talk of Show," *Ludington Daily News,* February 9, 1926. Additional sources include "Stearns Motor Co. Foundry Completed," *Ludington Daily News,* February 25, 1920; "Stearns Products in World Demand," *Ludington Daily News,* November 15, 1925; "Stearns Engine Has High Rating," *Ludington Daily News,* August 31, 1927. The actual results of the test conducted at the University of Nebraska can be found in University of Nebraska Agricultural Engineering Department, Copy of Report of Official Tractor Test No. 135, Stearns Box, Gile Boat and Engine Co. Folder, Mason County Historical Society Archive, Ludington, Michigan; Diary of Robert L. Stearns, April 14, 1924; April 15, 1924; April 19, 1924. Additional quotations from Robert Stearns can be found in Diary of Robert L. Stearns, November 6, 1927; November 7, 1927; December 14, 1927; and December 18, 1927, Stearns Archive, McCreary County Museum. The "several times a millionaire" quotation is from "Stearns Stays In," *Grand Rapids Press,* 1, December 15, 1899.

20. Justus Stearns letter to William Stearns, March 27, 1930, Mason County Historical Society Archive, Ludington, Michigan; "Stearns Motor to See Biggest Year in History, Predicts F. R. Stearns," *Ludington Daily News,* February 19, 1928; Hawley, *Historic Mason County,* 515; "Stearns Motor Manufacturing Company—A Brief History"; "Stearns Motors Will Continue Plant Operations," *Ludington Daily News,* November 6, 1929; "Will Auction Off Property Former Stearns Motor Co.," *Ludington Daily News,* July 15, 1930, available at http://news.google.com/newspapers, accessed November 21, 2012; "Bidding Is Spirited at Opening of Sale of Local Factory," *Ludington Daily News,* July 16, 1930, available at http://news.google.com/newspapers, accessed November 21, 2012; "Motor Plant Pays 2 Million Dollars Wages in 10 Years," *Ludington Daily News,* February 7, 1930.

21. Sage's biographer, Anita Shafer Goodstein, argues the "building, lot, books and furniture [at the Sage Library] were estimated to have cost $50,000," while Charles Hackley's biographer, Richard Harms, argues that Sage gave $25,000 for the library. It is likely that Sage contributed $25,000 to the construction of the building, while other costs, including the property, books, and furniture, may have included an additional $25,000. For more detail, see Goodstein, *Biography of a Businessman,* 132; and Harms, *Life after Lumbering: Charles Henry Hackley and the Emergence of Muskegon, Michigan,* 286. Additional sources include Kilar, *Michigan's Lumbertowns,* 147; Goodstein, *Biography of a Businessman,* 221; Harms, *Life after Lumbering: Charles Henry Hackley and the Emergence of Muskegon, Michigan,* 285–99.

22. The early history of Epworth Heights is chronicled in Hawley, *Historic Mason County,* 234, 235; *Epworth: The First One Hundred Years* (Ludington, MI: Epworth Board of

Trustees, 1994), 2–4; Peterson, *Story of Ludington,* 75–76. Another useful source is a memoir by Helen Putnam Shaver, who devotes an entire chapter to Stearns's contributions to Epworth. See Helen Putnam Shaver, *Steps to the Heights* (New York: Authors Choice Press, 2009), 85–94. Additional sources include "Program of 1899," *Epworth Assembly Quarterly* 5, no. 3 (1899): 8; "Program Talent," *Epworth Assembly Quarterly* 7, no. 3 (1901): 12–13; "General Program," *Epworth Assembly Quarterly* 12, no. 2 (1906): 9; *Epworth Assembly Quarterly* 6, no. 3 (1900): 6. The first quotation is from "Fine Prospects Ahead for the Epworth Assembly, Hon. Justus S. Stearns, of Ludington, Greatly Interested," *Epworth Assembly Quarterly* 7, no. 1 (1901): 7; much of the January 1901 article was reprinted in "Stearns' Great Work," *Ludington Chronicle,* January 17, 1901. The quotation from Stearns is from "Mr. Stearns and Epworth," *Epworth Assembly Quarterly* 7, no. 3 (1901): 7; Duane Wolf, e-mail message to author, July 19, 2013.

23. "Ludington and Northern," *Ludington Chronicle,* July 18, 1901; "Fine Prospects Ahead for the Epworth Assembly, Hon. Justus S. Stearns, of Ludington, Greatly Interested, *Epworth Assembly Quarterly* 7, no. 1 (1901): 6–7; James L. Cabot, "Dummy Train Carried Vacationing Passengers," *Ludington Daily News,* July 17, 1999.

24. The "generously donated" quotation is from "Fourteenth Annual Report of the President of the Epworth Assembly," *Epworth Assembly Quarterly* 14, no. 4 (1908): 5; "Fine Prospects Ahead for the Epworth Assembly, Hon. Justus S. Stearns, of Ludington, Greatly Interested," *Epworth Assembly Quarterly* 7, no. 1 (1901): 7, and 16–17; *Epworth Assembly Quarterly* 9, no. 2 (1903): 11; "Secretary E. Swarthout's Report," *Epworth Assembly Quarterly* 12, no. 3 (1906): 6–7; "Epworth Heights," *Epworth Assembly Quarterly* 15, no. 2 (1909): 4; *Epworth Assembly Quarterly* 8, no. 3 (1902): 22; *Epworth Assembly Quarterly* 8, no. 4 (1902): 11; *Epworth Assembly Quarterly* 8, no. 1 (1902): 17–19; "Mrs. Stearns' New Cottage," *Ludington Chronicle,* July 18, 1901; "More Buildings Than Ever," *Epworth Assembly Quarterly* 9, no. 1 (1903): 12; "Gift by Stearns," *Ludington Chronicle,* September 18, 1907; "The New School of Music," *Epworth Assembly Quarterly* 13, no. 4 (1907): 2–3. The estimate that Stearns built eleven cottages is based on the research of an Epworth cottager and can be found in Steve Hunt, e-mail message to author, January 23, 2013. Both Mr. Hunt and the author were surprised the number wasn't larger. It is possible Stearns built as many as one dozen more, but it is unclear. It is clear that he built at least eleven and that he owned several pieces of property on the Epworth grounds. Information concerning the cottage built by Congressman Bishop is from Duane Wolf, e-mail message to author, July 19, 2013. Bishop sold his cottage to George Fuller in 1903, and as of 2013 it was known as Pine Cliff cottage.

25. Men would be allowed to serve as members of the Hospital Association beginning in 1928 when the by-laws were amended to allow for their participation. The quotation is from Fran Schauer, "The Hospital's 75 Years," File Drawer M–N, Medical-Hospital, Mason County Hospital Assn. Folder, Mason County Historical Society Archive, Ludington, Michigan. Other sources include Articles of Association of the Mason County Hospital Association, Medical Box, Paulina Stearns Folder, Mason County Historical Society Archive, Ludington, Michigan; "Need It Badly," *Ludington Chronicle,* November 14, 1906, available at http://news.google.com/newspapers, accessed January 18, 2013. The early history of Paulina Stearns Hospital is chronicled in a series of excellent articles written by David K. Petersen. These include "Attempts to Organize Mason County's First Hospital Met with Resistance," *Ludington Daily News,* February 25, 2006; "Train Wreck Helps Focus the Community on a Hospital," *Ludington Daily News,* March 4, 2006; "Stearns Hospital Sets Its Course," *Ludington Daily News,* March 11, 2006; "The Conclusion of the Stearns Hospital Saga," *Ludington Daily News,* March 18, 2006. Many of the same articles are reproduced in a special insert, "Memorial Medical 100 Years," *Ludington Daily News,* May 8, 2006.

26. Schauer, "The Hospital's 75 Years"; "Fitting Tribute," *Ludington Chronicle,* October 16, 1907; "New Hospital Open to Public," *Ludington Chronicle,* November 13, 1907; "Stearns Makes Handsome Gift," *Ludington Chronicle,* February 5, 1908. The home of Justus Stearns served as Mason County's hospital until 1940 when a new brick building was built, just across the street from his old residence; it also was named Paulina Stearns Hospital. Stearns's original home was demolished in November 1940, and the location was used as a parking lot.

27. Schauer, "The Hospital's 75 Years"; "$15,000 Hospital Gift Made by Benefactor," *Ludington Chronicle,* April 19, 1911; Story and Plans of the New Hospital for Mason County, Mich., Medical Box, Medicine-Hospitals, Paulina Stearns Folder, Mason County Historical Society Archive, Ludington, Michigan.

28. "Will Build New Church," *Ludington Record-Appeal,* March 19, 1903, 1, available at http://news.google.com/newspapers, accessed November 21, 2012; "Things Told of Us," *Ludington Record-Appeal,* July 23, 1903, 1, available at http://news.google.com/newspapers, accessed November 21, 2012; "They Favor a New Church," *Ludington Chronicle,* March 25, 1903; Dedication of the New Educational Building for The Community Church Ludington, Michigan November 22, 1959, Religion A–L Box, Churches, Community Church Folder #1, Mason County Historical Society Archive, Ludington, Michigan. Members of the Stearns family continued to attend Community Church for many years, and in 1947, Laura Freeman Stearns, Robert Stearns's wife, donated the Stearns Memorial Organ to the church. Paulina Stearns Bennett, Robert Lyon Stearns Jr., and Freeman R. Stearns also contributed to the cost of the organ, which is still in use. In January 2013, Mary Carlson, from Community Church, gave the author a tour of the building and provided some helpful historical background to the church, and then in June 2014 longtime pastor Bill Collins was gracious enough to provide another tour. "Stearns Makes Library Handsome Book Gift," *Ludington Chronicle,* March 2, 1910; "J. S. Stearns Presents Rich Gift To Library," *Ludington Daily News,* November 2, 1924; "Stearns Employees Who Go to War Are Assured of Jobs," *Ludington Daily News,* May 11, 1917; "Stearns Co. Takes $50,000 of Second Liberty Loan Bonds," *Ludington Daily News,* October 25, 1917; Peterson, *Story of Ludington,* 42, 43; Ludington City Council Minutes, September 5, 1922, available at www.minutesondemand.com/mod/index.html?client=ludingtoncitymi#, accessed February 3, 2012; "Wants Boulevard on West Ludington," *Ludington Daily News,* September 6, 1922.

29. "J. S. Stearns Gives Cash Prizes Again to High Pupils," *Ludington Daily News,* October 23, 1917. The quotations concerning the Boy Scouts are found in "Will Discuss Ways to Interest Boys in Scouting," *Ludington Daily News,* August 13, 1926. The "substantial contributions" quotation is from "Col. Stearns Aids in Dedication," *Ludington Daily News,* July 18, 1932.

30. "Purchase Lake Front," *Ludington Record-Appeal,* July 22, 1909, 1, available at http://news.google.com/newspapers, accessed February 3, 2012.
31. Ibid.
32. "Vote the Bonds," *Ludington Chronicle,* August 11, 1909, 2, available at http://news.google.com/newspapers, accessed February 3, 2012. The quotation is from "Vote the Bonds." Additional sources include "Gains in Favor," *Ludington Chronicle,* August 4, 1909, 1, available at http://news.google.com/newspapers, accessed February 3, 2012; "Board of Trade Should Have the Bonds," *Ludington Chronicle,* August 11, 1909, 2, available at http://news.google.com/newspapers, accessed February 3, 2012; "Bonds Are Voted," *Ludington Chronicle,* August 25, 1909, 1, available at http://news.google.com/newspapers, accessed February 3, 2012.
33. Ludington City Council Minutes, January 3, 1910, Ludington City Hall, Ludington, Michigan; "Stearns Gives City $50,000," *Ludington Record-Appeal,* January 27, 1910, 1, available at http://news.google.com/newspapers, accessed February 2, 2012. The quitclaim deed for the property that became Stearns Park can be found at Record of Deeds Book 68, 265, Mason County Courthouse, Ludington, Michigan. The steps Stearns took to "sell" property to the city and use the proceeds to attract new industries to Ludington were not unprecedented. In 1892 voters in Muskegon, Michigan, voted to raise $100,000 in bonds to "purchase" about eighty acres of land from Newcomb McGraft, a leading businessman. When the bonds were approved he deeded the property to the city and then turned over the $100,000 in city bonds to the chamber of commerce. The money was used to attract several firms to relocate to Muskegon over the next ten years. See Kilar, *Michigan's Lumbertowns,* 281, 282, and Harms, *Life after Lumbering: Charles Henry Hackley and the Emergence of Muskegon, Michigan,* 267, for more detail.
34. Ludington City Council Minutes, May 7, 1923, available at www.minutesondemand.com/mod/index.html?client=ludingtoncitymi#, accessed February 3, 2012. The quotation is from Ludington City Council Minutes, September 17, 1923, available at www.minutesondemand.com/mod/index.html?client=ludingtoncitymi#, accessed February 3, 2012. Much of the same information is repeated in "Name of Stearns Given to Park," *Ludington Daily News,* September 18, 1923, 1, available at http://news.google.com/newspapers, accessed February 3, 2012.
35. Ludington City Council Minutes, October 1, 1923, available at www.minutesondemand.com/mod/index.html?client=ludingtoncitymi#, accessed February 3, 2012.
36. Stearns Park Property Deed, Ludington City Hall, Ludington, Michigan; Ludington City Council Minutes, September 20, 1948, available at www.minutesondemand.com/mod/index.html?client=ludingtoncitymi#, accessed February 3, 2012; "To Give City Park Addition," *Ludington Daily News,* September 21, 1948, available at http://news.google.com/newspapers, accessed February 3, 2012; Lenore P. Williams, "Stearns Park One of State's Most Beautiful Lake Sites," *Ludington Daily News,* June 27, 1956; Lenore P. Williams, "Stearns Park Queen of Lake Michigan Shore," *Ludington Daily News,* August 22, 1956; "Just for Summer: 51 Great American Beaches," *USA Today,* May 29, 2012, available at http://travel.usatoday.com/destinations/story/2012–05–27/Just-for-summer-51-great-beaches/55220960/1, accessed October 5, 2012.
37. "J. S. Stearns Home Now Redecorated," *Ludington Daily News,* October 19, 1920; United States Census, 1920, Ludington City, Mason County Michigan, sheet no. 2,

available at www.ancestry.com, accessed March 9, 2012; United States Census, 1930, Ludington City, Mason County Michigan, sheet no. 12, available at www.ancestry.com, accessed March 9, 2012. Both sets of quotations are from "Townsfolk Give Dinner in Honor of Hon. Justus S. Stearns," *Ludington Daily News,* April 11, 1923. The tribute booklet is an excellent source of information describing the life of Stearns; it includes a total of nineteen printed pages. A full citation can be found in the endnotes for chapter 1, but will be referred to here as "A Tribute: A Dinner Commemorating," Mason County Historical Society Archive.

38. "Says His 83d Birthday Anniversary Happiest; Feted at Stearns, Ky." *Ludington Daily News,* April 18, 1928.

39. "Ludington's Foremost Citizen Is Honored," *Ludington Chronicle* May 14, 1916; "Stearns Elected National Delegate," *Ludington Daily News,* April 18, 1928; "J. S. Stearns Is Honored Signally by Executive to Represent Michigan," *Ludington Daily News,* July 16, 1925; "J. S. Stearns Attends Meeting in Philadelphia," *Ludington Daily News,* February 7, 1928; "Col. Stearns Appointed Member of Washington Bicentennial Commission," *Ludington Daily News,* January 24, 1932. The quotations are from "Hon. J. S. Stearns Highly Honored by Gov. Sampson," *Ludington Daily News,* June 18, 1930.

40. "Stearns Pres't," *Ludington Chronicle,* November 3, 1909; "City Bank Elections," *Ludington Daily News,* January 13, 1932; "Scores Send Greetings to Hon. J. S. Stearns; Is 84 Years Old Today," *Ludington Daily News,* April 10, 1929; "Passes 87th Birthday," *Ludington Daily News,* April 11, 1932; "New Farm, Hotel Call J. S. Stearns, Held by Hurt Leg," *Ludington Daily News,* October 30, 1928.

41. "New Farm, Hotel Call J. S. Stearns, Held by Hurt Leg." The quotations are from "Pays Tribute to J. S. Stearns, Foremost Citizen of City," *Ludington Daily News,* August 9, 1926.

42. "Death Takes City's Foremost Citizen Today," *Ludington Daily News,* February 14, 1933; "Ludington's Grand Old Man Is Summoned by Death Today," *Ludington Daily News,* February 14, 1933.

43. "Death Takes City's Foremost Citizen Today"; "Places of Business Requested to Close At 1:30," *Ludington Daily News,* February 15, 1933; "Testimonials in Memory of Honorable J. S. Stearns," *Ludington Daily News,* February 15, 1933; "He Was Loyal," *Ludington Daily News,* February 15, 1933.

44. "Justus S. Stearns," *Grand Rapids Herald,* February 15, 1933, 4.

45. "Son Gets Entire Stearns Estate," *Ludington Daily News,* February 1913; "He Was Loyal"; Last Will and Testament of J. S. Stearns, Mason County Probate Court, File #4692, Mason County Courthouse, Ludington, Michigan. The other individuals identified in the codicil to Stearns's will and who were to receive the money were Mr. Allen H. Burch and Mr. Harold F. King. Additional sources include "The End Comes to Big Part of Local History," *Ludington Daily News,* December 17, 1971; Dickey's obituary can be found in "Elizabeth Dickey," *Ludington Daily News,* February 23, 1983. This was retrieved from "Elizabeth Dickey," Obituary Files, Mason County Historical Society Archive, Ludington, Michigan.

Chapter 9

1. "Townsfolk Give Dinner in Honor of Hon. Justus S. Stearns," *Ludington Daily News,* April 11, 1923. A willingness to take risks was a trait held by other industrialists in this era. In his study of entrepreneurs in Scranton, Pennsylvania, Burton Folsom notes, "the more effective the businessman, the more he seemed to court failure" by taking risks. See Folsom, *Urban Capitalists,* 65.

2. Both Rockefeller's and Carnegie's views concerning costs are described in Brands, *American Colossus.* Rockefeller is addressed in pages 75–76, while Carnegie's views are covered in 92–93. The quotation concerning Carnegie is from Joseph Frazier Wall, *Andrew Carnegie* (New York: Oxford University Press, 1970), 342.

3. Goodstein, *Biography of a Businessman,* 84.

4. "Reforestation Should Be a Major Function," Mason County Historical Society Archive; an additional source is Edmund Morris, *Theodore Rex* (New York: Random House, 2001), 231, 516–17.

5. An example of Ludington's "foremost citizen" label for Stearns is seen in "Ludington's Foremost Citizen," *Ludington Daily News,* July 22, 1915; it continued with "Ludington's Foremost Citizen Is Honored," *Ludington Daily News,* May 4, 1916.

6. "He Was Loyal," *Ludington Daily News,* February 15, 1933.

Selected Bibliography

Unpublished Sources

Barthell, Edward. "Mountain Stories," 1933.

Birdwell, Michael E. "The Stearns Company, a History, 1902–1975." Prepared for the Big South Fork Scenic Recreation Area by the Upper Cumberland Institute, Tennessee Technological University, 1988.

Jensen, James. "Ludington's Angels: Antoine Cartier and Justus Stearns." Unpublished manuscript, 2010.

Petersen, David K. "Justus S. Stearns." Unpublished manuscript, 2008.

McBride, Kim A. "A Background Archival and Oral Historical Study of the Barthell Coal Camp, McCreary County, Kentucky." Report 280, 1993.

"A Tribute: A Dinner Commemorating the Seventy-Eighth Birthday Anniversary of Justus S. Stearns." Mason County Historical Society Archive, Ludington, Michigan, 1923.

Archives

Bentley Historical Library, Ann Arbor, Michigan

Darwin R. Barker Historical Museum, Fredonia, New York

Lake County Historical Society, Baldwin, Michigan

Library of Congress, Washington, DC

Ludington City Hall, City Clerk's Record Office, Ludington, Michigan

Mason County Courthouse, Ludington, Michigan

Mason County District Library, Local History Special Collection, Ludington, Michigan

Mason County Historical Society Archive, Ludington, Michigan

Michigan State Archives, Lansing

National Archives and Records Administration, Atlanta, Georgia

National Archives and Records Administration, College Park, Maryland

National Archives and Records Administration, Washington, DC

Special Collections, University of Kentucky Libraries, Lexington, Kentucky

Stearns Archive, McCreary County Museum, Stearns, Kentucky

Personal Collections

Bellinger, Donald, Kalkaska, Michigan

Bosley, Bruce and Cindy, Branch, Michigan

Gable, Robert E., Lexington, Kentucky

Hankwitz, Mike, Evanston, Illinois

Holcomb, John, Ludington, Michigan
Petersen, David K., Ludington, Michigan

Personal Interviews

William "Doc" Coffey. Personal interview with author, March 27, 2012. Stearns, Kentucky.
Robert E. Gable. Personal interview with author, July 9, 2013. Ludington, Michigan.

Newspapers

Arizona Daily Star
The Bee
Bourbon News
Crossville Chronicle
Daily Public Ledger
Detroit Free Press
Fredonia Censor
Grand Rapids Press
Grand Rapids Herald
Hazel Green Herald
The Interior Journal
Louisville Post
Ludington Appeal
Ludington Chronicle
Ludington Daily News
Ludington Record
Ludington Record-Appeal
Marion Daily Mirror
Mason County Enterprise
Mason County Record
Milwaukee Journal
Mount Vernon Signal
Mt. Sterling Advocate
New York Times
Paducah Evening Sun
Pensacola Journal
The Richmond Climax
San Francisco Call
Spokane Spokesman-Review
USA Today
Winchester News

Government Documents

Last Will and Testament of Justus S. Stearns. Mason County Probate Court, File #4692. Mason County Courthouse, Ludington, Michigan.
President's Commission on Coal. John D. Rockefeller IV, Chairman. *The American Coal*

Miner: A Report on Community and Living Conditions in the Coalfields. Washington, DC: Government Printing Office, 1980.

Stearns, Justus S., ed. *Michigan Legislative Manual.* Lansing: Robert Smith Printing, 1899.

Twentieth Annual Report of the Executive Committee of the Indian Rights Association, For the Year Ending December 10, 1902. Philadelphia: Office of the Indian Rights Association, 1903.

United States Census, 1870, 1880, 1900, 1920, 1930.

US Coal Commission. *Report of the US Coal Commission.* Washington, DC: Government Printing Office, 1923–25.

US Department of the Interior. Directed by Rear Admiral Joel Boone. *A Medical Survey of the Bituminous-Coal Industry.* Report of the Coal Mines Administration. Washington, DC: Government Printing Office, 1947.

———. *Report on Indians Taxed and Indians Not Taxed in The United States (Except Alaska) at the Eleventh Census: 1890.* Washington, DC: Government Printing Office, 1894.

———. *Twenty-Seventh Annual Report of the Board of Indian Commissioners 1895.* Washington, DC: Government Printing Office, 1896.

US House of Representatives. *Annual Reports of the Department of the Interior for the Fiscal Year Ended June 30, 1897, Report of the Commissioner of Indian Affairs.* Washington, DC: Government Printing Office, 1897.

Woodrow Wilson Papers. Presidential Papers Microfilm. Library of Congress, Washington, DC.

Books, Journal Articles, and Magazine Articles

Adams, Robert P. *The Thirteenth River.* Manistee, MI: Robert P. Adams, 2002.

American Lumbermen: The Personal History and Public and Business Achievements of One Hundred Eminent Lumbermen of the United States, Second Series. Chicago: American Lumberman, 1906.

"Ashland County's Largest Town—Sanborn; Its Resources and Advantages." *Wisconsin Municipality* 14, no. 4 (1914): 874–80.

Barris, Lois, and Donna Johnson. *Selected Information from the 1855 New York State Census for the County of Chautauqua.* Vol. 2, *Harmony thru Westfield.* Fredonia, NY: Chautauqua County Genealogical Society, 2008.

Barris, Lois, and Norwood Barris. *Selected Information from the 1860 United States Census for the County of Chautauqua, New York, Vol. II, Towns of Hanover thru Westfield, plus Deaths by Towns.* Fredonia, NY: Chautauqua County Genealogical Society, 2003.

Benson, Barbara E. *Logs and Lumber: The Development of Lumbering in Michigan's Lower Peninsula, 1837–1870.* Mount Pleasant, MI: Clarke Historical Library, Central Michigan University, 1989.

Biographical History of Northeastern Ohio, Embracing the Counties of Ashtabula, Trumball, and Mahoning. Chicago: Lewis Publishing, 1893.

Blackburn, George M., and Sherman L. Richards. "The Timber Industry in Manistee County, Michigan: A Case History in Local Control." *Journal of Forest History* 18 (April 1974): 14–21.

Boyer, Paul. *The Enduring Vision.* Boston: Wadsworth, Cengage Learning, 2013.

Brands, H. W. *American Colossus: The Triumph of Capitalism, 1865–1900.* New York: Doubleday, 2010.

Cabot, James L. *Images of America, Ludington 1830–1930.* Chicago: Arcadia, 2005.

Catalogue of the Olivet College for 1904–1905. Olivet, MI: Frank N. Green, 1905.

Catlin, George B. *The Story of Detroit.* Detroit: Detroit News, 1923.

Caudill, Harry M. *Night Comes to the Cumberlands: The Biography of a Depressed Area.* Ashland, KY: Jesse Stuart Foundation, 2001.

———. *Theirs Be the Power: The Moguls of Eastern Kentucky.* Urbana: University of Illinois Press, 1983.

Chapple, Will H. "Practical Help for Reservation Indians." *National Magazine* 17, no. 6 (1903): 717–22.

Chernow, Ron. *Titan: The Life of John D. Rockefeller, Sr.* New York: Random House, 1998.

Clark, Thomas D. *A History of Kentucky.* Ashland, KY: Jesse Stuart Foundation, 1988.

Coleman, McAlister. *Men and Coal.* New York: Arno and the New York Times, 1969.

Collins, Robert F. *A History of the Daniel Boone National Forest, 1770–1970.* 1975; Forest History Society, 2010.

Condee, William Faricy. *Coal and Culture: Opera Houses in Appalachia.* Athens: Ohio University Press, 2005.

Cox, Thomas R. "Frontier Enterprise versus the Modern Age." *Pacific Northwest Quarterly* 84, no. 1 (1993): 19–29.

Danziger, Edmund Jefferson, Jr. *The Chippewas of Lake Superior.* Norman: University of Oklahoma Press, 1978.

———. *Great Lakes Indian Accommodation and Resistance during the Early Reservation Years.* Ann Arbor: University of Michigan Press, 2009.

Dondero, George A. *Why Lincoln Wore a Beard.* Springfield, IL: Journal Printing Company, 1931. Reprinted from *Journal of the Illinois State Historical Society* 24, no. 2 (1931).

Drutchas, Geoffrey G. "Gray Eminence in a Gilded Age: The Forgotten Career of Senator James McMillan of Michigan." *Michigan Historical Review* 28, no. 2 (2002): 79–113.

Dunbar, Willis F. *Michigan through the Centuries.* New York: Lewis Historical Publishing, 1955.

Dunbar, Willis F., and George S. May. *Michigan: A History of the Wolverine State.* Grand Rapids, MI: Eerdman, 1995.

Eller, Ronald D. "The Coal Barons of the Appalachian South, 1880–1930." *Appalachian Journal* 4, no. 3/4 (1977): 195–207.

———. *Miners, Millhands, and Mountaineers: Industrialization of the Appalachian South, 1880–1930.* Knoxville: University of Tennessee Press, 1982.

Ellis, Mabel Brown. "Children of the Kentucky Coal Fields." *American Child* 1, no. 4 (1920): 285–405.

Epworth: The First One Hundred Years. Ludington, MI: Epworth Board of Trustees, 1994.

Flanelly, M. J. "Ashland County's Retail Establishments." *Wisconsin Municipality* 14, no. 4 (1914): 855–56.

Folsom, Burton W. *Urban Capitalists, Entrepreneurs, and City Growth in Pennsylvania's Lackawanna and Lehigh Regions, 1800–1920.* Baltimore: Johns Hopkins University Press, 1981.

Forty Years of Industry. Stearns, KY: Stearns Coal and Lumber Company, 1938.

Fox, Jean M. *Fred M. Warner: Progressive Governor.* Farmington Hills, MI: Farmington Hills Historical Commission, 1988.

Gansser, Augustus H. *History of Bay County, Michigan, and Representative Citizens.* Chicago: Richmond and Arnold, 1905.

Gile Boat and Engine Co. Catalog. Grand Rapids, MI: Etheridge Press, ca. 1911.

Godfrey, Anthony. *A Forestry History of Ten Wisconsin Indian Reservations under the Great Lakes Agency, Precontact to the Present.* Salt Lake City: U.S. West Research, 1996.

Goodstein, Anita Shafer. *Biography of a Businessman: Henry W. Sage, 1814–1897.* Ithaca, NY: Cornell University Press, 1962.

Hamilton, Raphael N. "The Marquette Death Site: The Case for Ludington." *Michigan History* 49 (September 1965): 228–48.

Hannah, Frances Caswell. *Sand, Sawdust, and Saw Logs: Lumber Days in Ludington.* Ludington, MI: Frances Caswell Hannah, 1955.

Harms, Richard Henry. *Life after Lumbering: Charles Henry Hackley and the Emergence of Muskegon, Michigan.* New York: Garland, 1989.

Harrison, Lowell H. *Kentucky's Governors.* Lexington: University Press of Kentucky, 2004.

Harrison, Lowell H., and James C. Klotter. *A New History of Kentucky.* Lexington: University Press of Kentucky, 1997.

Hawley, Thomas A., ed. *Historic Mason County.* Ludington, MI: Mason County Historical Society, 1980.

Hevener, John W. *Which Side Are You On? The Harlan County Coal Miners, 1931–39.* Urbana: University of Illinois Press, 2002.

History of Manistee County Michigan, with Illustrations and Biographical Sketches of Some of Its Prominent Men and Pioneers. Chicago: H. R. Page, 1882.

History of Mason County Michigan, with Illustrations and Biographical Sketches of Some of Its Prominent Men and Pioneers. Chicago: H. R. Page, 1882.

Howell, Benita J. *Folklife along the Big South Fork of the Cumberland River.* Knoxville: University of Tennessee Press, 2003.

Hudson, E. R. "Dead Timber in the National Forests." *Forestry and Irrigation* 13, no. 7 (1907): 363–66, 383.

Husband, Joseph. *A Year in a Coal-Mine.* New York: Arno Press, 1977.

"Immense Lumber Deal Closed in the Northwest." *Lumber Manufacturer and Dealer* 64, no. 26 (1919): 31.

"The Influences That Made Ludington Come Back." *Michigan Manufacturer and Financial Record* 15, no. 10 (1915): 4–6.

Inman, Doyle, B. "In the Hills of Kentucky." *Trains* 9, no. 9 (1949): 12–13.

Karamanski, Theodore J. *Deep Woods Frontier: A History of Logging in Northern Michigan.* Detroit: Wayne State University Press, 1989.

Kaufman, Jo Ann, compiler, and Lois Barris, transcriber. *Directory of Students Who Attended the Fredonia Academy during the Years 1826–1867.* Fredonia, NY: Chautauqua County Genealogical Society, 1990.

Kilar, Jeremy. *Michigan's Lumbertowns: Lumbermen and Laborers in Saginaw, Bay City, and Muskegon, 1870–1905.* Detroit: Wayne State University Press, 1990.

King, M. Luther. *History of Santa Rosa County, a King's Country.* Milton, FL: Micanopy, 1973.

Kinne, W. A. *The Gum Tree Story.* Stearns, KY, 1929.

Kinney, J. P. *Indian Forest and Range: A History of the Administration and Conservation of the Redman's Heritage.* Washington, DC: Forestry Enterprises, 1950.

Kohlmeyer, Frederick W. "Northern Pine Lumbermen: A Study in Origins and Migrations." *Journal of Economic History* 16, no. 4 (1956): 529–38.

Lake County Historical Society. *Images of America, Lake County, 1871–1960.* Chicago: Arcadia, 2009.

Lantz, Herman R. *People of Coal Town.* Carbondale: Southern Illinois University Press, 1971.

Levi, Carolissa. *Chippewa Indians of Yesterday and Today.* New York: Pageant Press, 1956.

Lewis, Ronald L. *Black Coal Miners in America.* Lexington: University Press of Kentucky, 1987.

Livingstone, William. *Livingstone's History of the Republican Party.* Vol. 2. Detroit: Livingstone, 1900.

Loew, Patty. *Indian Nations of Wisconsin: Histories of Endurance and Renewal.* Madison: Wisconsin Historical Society Press, 2001.

———. *Native People of Wisconsin.* Madison: Wisconsin Historical Society Press, 2003.

———. "Natives, Newspapers, and 'Fighting Bob': Wisconsin Chippewa in the 'Unprogressive' Era." *Journalism History* 23, no. 4 (1998): 149–58.

"Ludington Concern Revives." *Michigan Manufacturer and Financial Record* 15, no. 18 (1915): 38–39.

Ludington, Gateway of the Northwest. Ludington, MI: Record-Appeal, ca. 1908.

Lyon, Sidney Elizabeth, ed. *Lyon Memorial.* Detroit: Press of William Graham Printing, 1907.

Maierhauser, Fran. "They Printed Their Own Money . . . and Got Away with It!" *Rural Kentuckian Magazine,* November 1975, 14–15.

Maybee, Rolland H. *Michigan's White Pine Era, 1840–1900.* Lansing: Michigan Historical Commission, 1960.

McCracken, S. B. *Men of Progress: Embracing Historical Sketches of Representative Michigan Men with an Outline History of the State.* Detroit: Evening News Association, 1900.

Moore, Charles. *History of Michigan.* Vol. II. Chicago: Lewis Publishing, 1915.

Morris, Edmund. *Theodore Rex.* New York: Random House, 2001.

Mountain Herald. "How A Friend Remembers Lincoln."

The National Cyclopaedia of American Biography. Vol. 31. New York: James T. White, 1944.

The Northwestern Reporter, Containing All the Decisions of the Supreme Courts of Minnesota, Wisconsin, Iowa, Michigan, Nebraska, North Dakota, South Dakota. Vol. 76. St. Paul: West Publishing, 1898.

Perry, L. E. *McCreary Conquest: A Narrative History.* Whitely City, KY: L. E. Perry, 1979.

Perry, Samuel. *South Fork Country.* Detroit: Harlo Press, 1983.

Peterson, Paul. *The Story of Ludington.* Ludington, MI: Mason County Historical Society, 2011.

Pond, J. M. "Fred Herrick, The Story of One of The Most Colorful Careers in the Lumber Industry of This Country." *Four L Lumber News* 12, no. 23 (1930): 18, 42–43.

Powers, Perry F. *A History of Northern Michigan and Its People*. Chicago: Lewis Publishing, 1912.

Reimann, Lewis C. *When Pine Was King*. Ann Arbor: Edwards Brothers, 1953.

Rubenstein, Bruce A., and Lawrence E. Ziewacz. *Michigan: A History of the Great Lakes State*. Wheeling, IL: Harlan Davidson, 2002.

Schneider, Dorothy, and Carl J. Schneider. *American Women in the Progressive Era*. New York: Facts on File, 1993.

Shaver, Helen Putnam. *Steps to the Heights*. New York: Authors Choice Press, 2009.

Shifflett, Crandall A. *Coal Towns: Life, Work, and Culture in Company Towns of Southern Appalachia, 1880–1960*. Knoxville: University of Tennessee Press, 1991.

The Southwestern Reporter, Containing All the Current Decisions of the Supreme and Appellate Courts of Arkansas, Kentucky, Missouri, Tennessee, and Texas. Vol. 164. St. Paul: West Publishing, 1914.

"Stearns Plants Do Big Business." *Michigan Manufacturer and Financial Record* 15, no. 1 (1915): 15.

Stearns, Robert L. *The Ass and the Barnacles*. Stearns, KY: Stearns Coal and Lumber, 1921.

Stebbins, Catherine L. "The Marquette Death Site." *Michigan History* 48 (December 1964): 333–68.

Steen-Adams, Michelle M., Nancy E. Langston, and David J. Mladenoff. "Logging the Great Lakes Indian Reservations: The Case of the Bad River Band of Ojibwe." *American Indian Culture and Research Journal* 34, no. 1 (2010): 41–66.

Sulzer, Elmer G. *Ghost Railroads of Kentucky*. Bloomington: Indiana University Press, 1998.

Teholiz, Leo. "Ludington's Robert Lyon Stearns: The Mark Twain of Art." *Great Lakes Review* 5, no. 1 (1978): 28–41.

Thomas, Frank. "Louie Bryant—A Visionary Scott Countian." *First National Bank Chronicle* 3, no. 2 (1992): 1–2.

Thomas, J. Patrick. *Lore and Legend*. Stearns, KY: J. P. Thomas, 1989.

Van Wagenen, Avis Stearns. *Genealogy and Memoirs of Charles and Nathaniel Stearns, and Their Descendants*. Vol. 2. Syracuse, NY: Courier Printing, 1901.

Victor, Arthur Earl. "Fred Herrick and Bill Grotte: Idaho's Paul Bunyan and His Bull of the Woods." *Pacificnorthwesterner* 16, no. 3 (1972): 33–48.

Wall, Joseph Frazier. *Andrew Carnegie*. New York: Oxford University Press, 1970.

Wargo, Justin. "A Case without Parallel: The Sensational Battle over Eber Brock Ward's Will and Subsequent Legacy of Detroit's First Great Industrialist." *Michigan Historical Review* 39, no. 2 (2013): 77–103.

Warren, Louis A., ed. "Lincoln's Beard." *Lincoln Lore* 98 (February 1931): 1.

Weeks, Philip. *Farewell, My Nation: The American Indian and the United States, 1820–1890*. Arlington Heights, IL: Harlan Davidson, 1990.

Periodicals

American Child

American Indian Culture and Research Journal

Epworth Assembly Quarterly

First National Bank Chronicle
Forestry and Irrigation
Four L Lumber News
Great Lakes Review
Journal of Economic History
Journal of the Illinois State Historical Society
Journalism History
Lincoln Lore
Lumber Manufacturer and Dealer
Michigan Historical Review
Michigan History
Michigan Manufacturer and Financial Record
Mountain Herald
The National Magazine
Pacificnorthwesterner
Pacific Northwest Quarterly
Pick and Powder
Rural Kentuckian Magazine
Stearns Co-Operator
Trains
West Virginia History
Wisconsin Municipality

Websites

http://bioguide.congress.gov
http://chroniclingamerica.loc.gov
http://college.cengage.com/history/lecturepoints
http://content.wisconsinhistory.org/cdm/ref/collection/tp/id/26289
http://en.wikipedia.org
http://freepages.folklore.rootsweb.ancestry.com/~smokymtnman/stories/mountainstories.html
http://kyknfolk.com/mccreary/coalmining/coalmining.htm
http://lsc.wisc.edu/faculty/patty-loew/
http://michigan.maripo.com/justus_1.htm
http://name.umdl.umich.edu/BAD6035.0001.001
http://news.google.com/newspapers
http://proquest.com
http://ukcc.uky.edu/census
www.ancestry.com
www.foresthistory.org/ASPNET/Publications/region/8/daniel_boone/contents.htm
www.friendsofpacelibrary.org/History/King%20History/Bagdad.htm
www.heritagequest.com
www.michigan.gov
www.minutesondemand.com/mod/index.html?client=ludingtoncitymi#

www.olivetcollege.edu/about/history.php
www.rootsweb.ancestry.com/~nychauta/CHURCH/FredoniaPresby/FPCRosterBookA.html#Top
www.rootsweb.ancestry.com/~nychauta/CHURCH/FredoniaPresby/FPCRosterBookB.html#Top
www.royalarcanum.com
www.senecakids.org/SenecaProject/Herrick/FredHerrickHome.html
www.timeanddate.com
www.wisconsinhistory.org

Index